THE
HEALING
WATERFALL

ALSO BY MAX HIGHSTEIN

GUIDED IMAGERY AUDIO PROGRAMS

All the scripts included in this book and more can be obtained as beautifully recorded audio programs at TheHealingWaterfall.com, and elsewhere online. **Some of the most popular include:**

- The Healing Waterfall
- Morning Meditation
- Sleep Well Tonight
- Visiting Mother Mary
- Good Boundaries
- Self Esteem
- Saying Goodbye (Grief and Loss)
- Guided Imagery for PTSD
- Sanctuary of Peace
- Meet Your Guardian Angel
- Magic Island (with Betty Mehling)

ONLINE COURSES

- Intuition Retreat: Develop Your Intuitive & Psychic Ability
- Open Your Heart with Saint Francis (With Mirabai Starr)
- Heart Meditations
- Master The Art Of Deep Listening
- Awaken To Miracles With Padre Pio
- Opening Doors For The Spiritual Creative
- Releasing Fear: Say Goodbye to Anxiety
- Say Goodbye To Anger
- Attracting A Great Relationship
- 12-Step Guided Meditations
- Car Peace: Make Your Car A Stress-Free Sanctuary

MUSIC CDS

- Touch The Sky
- Stars
- Path Of The Heart
- Intuition: Music To Guide You Deeper
- Daydreams
- Flight Plans
- Sacred Journeys
- Healing Journey
- Gentle Music for Massage

WORKSHOPS, CLASSES, AND SERVICES

Max Highstein offers live workshops, intuitive counseling sessions, custom made guided imagery recordings, and custom music composing.

Visit TheHealingWaterfall.com and MaxHighstein.com for information about all of Max Highstein's work.

THE
HEALING
WATERFALL

ONE HUNDRED
GUIDED IMAGERY SCRIPTS FOR
COUNSELORS, HEALERS, & CLERGY

MAX HIGHSTEIN

Desert Heart Multimedia
Santa Fe, New Mexico, USA

GRATITUDE & APPRECIATION

This book was made possible by the generous support of the following kind and lovely people, to whom I am most grateful!

Betty Mehling
Hope Suzanne
Sherry Geyer
Lu Bernstein
Lesley Urquhart
Marsha Craven
Angela Rose Pate
Tabu M. Kunzl
Kathleen H. Danz
Rick Hunt
Gary Hanick
Rev. D. Jeep Ries
Ann E. Kurtzman
Jill Singer
Adrienne Bramhall
Bill Good
Barry Allen
Lisa Mertz
Janine Peterson
Melinda Gittleman
Nina Peacock
...and the many, many others who have supported this book, and all of my work, through the years.

With extra special thanks, gratitude, appreciation and love to my wife and forever friend, Michele Flynn.

CONTENTS

EMOTIONAL WELLBEING & HAPPINESS

ELEVATE YOUR ATTITUDE

VISUALIZATION FOR SUCCESS

LEARN TO MEDITATE

HIGHER GUIDANCE & HEALING

CONNECTING WITH SPIRITUAL FIGURES

FOR KIDS & FAMILY

12-STEP GUIDED MEDITATIONS

INTRODUCTION

IN THE BEGINNING

I was a spiritual psychology student and musician when I wrote my first guided meditation, or guided imagery program, as they are also called. I was captivated by the idea that words and music could heal. And I knew that progressive medical clinics had begun using guided imagery to alleviate pain, and to even treat cancer.

That first guided meditation of mine led the listener on a journey through the twelve signs of the zodiac, and with its background music connected twelve musical key signatures to different parts of the body. Well, *12 Cosmic Healers* didn't exactly sell like hotcakes. But my more eccentric listeners seemed to enjoy it a great deal, and by then I was hooked on guided imagery.

THE RIGHT COMBINATION

For my second project I tried to address a wider audience. I made a program called *The Healing Waterfall*, and that one really struck a chord. It was as much a hit as a guided meditation program could possibly be, going into thousands of small bookstores and reaching a rather sizable audience. And it's had staying power! 30 years later, people who first bought it on cassette still seek it out, and purchase it again as a download from my website.

The Healing Waterfall had a number of things going for it, all of which combined to make it an effective and popular guided imagery recording:

- *A compelling story that one could easily become engrossed in*

- *A relaxation process that went progressively deeper*
- *A highly skilled narrator, who gave a gentle yet expressive delivery*
- *Beautiful music, speci fically composed to underpin the narration*

I have followed that same recipe ever since, in all the programs I've developed over the years. Based on the feedback I receive, it's a winning combination. However, I think *you* can take it a step further.

THE MISSING INGREDIENT

As professionally polished as my recordings may be, they are all missing one ingredient; the one thing that can make them especially meaningful to your clients, patients, students, or congregation: *Your voice.*

If your potential listeners already know and trust you, reading these scripts aloud to them will help them connect to the material more powerfully than any recording can. And if you are new to your audience, you can use these scripts as a way to introduce your own personality, soul, and spirit to your listeners.

I encourage you to make these scripts you own. Modify them to suit your needs, and let them be a bridge from your heart, to the heart of your own listeners.

I hope you'll enjoy this work, and find it helpful.

Max Highstein, July 4, 2016

A FEW SUGGESTIONS

Over the years I have learned a few things about effectively voicing a guided meditation that I will happily share with you. Follow these tips, and your listeners will thank you.

1) TAKE YOUR TIME

Read at a fairly slow pace to help your listeners settle into a nice, deep relaxed state of mind. Go slower than you think you should, and that will probably be about the right speed.

2) SPEAK SOFTLY

So that you can speak softly and still be heard, sit close to your listeners if you can, or use a microphone if you need to address a large audience. Speaking in a soft voice can establish a tone of intimacy that will help your listeners feel welcome, safe and relaxed. If you feel as though you must speak in a loud, booming "voice of authority" to be heard and respected, well then this might not be your gig!

3) PAUSE BETWEEN THOUGHTS

These scripts are full of ideas, imagery, colors, descriptions. That's what makes them rich and engaging. So give your listener time to absorb what you're reading. If you say, "Imagine you're walking along a forest path, early in the morning," pause, and give them a moment to fill in the picture, feel their feelings, and hear the stream in the background, in their mind's ear. Then continue on to the next thought.

As a general rule, pause a bit between sentences, and pause a bit longer between paragraphs.

Adapt your delivery according to the content, and establish a rhythm, so your listener will know what to expect. Knowing what to expect will help them relax further.

Beyond that, in almost all the scripts there are places where you'll want to give your listeners extra-long pauses. Whenever the script indicates "Take some time with this", or something similar, give your listener a full minute or more to process what's been introduced. It may feel like a long time to you, but they will be busy, engaged in their own inner story. So allow them all the time they need before going on.

4) READ AS IF YOU ARE TELLING A STORY

Most of the meditations on these pages have some kind of story in them. I encourage you to read as if you were telling a story. Put some expression into your voice! It's true that some people who do hypnosis deliver their material in a dull monotone, intending to thereby lull their subject into a deep trance. But that's not necessary. The idea here is not to put someone to sleep (unless it's a guided meditation for sleep), but to help them have a rich inner experience. Putting some color in your voice helps the listener go deeper into the story, and into their experience. As long as you speak softly, and read at a fairly slow, steady pace, your client will go inward just fine, even while you include some expression. No need to sound like a hypno-drone!

5) INTROS & OUTROS

The guided meditations in this book were written between 1984 and 2016. Despite the long time range, you'll find many similarities. For example, all of the scripts begin with a similar "induction."

An induction is the initial part of the meditation that helps the listener shift from their normal waking consciousness, to a more relaxed, trance-like state. That state of deep relaxation is helpful in itself for most people, since we tend to be over-stressed, and need more rest than we get. But beyond that, the deep relaxation state also allows us to take in and assimilate the ideas in these meditations about healing, change, and transformation.

Most of these scripts include several lines at the beginning about taking slow, deep breaths. Never underestimate the power of a few deep breaths! There's no faster, simpler, easier, or less expensive way to relax and shift gears. Indeed, if pharmaceutical companies could somehow package deep breaths, you would be seeing ads for them everywhere. Please don't skip this part of the meditation, no matter how familiar or repetitive it may seem.

Likewise, all the scripts include a virtually identical "outro" or re-entry segment. That final part is designed to help the listener make a gentle transition back to their normal state of consciousness. In many cases the listener will have gone very deep within. Help them make a smooth re-entry by giving them ample time to transition back.

6) USE QUALITY BACKGROUND MUSIC

Use good quality, gentle music or nature sounds in the background, behind your narration. Any music you use should be quiet, and soft. You can find music I've composed just for this purpose at The Healing Waterfall website (www.TheHealingWaterfall.com).

7) CARING IS KEY

Most importantly, your attitude toward your listener is crucial. If you are feeling patient, kind, and caring, it will come across in your voice, and your listener will feel it. It will help them feel safe and cared for. More than anything, your caring will allow them to relax, open up, heal and transform.

Simply put, love heals. I would encourage you to do whatever you need to do to get in touch with your own love before you guide someone through a script like the ones included here. Your love will make the work much, much more effective.

PART ONE

DEEP RELAXATION
& HEALING

THE HEALING WATERFALL

Find a comfortable place, where you'll not be disturbed, and close your eyes. Take in a slow deep breath, and as you release this breath, let your body completely relax. Take another slow deep breath, and breathe out any burdens or fears. And take another breath, and release all your thoughts, leaving your mind completely free.

Picture the most crystal clear, pure white light you can imagine, and see this light gently swirling and flowing all around you, until it begins to form itself into a beautiful, clear bubble.

This bubble of light will provide you with comfort, safety, and perfect protection upon your journey, so that only that which is for your highest good may take place.

Imagine that you're suspended in mid-air, within the protection of this bubble, and feel yourself becoming lighter, and lighter… so light that you begin to float up, above your chair, through the ceiling, and into the sky.

Feel yourself float and drift freely, as your bubble carries you above lush forests, and rolling hills. Allow your gaze to focus upon a beautiful green meadow, far below, and notice how it seems to sparkle like an emerald, beaconing your toward it. Feel yourself begin to float down, and approach this meadow, coming closer, and closer.

As you lightly touch down, look around at the grass and wildflowers, the old shade trees, and the brook winding it's way into a nearby forest. Everything about this setting seems perfect, almost magical, as if it had been created just for you.

Take a walk over to the edge of the forest, and you will find a path leading in.

Stepping upon this path, sense the cool, peaceful feeling in the air. And looking above you at the canopy of trees, see their leaves form beautiful patterns against the sky. Glimmers of sunlight shine through to the forest floor, and illuminate a carpet of rich moss, studded with all manner of wildflowers.

As you walk along, look down, and you'll notice that your path is composed of pebbles that are a brilliant color red. Red is the color of strength and vitality, and with each step, the vitality of the color red flows up into your feet, and throughout your entire body, leaving you stronger and more full of life's energy than before.

As you walk deeper into the forest, the pebbles become orange, the color of endurance. An orange glow now surrounds your body, charging you with the ability to remain healthy and vibrant.

As you continue upon this path, the pebbles turn a brilliant golden yellow, the color of mental clarity and understanding. And as you walk, a yellow star appears upon your forehead, with rays of pale light shining forth from the center of your mind.

Walking further into the center of the forest, the pebbles turn a deep emerald green, and all around you the plants and trees richly display this color of healing and balance. Take a moment to bask in the presence of this emerald green color, and allow it to awaken in you the ability to heal yourself on all levels.

As you walk along further still, the pebbles upon this path become blue. As your gaze falls upon this color, feel its cool serenity sooth your emotions, and lift your mind into the highest spheres.

As you near the end of this forest path, the pebbles become a deep, rich purple, the color of transformation. Imagine yourself being surrounded and filled with the color purple, awaking within you the ability to transform your body, mind, and emotions in whatever way you would like.

Stepping out into the clearing at the end of the forest, you find yourself once again flooded by the crystal clear, pure white light. And as the light lifts, you will see that you are standing at the base of a group of enormous mountains. Looking up at these mountains, you see that their majestic peaks extend so high that they disappear into the sky. Traces of brilliant color swirl and weave before you in the air, and reach up toward the mountain peaks, as if to form an aerial latticework for you to climb.

Bring your bubble of light back into your awareness, and it will lift you once again into the air. This time it carries you upon the latticework of color, like a magical conveyor. Higher and higher you go, leaving the world below far behind.

As the mountain peaks come into view, you can see they are covered with powdery white snow, glistening in the sun. Lower down the mountainside the snow is melting, and running into streams of sparkling clear water. One of these streams has caught your attention, and as your bubble brings you closer, you find that it is deeper and wider than the rest, turning into a beautiful waterfall.

As you gently touch down by the side of the waterfall, you are greeted by the sound of its rushing water, a sound that you hear not only with your ears, but with all of your body, as it resonates deeply within you.

This waterfall has a very special presence, a life of its own, nourished by the snow of the highest mountain peaks, and charged by the sun's powerful rays. It is apparent that here is a vessel of purest healing energy, waiting to be shared with you. To experience this energy directly, remove your clothing, and step into the shallow end of the pool, formed at the bottom of this waterfall.

This pool is the perfect temperature for you, and as your feet relax, you can feel them begin to receive the comforting, healing essence of the water, penetrating your muscles and bones.

Slowly walk forward into the pool, as this healing water caresses your ankles, your calves, and your knees, as they too absorb this gentle energy, and completely relax.

As you run your hands across the surface of the water, you find yourself more and more comfortable, and at home in this pool, and you have the feeling that you're completely safe, and totally free to be yourself. Let your body know that this is an opportunity to let go of any tension, release any imbalance, and be completely cleansed, purified, and renewed.

Allow yourself to totally experience all the healing energy this pool has to offer, as you dip below its surface, and gently float up again. Feel the essence of the water permeating every part of you, until your entire being becomes one with it.

Take time now to experience yourself in this way, and if there is any part of you that you feel needs particular attention, see the water's loving essence flowing there now, touching into the very nucleus of each cell, and leaving it filled and pulsating with pure, vital energy.

If you would like, step beneath the waterfall, and let it shower down over you. Listen carefully to the sound of its music, and as it cascades down, splashing into the pool, and hear whatever message it may hold for you at this time.

It will soon be time to begin your return home. Slowly swim over to the edge of the pool, and gently lift yourself out of the water. Finding your clothes, you will see that even they seem to be fresh and new. And with them, you can put on any new self-image that you wish.

Once again, feel the bubble of light surrounding you. Know that this place is one that exists inside of you, and that you can return to it whenever you would like.

Let your bubble lift you up into the air, above the waterfall, over the forest, the meadow, and through the sky, until you find your way back to the place where your journey began.

Settle down gently into your body, and begin to be aware of your body.

Feel your physical energy becoming more and more present, and prepare to return to your full waking consciousness.

Let all the benefits of this experience stay with you, and when you're ready, open your eyes, and feel completely awake, alert, and refreshed.

GATEWAY TO PEACE

Place your body in a comfortable position, and close your eyes. Take a slow, deep breath, and as you release it, feel your body settle in, as you become still more comfortable, and relaxed.

Allow your awareness to drop down into your body's center—your lower abdomen—and notice that your breathing there has become steady and peaceful. In this moment, all you need do is gently breathe in, and out, and everything else can wait. You're entirely safe and secure, and in this moment, all is well.

Imagine you're walking down a quiet lane. The weather is perfect, and you're enjoying the steady rhythm of your footsteps, as you move along at an easy, comfortable pace. It must have rained here recently, because the air is crisp and clear, and you can smell the fresh fragrance of flowers on the gentle breeze. There are tall, old trees along this lane, and you're enjoying their shade, and the soft rustle of their leaves.

As you continue walking, you come alongside a weathered, wooden fence, its slats all shades of silver and gray. This fence seems to go on for quite a distance, and it's too tall to see over, so you begin to wonder what could be on the other side. Pretty soon, you come to a wooden gate, closed securely. A paper note is pinned to the gate, and the paper has your name neatly written upon it.

Take the note off the gate, and turn it over, and you'll see that it simply says, "Come in."

Put the note in your pocket, and open the gate. As you step through to the other side, you're greeted by a field of waving grass, some beautiful shade trees, and a small meandering brook. There's a comfortable looking old wooden chair waiting under a tree by the brook, and that's where you're headed. As you walk toward the chair, you begin to take in the lovely essence of this place. The gentle movement of the grass, the warmth of the sun, and the riffles on the water's surface all seem to be telling you a story, one you've been longing to hear.

Sitting in this comfortable old chair, you feel a familiar sense of warmth and peace, as if you had just been reunited with a dear, old friend, someone who knows you very well. There's nothing you'd keep from this person, and anything you do, say, or feel is just fine.

Allow this feeling of warmth and peace to completely surround you now, as it communicates its healing presence to every part of you, inside and out.

Feel this healing presence touching your shoulders and back, as any tension there melts away. And feel it in your arms, and hands, and in your chest, abdomen, and hips.

And feel this relaxing, healing presence in your legs and feet.

And allow this gentle, healing presence to touch your face, head and neck, as it connects and flows throughout your entire body.

Take a few moments to absorb and enjoy this feeling of warmth and peace.

From the other side of the brook, an animal has come to drink, attracted by the delicious smell of the water, and the inviting peacefulness of this place. As you observe this simple, beautiful occurrence, a leaf falls from the tree overhead, and lands in the brook. And as you watch the leaf float downstream, perhaps it occurs to you that some of the concerns you may have been carrying are not really necessary, and you can release them as well. And so as the leaf floats away out of sight, your heart seems to become lighter, and your breathing freer.

Now the animal that has visited the stream to drink picks up its head, and looks directly into your eyes, making a deep connection with you. And in this moment, you recognize that this creature is a mirror of yourself. You understand that in drinking here, it expresses its need, nurtures itself, and fulfills its own destiny. And in knowing this, you also feel nurtured, and fulfilled. Take a few moments to more deeply enjoy this awareness.

Before you leave the stream, take the note out of your pocket, the one with your name on it. Examine this note a second time, and you may find another message written there, one you didn't notice earlier. Perhaps even the handwriting looks familiar now.

Well, it's time to begin your return, so take your time, and let all you've learned stay with you, as you gradually bring your focus back to your physical surroundings.

When you're ready, open your eyes, and feel awake, alert and refreshed.

GUIDED MEDITATION FOR INNER PEACE

Make yourself comfortable, and close your eyes. Inner peace is all about letting go, relaxing, letting go more, and relaxing more. You can do this now.

Take a slow, deep breath, and let go of any tension, as you feel yourself sinking into the surface you're resting on, becoming still more comfortable and relaxed. Take another slow, deep breath, and release your thoughts, letting them drift far away. And take another slow, deep breath, and know that in this moment, all is well.

Notice your connection to the ground, either through the bottom of your feet, or your the bottom of your seat, as you feel the energy of the earth softly flowing into you, supporting you, and grounding you.

And imagine the energy of life is flowing into you through the top of your head, your hands, and your heart, softly and peacefully.

Picture this energy of life as a soft green-colored light, filling your body, mind, and emotions.

Now notice your breathing, and allow it to become deeper, and slower. As you breath in, breath in the word "deep." And as you breathe out, breathe out the word, "peace."

Take a few moments to continue to follow your breath, in, and out, with the words, "deep... peace." If other thoughts come in, simply let them go, and refocus on "deep" and "peace," breathing in, and out. Do this for a time now.

Consider one thing in your life that tends to disturb you, and imagine you are holding that situation gently in your heart, surrounded by the soft green light. Without trying to analyze, change, or control that situation, just hold it softly in your heart, and breath the words, deep, and peace, in and out of that situation.

Very often, the things that disturb us either change, dissolve, or cease to disturb us, if we lighten the way we think about them. So for now, for the sake of your own inner peace, just continue to hold that situation softly in your heart, in the green light, and breath the words "deep" and "peace," in and out. Do this for a time.

Now allow that situation to fade, and focus only on the soft green light, and breathing it in, and out, with the words "deep," and "peace."

It will soon be time to bring this inner journey to a close. So take a moment to thank yourself for giving yourself this gift.

Bring your awareness gently back to your physical surroundings. Take your time, and when you're ready, open your eyes, and feel awake, alert, and refreshed.

STEP INTO SERENITY

Make yourself comfortable, and close your eyes. Take a slow deep breath, and let go of any tension, as you feel yourself sinking into the surface you're resting on, becoming still more comfortable and relaxed. Take another slow, deep breath, and release your thoughts, letting them drift far away. And take another slow, deep breath, and know that in this moment, all is well.

Bring your awareness into your heart, in the center of your chest, and notice a softness there, a feeling of peace. Take a moment to enjoy this feeling, as you quietly focus in your heart, and follow your breath, in, and out.

Bring yourself more fully into your heart, as if you were standing there now, inside a cozy room. And as your eyes adjust, you'll find a doorway, one that seems to be calling you to enter.

As you pass through the door, you find yourself walking alongside a mountain stream, on a crisp fall afternoon. The path you're on is well worn, and has been walked by many before. People often come here to find comfort and peace. And this setting, this stream, and this path have the power to soothe and heal even the most troubled mind.

Let the sound of the stream fill you. It speaks to you in a language your body and mind can hear, and understand. As you listen, it will bring you peace, and healing. Take some time to simply relax, walk along this path, listen, and be restored.

Soon you come to a large, smooth rock, a resting place at the edge of the water. Here you can sit, take off your shoes, and rest your feet in the cool water. As you do, the water begins to turn into silver colored light. Let the light flow up into your feet, into your legs, through your hips and up into your torso, through your shoulders, arms, neck and head, until it's flowing all through you.

Let this silver light clear away any distress, leaving you calm, peaceful, and serene. Take some time with this now.

If there is a situation in your life that causes you great distress, imagine bringing the sound of the mountain stream into that situation, and send forward to yourself in time some of the serenity and peace you're experiencing now. See and feel yourself surrounded and filled with that light, and that deep feeling of peace. Take some time with this, now.

Listen to the following affirmations, and allow them to resonate deep within.

I am letting go of anything that might disturb me, and allowing serenity to come forward into my mind.

Serenity is always available to me, and I am training my mind to easily experience it.

Peace is a natural state of being for me, and I settle down into it easily.

All disturbances are temporary illusions on the surface of my mind, and they sail away as I connect to peace within.

It will soon be time to bring this inner journey to a close. But first, take a moment to thank yourself for giving yourself this gift.

Let all the benefits of this experience stay with you, as you bring your awareness gently back to your physical surroundings.

Take your time, and when you're ready, open your eyes, and feel awake, alert, and refreshed.

RELAX ON A TROPICAL BEACH

Make yourself comfortable, and close your eyes. Take a slow deep breath, and let go of any tension, as you feel yourself sinking into the surface you're resting on, becoming still more comfortable and relaxed. Take another slow, deep breath, and release your thoughts, letting them drift far away. And take another slow, deep breath, and know that in this moment, all is well.

Imagine you're taking a walk along a tropical beach, on a summer day. You're on vacation, and you have all the time in the world. And today, you have the beach all to yourself. There weather is perfect, and as you walk along, you can smell the salt air, and feel the light ocean mist on your face. Perhaps you're walking barefoot, on the packed sand just by the water's edge. And as you walk, you can feel your heels pushing into the sand a little with each step. And now and then the warm water just barely laps up to kiss your feet.

Sandpipers dart here and there, at the edge of the water. And out beyond the breakers, a small flock of pelicans soar just above the water. Take a moment to simply walk along, take in the scenery and the sounds, and enjoy.

Soon you come to an inviting lounge chair that's been set up for you on the sand, and you decide this would be a good time to take a rest. So you settle down and get comfortable, shading your eyes with a nice big straw hat. Now you're completely content to simply lie back, relax, and listen to the sound of the waves.

Your body is loving this restful feeling, and a wonderful wave of deep relaxation begins to gradually make its way all through you. The relaxation moves through your body easily, beginning with your toes, moving up through your feet, and ankles, and into your calves and your knees. And it makes its way up into your upper legs and hips.

Now your legs and hips are completely comfortable, and deeply relaxed. And this wave of peaceful relaxation moves on into your abdomen, and lower back, and your chest and upper back… and they're also feeling completely comfortable, and deeply relaxed. And this wave of peaceful relaxation flow up into your shoulders, and down your arms, into your hands, and out your fingertips. You're feeling wonderfully calm, and settled.

And so this wave of peaceful energy flows up through your neck, throughout your head, and face, and right out the top of your head. Now your whole body is as relaxed, comfortable, and peaceful as it can be.

As you listen to the gentle rhythm of the waves, begin to notice the rhythm of your breath. It's a lot like the ocean; wave after wave, peaceful breath after breath.

Begin to follow your breath a little more closely now, and between each breath, pause just for a moment, to enjoy the feeling. Breathe in, pause just a bit, breathe out, pause just a bit, in the timing that's comfortable for you. This little pause helps you to really savor each breath. Notice how good each breath feels, and how it nourishes you.

Your body loves this peaceful, relaxing rhythm, like the ocean loves the waves, so perfectly natural and satisfying. To enjoy this feeling even more, with each breath in, inwardly say the word, "deep," and with each breath out, inwardly say the word, "peace." If that feels good to you, repeat it for some time, as you lie on your comfy lounge chair on the beach, on this beautiful summer day, and enjoy the peaceful, relaxing comfort. Stay as long as you like.

DOLPHIN DAY

Make yourself comfortable, and close your eyes. Take a slow, deep breath, and let go of any tension, as you feel yourself sinking into the surface you're resting on, becoming still more comfortable and relaxed. Take another slow, deep breath, and release your thoughts, letting them drift far away. And take another slow, deep breath, and know that in this moment, all is well.

Imagine you've come to a secluded beach, early in the morning, and you're sitting barefoot on the sand, with your arms around your knees, watching the sunrise. The rhythmic sounds of the waves and the sea birds soothe and comfort you, and all the sights, sounds, and feelings here convey a deep sense of peace, and harmony with nature.

The ocean mist is cool on your face, and you can smell the salt air, the seaweed, and the clean scent of the sand. It's a magical time, as the sun rises gradually from the sea, changing the sky from dark blue to yellow, rose, and lighter blue above. A line of pelicans takes their first flight across the horizon, as if opening the day for what's to come.

Standing up, you begin walking toward the water, your feet sinking down deeply at first, then less so as you approach the wet packed sand. Here the foam thins out, coming in to cover shells and bits of seaweed, before retreating back into the ocean, only to come forward again. A sandpiper joins this hypnotic dance, running along the edge, finding hidden meals in the sand.

Now you're letting the water softly lap up to your ankles, each time offering a caress, and an invitation to wade in a bit more, as the surf seems to pull you gently forward.

Whatever burdens you may have brought with you today are loosening inside, and as you watch the ocean you feel more and more drawn to its warm support. Soon you find yourself wading in among the gentle waves, as each swell helps you feel more welcome and at home in the water, until you find a comfortable place to float peacefully on your back.

Buoyed by the warm saltwater and caressed by the sun, you feel completely safe, totally free, and ready to let go. Layer upon layer of tension seems to be melting away from your body, dissolving in the sea. Take some time to float, relax, and enjoy this.

Looking around, you see the shore, well within reach, and notice you've got company. A group of dolphins have come to visit, forming a circle around you. The light has changed, and there's a magical glow all around. The energies of the sea, the sun, and your new friends seem to have converged to create this enchanted experience, created just for you. The dolphins are enjoying themselves, and they're celebrating your healing by playing and swimming all around. It feels as if you've left your body, and are pure energy, floating free. Take some time to experience this, and enjoy.

One of the dolphins comes close, inviting you on its back. Say yes, and you'll find yourself speeding happily along, enjoying an exhilarating feeling like flying in a dream. Soon you're flying together through the night sky, high in the heavens. Take some time to go as high as you wish, see whatever's there for you to see, and know whatever is there for you to know.

You find yourself back on the beach now, resting on the sand, watching the waves, and reflecting on your experience. Soon other people begin to come, and before long, you're one among many, each enjoying their own experience of life at the beach. Still, you're glad you took the opportunity to come early, have some time all to yourself, connect within, and heal.

It will soon be time to bring this journey to a close. But first, ask for a sphere of light to be placed all around you, and this experience, so that all the positive benefits will stay with you, and anything that you've released can be left behind.

Take a moment to thank yourself for giving yourself this gift.

Bring your awareness gently back to your physical surroundings. Take your time, and when you're ready, open your eyes, and feel awake, alert, and refreshed.

THE HEALING WELL

Place your body in a comfortable position, and close your eyes. Take a slow, deep breath, and as you release it, feel yourself begin to relax. Take another deep breath, and gradually feel your breathing begin to slow. Your body is relaxing further, and you can feel yourself settle deeper into the surface you're resting on.

As you relax, a feeling of peace and calm makes its way through your body, beginning with your feet, your ankles, and your calves. Tension is leaving, as all the muscles begin to relax.

Allow this relaxation to extend to your knees, your thighs, and your hips.

And feel this relaxation extend into your lower back and abdomen, and into your chest and upper back, as you become still more comfortable and at peace.

Imagine all your internal organs enjoying this good, calm feeling. You're letting every part of you know that this is an opportunity to rest, relax, and heal.

And feel this comfortable, peaceful feeling moving throughout your shoulders, arms, and hands, and let it flow out your fingertips.

Feel your neck relax, and allow this feeling of comfort to move into the back of your head, your ears, all through your face, your forehead, and the top of your head.

Now your entire body is completely comfortable, relaxed, and ready to receive positive energy and healing. You're in a deep state of peaceful relaxation, open to good things, and ready for an adventure.

It's time to gather support for your journey, so inwardly call upon any allies you'd like to have with you, to assist in your healing. These might include spiritual figures, angels, friends, or loved ones. Even animals can be allies on your inner journey. Inwardly ask anyone who's presence gives you strength and support to be with you now in spirit.

And so, as your journey begins, imagine you're walking in a beautiful meadow, on a fine spring morning. The weather is perfect, the sky is blue, with a few fluffy white clouds, and there's just a hint of a breeze. You can smell the subtle scent of wildflowers, and hear a bird's song. The ground feels soft beneath your feet, and your steps are light and easy.

No one else is around this morning, and that feels just fine, because you're enjoying having this day all to yourself. You deserve this, and are appreciating every moment of it.

A little way ahead, there's a pretty garden, and in the center of the garden is a well. As you walk closer, you find that the path to the well is made of brightly colored stones, a rainbow of color unfolding beneath your feet.

At first the stone path is red, and as you step upon the red stones you feel a boost of positive energy moving up through your feet, and all the way through your body.

Walking further, the stones become orange, and as you step forward, you feel a wave of support from your inner allies.

Further along the stones are yellow, and you find your mood brightening, with a sense of optimism, and joy.

As you step upon the green part of the path, you heart softens, as past hurts or hard feelings within you begin to dissolve, and melt away.

As you continue, the path beneath your feet becomes blue, and you find you mind opening, with a pleasant sense of wonder.

As you draw close to the well, the path changes to purple. Your senses heighten, your spirit awakens, and all the cells in your body anticipate receiving something pure, precious, and life-giving.

Coming up to the well, you notice that it is an ancient one, constructed of rocks and mortar. It has a little pitched roof above, and a pulley, a crank, and a wooden bucket. The bucket is attached to a strong rope, and is weighted with stones, so it will sink down into the clear water below.

Since the beginning of time, people have tapped into the earth for pure water. When we drink from such a well, it connects us with the living spirit of the earth. As you realize this, you notice that this well, and indeed the whole garden surrounding it, is filled with the most beautiful golden light imaginable, and you can sense the light touching you with its beauty and grace. Take a moment to experience this, as you receive its blessing.

You will use the crank to gently lower the bucket into the water below. Take a deep breath, and as the bucket descends, feel yourself going deeper within your own heart.

Take another deep breath and let the bucket go deeper. As you exhale, release any remaining cares.

And take another deep breath, and as the bucket finds the water, deep in the well, know that you are connecting deep inside, with the strong, loving being that you truly are.

The bucket fills, and you begin to turn the crank to bring it back up. It's heavier now, but you find it easy to lift, as your body senses that it's about to receive a new level of love and support.

Raise the bucket further up as you experience a feeling of warmth and comfort; a sense that everything is being taken care of, and all is well.

And raise the bucket higher, and feel your heart open to accept healing from deep within, and from the allies who have gathered around you.

Bring the bucket up to the top, set it down carefully, and look at the water. It's clear, and alive, and reflects the sky above. This water comes from the sacred source of all living things, and is charged with pure, loving energy. There is a cup just by your hand. Pick it up and dip into the bucket, making ripples in the reflected sky.

Take a long, slow drink of the cool water. As soon as the water touches your lips, you feel a gentle burst of energy that seems to bring new life all through you. Feel the cool, healing water flowing down your throat. Your body is so open to receive, and all the cells seem to welcome this positive force.

Drink deeply, and notice the energy of this clear water moving throughout your body, going wherever needed. Everywhere within you the effect of this water can be felt, touching the center of every cell, clearing away any negativity or pain, and bringing new life. Take some time to experience this gentle transformation, paying special care to anywhere within you that you feel needs particular attention. Drink all you need.

Stay here a little longer, and feel the golden light that fills the garden touching your skin, warming you, bestowing its gifts. If there's anything you believe you need for your healing, ask for it now, and know that you will receive whatever is for your highest good.

It will soon be time to bring this inner journey to a close. But first, take a moment to thank yourself for giving yourself this gift.

Let all the benefits of this experience stay with you, as you bring your awareness gently back to your physical surroundings.

Take your time, and when you're ready, open your eyes, and feel awake, alert, and refreshed.

PATIENCE

INTRODUCTION

Patience allows us to meet challenges peacefully, get along easily with others, accomplish long term goals, and enjoy life. With patience we can handle bad drivers and computer glitches without tearing out our hair, master a musical instrument, or raise a child with our sanity intact.

In childhood, if we're treated with patience, and raised in an environment where long term effort is modeled, and delayed gratification is valued, we'll tend to learn patience automatically. But most of us also absorb a variety of negative patterns and beliefs that undermine our patience. Some of these include:

- Fear of being punished or criticized for being too slow.
- Fear of being seen as stupid if we spend too much time on something and fail.
- Fear of falling behind in a real or imagined competition.
- Th e belief that "time is money."
- Or any judgment against our self and others about being slow, incompetent, or unintelligent.

As we grow older, these patterns and beliefs contribute to a state of mind in which we constantly pressure ourselves and others to think and move faster, and never allow ourselves to be comfortable with life as it is.

Use the following guided meditation to uncover and release old programming, and bring patience and peace into your most challenging situations, and all of your life. To gain the maximum benefit, you'll want to work with this program on a regular basis over time. To begin, I would recommend using it once a day for at least a week. Then you might begin to listen every other day, and so on. Use your own judgment, be patient, and make it work for you.

GUIDED MEDITATION

Make yourself comfortable, and close your eyes. Take a slow deep breath, and let go of any tension, as you feel yourself sinking into the surface you're resting on, becoming still more comfortable and relaxed. Take another slow, deep breath, and release your thoughts, letting them drift far away. And take another slow, deep breath, and know that in this moment, all is well.

Imagine you're walking in a lovely valley meadow on a beautiful fall day. The sun is warm on your back, and puffy white clouds float by lazily overhead in the soft blue sky. A little stream winds its way into the meadow from the hills nearby, and as you approach the stream, its gentle sounds begin to soothe and comfort you. You can smell the sweet scent of the stream, the grass, and the wildflowers scattered here and there across the meadow. You feel peaceful, and quite at home here, and find a comfortable place to sit by the stream and relax.

A little way upstream is a majestic oak tree in full fall colors, its leaves all shades of yellow, orange, red, and brown. Now and then a gentle breeze rustles the leaves, and sends one drifting down to the water. One by one the leaves float softly toward you on the current, until you can make out their shape and color, and then watch them float on their way downstream, far out of sight.

As you watch, you feel no concern about how long it takes for each leaf to reach you, no pressure over when it will finally pass out of sight. The current carries every one at nature's pace, and you're content to simply relax and watch.

As you continue to enjoy this lovely setting, take some time to reflect on the following question:

What demands do I place on myself and others that interfere with my ability to relax, enjoy the flow of life, and be at peace?

Leaves continue to fall and drift by, now a yellow one, now a red. And the stream continues to offer its music to accompany this play of nature. All is calm.

Consider a situation in your life where you might normally feel pressure or impatience. How could you modify your attitude or behavior to come into greater harmony with this situation? Use your imagination to observe yourself, and adjust your response. Watch as you allow things to unfold at their most natural pace, without any attachment to the speed or result of the outcome. If it's your job to participate in the process, imagine yourself doing so as simply and directly as possible, from a peaceful and neutral state of mind. Take some time to observe yourself as you soften your response, and notice how the results of this change might feel in your body, mind, and emotions.

Take a closer look, down into the water before you. If you concentrate on one spot for a while you'll begin to notice a few oblong shadows near the stream bed. You've spotted some fish, and now you can clearly see them facing upstream, holding in the current, now and then turning off to the side to feed upon something, before they resume their post. These creatures were born here in the water, and live this way. Their only job is to remain steady, wait for food to float by, and catch it as it comes.

Consider something you do that requires you to wait, perhaps for other people to do something, for circumstances to be ripe, or for an inspired idea to occur. Imagine that while waiting, you're able to drop down into a peaceful state of rest and relaxation, where you're perfectly comfortable to simply observe, reflect, and allow life to unfold in it's own timing. Take some time to notice how this peaceful state of mind might effect you, and feel it in your body, mind, and emotions.

Look across the stream to the other side, and you'll see a family of foxes making their way across the meadow, looking for their dinner. Softly and patiently they go, perhaps finding insects, mice, or other food to enjoy. And now and then they stop to play with each other, or look around at the stream or the hills in the distance, taking everything in.

Consider another situation in your life, one that involves a certain level of intensity, concentrated effort, or hard work over an extended period of time. Observe yourself and notice whether you tend to let tension mount to the point where you loose patience. Visualize yourself doing something to break up the tension in that situation, whether that means taking short breaks, switching tasks, using humor, taking slow deep breaths, or just relaxing into the work in some way. Take some time to watch yourself making this adjustment, and notice how it effects the way you feel.

Listen to the following affirmations, and allow them to resonate deeply within. Notice whether any of these affirmations bring up any resistance or discomfort, and if that happens, simply breathe deeply, and relax.

I make inner peace a top priority, and arrange my life accordingly.

I accept and appreciate myself as I am, and enjoy life at my own pace.

I accept others as they are, and allow them to go at their own pace.

When others try my patience, I relax, breath, and become peaceful.

When life tries my patience, I relax, appreciate, and let go. I expect the unexpected, and easily adjust to life as needed.

When tempted to rush, I relax and deepen my experience of each moment.

Time is a gift to be enjoyed, and I relax and enjoy the journey.

It will soon be time to bring this journey to a close. But first, ask for a sphere of light to be placed all around you, and this experience, so that all the positive benefits will stay with you, and anything that you've released can be left behind.

Take a moment to thank yourself for giving yourself this gift.

Bring your awareness gently back to your physical surroundings. Take your time, and when you're ready, open your eyes, and feel awake, alert, and refreshed.

SAY GOODBYE TO WORRY: HOT AIR BALLOON

Make yourself comfortable, and close your eyes. Take a slow deep breath, and let go of any tension, as you feel yourself sinking into the surface you're resting on, becoming still more comfortable and relaxed. Take another slow, deep breath, and release your thoughts, letting them drift far away. And take another slow, deep breath, and know that in this moment, all is well.

Imagine you're walking in a wide open grassy field in the country, just before dawn on a crisp fall morning. It's quiet, and there's some early morning fog rising from the ground. As you walk along, you can feel the uneven ground beneath your feet.

You're carrying a heavy backpack, and it's filled with all the worries that have been weighing on you lately. You could enjoy the morning so much more if you were to put that down, but you just haven't felt ready to do that yet. So you continue walking on, through the field.

Soon you begin to make out some kind of large, round shape coming up out of the fog, a little way ahead. And as you come closer, you see that it's a hot air balloon, just finishing filling up. The basket is tied down with 4 ropes, staked into the ground on all sides. There's a burner above the basket, heating the balloon. And the balloon itself is made of colorful sections of material, arranged in strips, running top to bottom. It's quite a sight to behold.

There's a brass plaque on the side of the basket, and as you take a closer look, you see that it has your name written upon it in ornate, scrolled letters. And printed below your name are the words, "Let the healing begin!" Well, that sounds promising! Now you know where you can put your backpack full of worries.

Better take a last look at them, just to make sure. Pull your heavy backpack off your shoulders, one strap at a time, and put it down. Take each worry out of the backpack, one at a time. What do worries look like? They could look like anything. Some people's look like globs of grey goop. Some look like spiky metal balls. Some peoples' look more like old musty encyclopedia volumes. Take each worry out of your backpack, take a look at it to be sure you know what it is, become certain you'd like to let it go, and toss it into the basket. Take a few moments to do this for each and every worry.

Once you've gotten all the worries out of the backpack, and tossed them into the basket below the balloon, go ahead and toss the backpack in there too. You won't be needing that now.

The basket is filled up, and now the balloon is completely inflated and ready to go. It's pulling hard against the ropes, and looks eager to take off. Look down to your right and you'll see a big knife in a leather sheath. Pick it up, and pull off the sheath. The blade is gleaming stainless steel, and very, very sharp. It's going to feel really good to cut those four ropes with this knife.

Go to the first rope, and cut it with the knife. It cuts like butter, and the balloon shakes a little, leaning a bit to one side. This is good.

Go to the opposite side of the balloon, and cut the rope there. Easy peasy. The balloon wobbles a bit.

Cut the third rope, and the balloon leans toward the side of the last one, straining hard and ready to take off.

You're ready too, to say bye-bye to your worries, and the balloon. Cut that last rope, and the balloon begins to rise.

As the balloon ascends, you begin to feel freer. And as it rises further, ties you may have still had to any worries become thinner. The balloon goes higher, and higher, gets smaller, and smaller till you can barely see it. And now… it's gone. Nothing in the sky but a few puffy white clouds, and a flock of geese, way up there, flying in a "V" formation, migrating toward their winter home.

You're free. Imagine everything ahead of you in your life working out perfectly. Visualize all your affairs going exactly the way you'd like them to go. Be happy, look forward to your life. Put your mind in good order. Take a few moments to do this now.

It's a little later in the morning now, and you walk on through the field to the other side. And as you come to the edge of the field, you notice the scene has changed to a setting somewhere in your every day life, one that is very positive, and enjoyable for you. Put yourself as fully as possible into this positive, happy scene, and take a few moments to enjoy it.

It's almost time to bring this inner journey to a close. But first, take a moment to thank yourself for giving yourself this gift.

Gradually bring your awareness back to your physical surroundings. Take your time, and when you're ready, open your eyes, and feel awake, alert, and refreshed.

PART TWO

WELL MIND & BODY

SLEEP WELL TONIGHT: COTTAGE BY THE SEA

Make yourself comfortable, in your favorite position for falling asleep, and close your eyes. Take a slow, full deep breath, and let it go. It's time to set the world aside, let go of your day, and begin your gentle transition into sleep. And take another slow, full, deep breath, and breathe out any tension in your body. All there is to do now is relax, rest, and be restored.

Imagine you're standing on the shore of a lovely tropical island. It's evening, and the sun is just now setting, and you watch as the orange ball begins to touch the horizon, casting a beautiful golden glow over the sea. The light blue sky is beginning to glow yellow and pink where it meets the ocean, deepening into shades of dark blue and purple, higher up.

A surfer is taking his last ride of the day, and a sentry of pelicans glides softly across the placid scene, heading for a place to rest for the night. Earth is ready to welcome the nighttime, and the sky has begun to draw its curtain on another day.

Your favorite spot, a little ways down the beach, is a little hideaway cottage with a screened in porch, where you can lie on a comfy bed, listen to the waves, and let the sounds rock you gently to sleep. And so you begin your walk home. Barefoot at the edge of the warm, tropical water, you love the way your heels sink in a little with each step. It's a wonderful rocking motion that seems to go so well with the way the water thins out onto the sand, and then recedes, and then returns to wash your feet with it's salty foam.

The ocean air feels so pleasant on your skin, and the smells of the ocean and the scents of the blossoming trees nearby are softly intoxicating, beginning to make you a little drowsy. Soon you come to your cottage, open the screen door, and sit on the edge of the bed looking out at the sea and the sky.

The first stars have begun to come out, and you take some time to just sit there, and watch them appear, one by one, as last light of day fades, and the sky darkens to a deep velvet. Perhaps you can see the sliver of the new moon, set just so, not far above the horizon.

You're in bed now, feeling your body relax from the day. Beginning with your feet, allow all the tension to go out of them now. They've worked hard for you all day, and deserve a rest.

And so the relaxation in your feet begins to find its way into your ankles, your calves, and your knees. And now relax your upper legs, your hips, and your buttocks. And feel this relaxation flowing up into your abdomen and lower back, and your upper back and chest. And feel this peaceful, relaxing feeling flowing down your arms, into your hands, and out your fingertips. And then up into your neck, head and face.

Now your whole body is perfectly calm, relaxed, and ready for sleep. And just to make sure there's nothing left between you and a gentle full night's rest, imagine that the very top of your head opens, and out float any thoughts that might still be trapped inside, to find their way into the beautiful, starry night sky, far above the sea, and drift out of sight.

Now you're all clear. Don't forget to close the top of your head!

Soon you'll be sound asleep, off on a peaceful journey into dreamland that will carry you all the way through until morning.

So as you continue to listen to the waves outside, begin to follow your breath, and intone the words, "soft... sleep... deep... peace... soft... sleep... deep... peace... soft... sleep... deep... peace..."

Have a wonderful soft sleep, deep, and peaceful...

SLEEP WELL TONIGHT: OVERNIGHT TRAIN

Make yourself comfortable, in your favorite position for falling asleep, and close your eyes. Take a slow, full deep breath, and let it go. It's time to set the world aside, let go of your day, and begin your gentle transition into sleep. And take another slow, full, deep breath, and breathe out any tension. All there is to do now is relax, rest, and be restored.

Imagine you're walking down a country lane, toward a little train depot, where you'll be boarding an overnight train. It's a crisp fall evening, and as you walk along, you feel the pavement beneath your feet, breathe in the cool autumn air, and take in the trees along the lane, their leaves turning all shades of gold, orange, and brown. It rained a little while ago, and you can smell the damp earth, and feel the moisture in the air, gently caressing your face.

And as you make your way along the lane, all the events of the day seem to release their hold, as you look forward to your gentle nighttime ride.

Soon you turn a corner, and see the station up ahead. It's an old building, painted dark green and blue, with a row of old fashioned lamp lights in front, a curved archway at the entrance, and a sign overhead that says "Train Depot" in beautiful gold lettering. The sidewalk in front is still a bit wet from the rain, and as you walk in, it glistens a little, softly reflecting the lights above.

Inside the depot are ornately carved old wooden benches in the waiting area, and on one wall, a ticket window. An old man behind the window is reading a newspaper, and when you come up to the window, he puts down his paper, smiles, and greets you by name. You hand him one dollar, and he hands you a ticket.

And so you take your ticket and go out the back door toward the tracks, just as your train is pulling in. It's an old one, but very clean and lovingly cared for. And as the train comes to a stop, the conductor steps out, greets you kindly by name, takes your ticket, and wishes you a good night. You nod to him, and climb aboard.

It's only a little way through the corridor to your sleeping compartment, so you walk down, open the door, and settle in. Your bed is waiting for you, and you sit down on the edge, and get comfortable. Everything you need is right here, so you lay down under the covers, just as the train begins moving. Now you can feel the gentle motion of the car, and hear the click of the wheels along the track.

Outside, your train is passing through open fields and wooded areas, alongside rivers, and past beautiful mountain landscapes off in the distance, all cloaked in darkness, and covered by a twinkling night sky. But here inside, you're cozy, and comfy, with nothing to do but drift off into dreamland.

So feel your body begin to relax. Starting with your feet, allow all the tension to leave them. They've worked hard for you today, and deserve a rest.

And so the relaxation in your feet finds its way into your ankles, your calves, and your knees. And now relax your upper legs, your hips, and your buttocks. And feel this relaxation flowing up into your abdomen and lower back, and your upper back and chest. And feel this peaceful, relaxing feeling flowing down your arms, into your hands, and out your fingertips. And then up into your neck, head and face.

Now your whole body is perfectly calm, relaxed, and ready for sleep. And just to make sure there's nothing left between you and a gentle full night's rest, imagine that the very top of your head opens, and out float

any thoughts that might still be trapped inside, to find their way out of the train and into the beautiful, starry night sky, where they drift out of sight.

Now you're all clear. Don't forget to close the top of your head!

Soon you'll be sound asleep, off on a peaceful journey into dreamland that will carry you all the way through the night. So as you continue to feel the gentle motion of the train, and hear the click of the wheels along the tracks, begin to follow your breath, and inwardly repeat the words "soft... sleep... deep... peace... soft... sleep... deep... peace... soft... sleep... deep... peace..."

Have a wonderful restful sleep, deep, and peaceful...

SLEEP WELL TONIGHT: UNDER THE STARS BY A MOUNTAIN STREAM

Make yourself comfortable, in your favorite position for falling asleep, and close your eyes. Take a slow, full deep breath, and let it go. It's time to set the world aside, let go of your day, and begin your gentle transition into sleep. And take another slow, full, deep breath, and breathe out any tension. All there is to do now is relax, rest, and be restored.

Imagine you're walking along a path by a mountain stream on a crisp fall afternoon. And as you walk along, you can feel the ground beneath your feet, and hear the gentle sound of the water, changing its song as you go further upstream. Where the water is shallow, and rushes over rocks, it's bright and bubbly. And where the stream is wider, and the water deeper, it becomes tranquil, and calm.

You can smell the scent of pine, and the sweet fragrance of the plants by the water's edge. Looking into the stream you can see a few small trout waiting for food in the current, or darting here and there.

In a shallow pool, a pretty stone catches your eye, reflecting the late afternoon sun through the water, and you reach into the water, to pick it up. Examining it more closely you see finely webbed patterns etched into its flat oval surface, and you consider whether it might be a fossil of some kind: evidence of life lived here ages ago. You put the stone in your pocket, and walk on.

Soon your path widens out onto a meadow by the stream, and you find your campsite waiting for you. It's a place you've visited many times before, to find peace, and quiet. And you always feel totally safe, comfortable and at home here.

There's a log fire surrounded by stones waiting for you, burning softly. And nearby is a soft bed of pine needles, the perfect place to unroll your sleeping bag.

It's starting to get late, and the sun has gone down, and the first stars have already begun to come out. And you're quite tired from your long hike today. So you sit down on your bed, and take in the deep feeling of peace that's here for you. Perhaps you take that stone out of your pocket, and look at it again in the firelight, admiring the patterns on its surface, as you get a bit more drowsy.

It's getting hard to keep your eyes open, so you climb into your sleeping bag, and settle into your comfy bed.

The stars have all come out now, and you can see the Milky Way painting the dark night sky. More stars than you could ever count. And just as you're closing your eyes, a bright shooting star crosses the sky above you, signaling the perfect end to your day.

It's time to go to sleep now, so feel your body begin to relax. Starting with your feet, allow all the tension to leave them. They've worked hard for you today, and deserve a rest.

And so the relaxation in your feet finds its way into your ankles, your calves, and your knees. And now relax your upper legs, your hips, and your buttocks. And feel this relaxation flowing up into your abdomen and lower back, and your upper back and chest. And feel this peaceful, relaxing feeling flowing down your arms, into your hands, and out your fingertips. And then up into your neck, head and face.

Now your whole body is perfectly calm, relaxed, and ready for sleep. And just to make sure there's nothing left between you and a gentle full night's rest, imagine that the very top of your head opens, and out float

any thoughts that might still be trapped inside, to find their way into the beautiful, starry night sky, where they drift out of sight.

Now you're all clear. Don't forget to close the top of your head!

Soon you'll be sound asleep, off on a peaceful journey into dreamland that will carry you all the way through the night. So you begin to follow your breath, and inwardly repeat the words "soft... sleep... deep... peace... soft... sleep... deep... peace... soft... sleep... deep... peace..."

Have a wonderful restful sleep, deep, and peaceful...

SLEEP WELL TONIGHT: COMFY OLD FARMHOUSE

Make yourself comfortable, in your favorite position for falling asleep, and close your eyes. Take a slow, full deep breath, and let it go. It's time to set the world aside, let go of your day, and begin your gentle transition into sleep. And take another slow, full, deep breath, and breathe out any tension. All there is to do now is relax, rest, and be restored.

Imagine you're walking along a country lane, late in the afternoon on a warm summer day. There are tall old trees lining the lane, and just beyond the trees are rolling fields of green grass and wildflowers. You can smell the delicate scent of flowers in the air, and hear a meadowlark calling in the distance. And just ahead, a pair of deer are crossing the lane, to the field on the other side.

As you come around a bend in the road, you approach the entrance of what used to be an old farm property, now a sanctuary for travelers like yourself. Turning in, you walk down the dirt driveway toward the house. There's no longer much farming going on here, but there's still a red barn standing off to one side, with its wide wooden doors open, an old windmill turning slowly, and a corral with a few horses, eating their evening hay. One of them looks up at you, twitches his ear, and then goes back to dinner.

The house is stone and wood, with green shutters on either side of the widows, and a wide front porch, with a comfy looking swing. An old dog is sleeping contentedly on the porch, and as you approach, he wags his tail once, but doesn't bother to get up. So you climb the porch steps, have a seat on the swing, and rest for a few minutes, to watch the sunset. Soon an orange tabby cat comes along, jumps up in your lap, and falls asleep, purring.

As the sun sets, and evening draws on, crickets begin chirping, and the air turns cooler. It's time to go inside, and get some sleep. The house is all yours tonight, and walking in, you find it's simply furnished, warm, and clean, with a sitting room off to one side, with soft couches and comfy chairs. There are braided rugs on polished wood floors, and a staircase with a wooden banister. You're quite tired now, so you climb the stairs, and find your room.

Your bedroom is simple and clean, with ivory colored walls, a soft tapestry, lacy curtains on the windows, and a polished wood floor. And there's a beautiful country quilt on the bed. The window is open a bit, and you can still hear the evening crickets, chirping in their soft rhythm.

Everything you need is here, and your favorite sleeping garments are already laid out for you. Sitting on the edge of the bed, you find it's really very comfortable. And so you get ready for bed, and lay down under the covers, as the last light of day fades. All is quiet and peaceful, and you're ready for a good night's sleep.

So feel your body begin to relax. Starting with your feet, allow all the tension to leave them. They've worked hard for you today, and deserve a rest.

And so the relaxation in your feet finds its way into your ankles, your calves, and your knees. And now relax your upper legs, your hips, and your buttocks. And feel this relaxation flowing up into your abdomen and lower back, and your upper back and chest. And feel this peaceful, relaxing feeling flowing down your arms, into your hands, and out your fingertips. And then up into your neck, head and face.

Now your whole body is perfectly calm, relaxed, and ready for sleep. And just to make sure there's nothing left between you and a gentle full night's rest, imagine that the very top of your head opens, and out float

any thoughts that might still be trapped inside, to find their way out of the house and into the beautiful, starry night sky, where they drift out of sight.

Now you're all clear. Don't forget to close the top of your head!

Soon you'll be sound asleep, off on a peaceful journey into dreamland that will carry you all the way through the night. So you begin to follow your breath, and inwardly repeat the words "soft... sleep... deep... peace... soft... sleep... deep... peace... soft... sleep... deep... peace..."

Have a wonderful restful sleep, deep, and peaceful...

RELEASING PAIN

Make yourself comfortable, and close your eyes. Take a slow deep breath, and let go of any tension, as you feel yourself sinking into the surface you're resting on, becoming still more comfortable and relaxed. Take another slow, deep breath, and release your thoughts, letting them drift far away. And take another slow, deep breath, and know that in this moment, all is well.

Imagine that within you is a control room, a place free of distractions, and filled with healing energy, where you can easily focus your thoughts, and influence your body's responses very efficiently, and effectively. And imagine you're about to walk up a flight of stairs, toward your control room now.

The first step is a brilliant ruby red color, and as you step upon it you feel yourself flooded with powerful, bright energies, bringing you a burst a strength to propel you forward.

Your second step is orange, and as the orange color flows through your body it helps you feel grounded and safe, with strong, sustaining support.

The third step is bright yellow, and as you step upon it, you become filled with joy and optimism, a sense that anything is possible, and you can succeed at whatever you put your mind to.

The fourth step is emerald green, and as you step upon it you're filled with a feeling of deep peace, balance, and an inner knowing that all is unfolding perfectly, just as it should.

The sixth step is a clear, bright blue, and as it flows through you it brings mental clarity and focus, and the feeling that you can know whatever you need to know.

Nearing the top of the staircase, you step upon the seventh step, a rich amethyst purple. As you become flooded with this color you can feel your higher mind open, and sense your connection with all the positive forces of the universe, and beyond.

Stepping forward onto the landing, you'll find yourself in a beautiful, dome shaped room, filled with golden white light, and delicate soft energy that seems to envelope and embrace you. This is your control room, a space designed to help you connect with all that is good, and create deep and lasting positive changes within you. The work you're about to do here will help you move through the world with more ease and comfort, and enjoy your life more fully.

There's a comfortable chair in your control room, and you know you've got a lot to do today, so you take a seat.

To begin, do a quick inner scan of your body, and notice the part that's highlighting, for you to release pain. That's where you'll be focusing today.

Imagine that the pain you experience wants to better reveal its identity to you, and is beginning to take on its own three dimensional appearance. Notice or imagine its size and shape. Imagine its color. Imagine the texture of its surface. If you were to touch it, would it feel solid, squishy, spongy, crinkly, or another way? And if it were to make a sound, what would it sound like?

We can assume that your pain exists for a reason, but the reason might not be what you think it is. Although it may be connected to something going on physically in your body, it might also be connected to something going on mentally, emotionally, in relationship to other people, or about some other aspect of your life.

First, ask your pain what it's been trying to tell you about your physical body, perhaps about something you've been doing or not doing, eating or not eating, and so on. Take a moment to listen carefully to what your pain has to say.

Now ask your pain what it's been trying to tell you about your feelings and emotions, and if anything's been bothering you that you might need to clear up.

Ask your pain if there's anything else it's been trying to tell you, that it thinks you need to know.

Now, ask your pain what you might need to do or change, in order for it to not need to get your attention so much. Take some time to receive this important information, and be very clear about any steps you'll be taking to make a change.

Imagine you are taking all the information you've just received, and placing it on one sheet of paper, entitled, *Information From My Pain*. Now imagine you're rolling that paper up, and placing it in a chute in the wall of your control room. There is a button next to the chute. Once you press that button, the paper, with all the information on it, will be sent up the chute, and filed away in your system, so you can access it again whenever you need to. Press the button now. The paper flies up the chute with a whoosh, and the information has been filed.

You've now received all the information your pain had to give you, filed it away, and are prepared to make any changes you need to make. So, your pain won't be needed nearly as much from now on. It's time to clear it out of your body, now.

Imagine that the clear, golden white light from your control room is beginning to shine on your pain. Soon your pain begins to change color, and take on that golden white hue, and before long, it begins to shrink, growing smaller and smaller. Take some time to watch, as the golden white light continues to shine on your pain, until it's so small you can hardly see it.

Now a gentle, rainbow-colored healing rain begins to fall on the area where your pain has been, dissolving and washing away any residue. Take some time to experience this gentle, healing rain as it clears and releases any remaining pain from your body, now.

From now on, any time you begin to experience pain, simply take a moment to listen to any message your pain may have for you, and then imagine that gentle, rainbow colored healing rain dissolving, clearing, and releasing the pain from your body.

It will soon be time to bring this journey to a close. But first, ask for a sphere of light to be placed all around you, and this experience, so that all the positive benefits will stay with you, and anything that you've released can be left behind.

Take a moment to thank yourself for giving yourself this gift.

Bring your awareness gently back to your physical surroundings. Take your time, and when you're ready, open your eyes, and feel awake, alert, and refreshed.

LOWER YOUR BLOOD PRESSURE

CAUTION

High blood pressure is a serious health issue. Follow your doctor's advice regarding medication, diet, and exercise, and monitor your blood pressure regularly.

Use this program as a supplement to your doctor's care. Individual results vary. Listen once or twice a day, and look for results after a few weeks. Then continue to monitor your blood pressure over time to keep tabs on how you're doing.

Blood pressure responds naturally to heart rate and breathing. As a general principal, as you slow down your breathing, your heart responds, as does your blood pressure. This program combines deep relaxation with a simple breathing exercise to help your body slow down, relax, and come into balance.

MEDITATION

Make yourself comfortable, and close your eyes. Take a slow deep breath, and let go of any tension, as you feel yourself sinking into the surface you're resting on, becoming still more comfortable and relaxed. Take another slow, deep breath, and release your thoughts, letting them drift far away. And take another slow, deep breath, and know that in this moment, all is well.

Imagine that all of the energy you've sent out into the world lately is coming gently back home to you, helping you feel more whole, and complete. Quietly receive this energy, and know there's nothing else you need to do right now. You can simply be here, relax, and receive.

Imagine you're in a grassy park, on a warm spring day. It's quiet, and the only sounds you hear are a songbird or two, the gentle rustle of the leaves in the trees nearby, and perhaps far in the distance, some children playing. The sky is bright blue, with a few puffy white clouds drifting slowly overhead. And you're walking casually along, enjoying the peace and beauty of this place.

Before long, you come to the top of a long, sloping hill. Gazing far down the hill, you notice an inviting shady spot at the bottom, and feel drawn there. So you decide to take a relaxing walk down toward it.

And as you walk down the hill a little way, you notice that you feel a little more relaxed and at peace than before. Continuing on down the hill, the further you go, the lighter you feel inside. And as you make your way down further, you become even calmer, happier, and lighter still. And by the time you get to the bottom of the hill, you feel completely carefree, and ready to bring healing into your body and mind.

There in that shady spot at the bottom, you find an inviting hammock stretched between two old trees, and you easily climb in and lie down. Ah… that's more like it. This is a great place to just rest, and relax.

Begin to follow your breath, as if each breath were an ocean wave coming into shore, and then going back out. Simply enjoy the gentle rhythm of your breathing for a few moments.

As you follow your breath, enjoying its rhythm, your breathing gradually begins to slow down. Continue to follow your breath for a while, and each time you breathe in inwardly say the word "slow," and each time you breathe out inwardly say the word, "even." Do this for a time now.

Continue to follow your breath, and now, each time you breathe in, inwardly say the word "lower," and each time you breathe out, inwardly say the word, "slower." Do this for a time now.

Listen to the following affirmations, and allow them to resonate deep within.

I am adjusting my habits and lifestyle to support healthy blood pressure.

I practice this simple breathing relaxation every day, and become peaceful.

I am learning to respond to life calmly and evenly.

I enjoy eating foods that support healthy blood pressure, and easily avoid food that doesn't serve me.

I make exercise that's right for me a regular part of my routine.

Health and wellbeing is a priority for me, and I easily make changes that support myself.

I have a life worth living, and a body worth taking good care of, and I appreciate everything.

Once again, follow your breath, and each time you breathe in inwardly say the word "slow," and each time you breathe out inwardly say the word, "even." Do this for a time now.

Continue to follow your breath, and each time you breathe in, inwardly say the word "lower," and each time you breathe out, inwardly say the word, "slower." Do this for a time now.

It will soon be time to bring this inner journey to a close. But first, take a moment to thank yourself, for giving yourself this opportunity to relax, and heal within.

Gradually bring your awareness gently back to your physical surroundings.

Take your time, and when you're ready, open your eyes, and feel awake, alert and refreshed.

HEAL YOUR BODY IMAGE

INTRODUCTION

A physical body is our very first possession here on Earth; some call it our "Earth Suit." Before we have clothes, a car, a house, a mate, or a dog, we have a body. As we grow and become conscious of ourselves, we look at our own body and instinctively compare it to other bodies, to help us define who we are, and understand how we fit into the world.

When we compare ourselves to others whom we admire, in some cases we can use the information to inspire ourselves to strive for improvement. But as often as not, when we compare, we feel "less than," and fall into disappointment and self-judgment.

Self-judgment sets up a negative energy within us that can lead to depression, and attract all sorts of other negative energies, situations, and people. And ironically, self-judgment can lock in the very thing we're unhappy about, making it harder to change.

In the cases where genetics and circumstance have dictated how our bodies must be, we need to let go of judgment and come to accept and appreciate our bodies as they are. This is a necessary step toward happiness and inner peace. And in cases where we may have the potential to change our bodies—for example by adopting healthier eating and exercise habits—letting go of judgment and coming into acceptance allows us to change more easily.

If you are interested in improving your health, recovering from illness, loosing weight, or becoming more fit, never underestimate the importance of your body image—the way you see yourself and your attitude about how you appear. And if you happen to be struggling with an eating disorder, you'll want to pay especially careful attention to this issue.

Use the following guided meditation to release self-judgment and negativity, and make peace with your own body image. Acceptance is always the first step toward change.

MEDITATION

Make yourself comfortable, and close your eyes. Take a slow deep breath, and let go of any tension in your body, as you feel yourself sinking into the surface you're resting on, becoming still more comfortable and relaxed. Take another slow, deep breath, and feel a sense of calm and peace begin to fill you, as you relax further. And take another slow, deep breath, and let your thinking begin wind down and smooth out.

Imagine you've been sleeping a deep, sound sleep for many hours, and you're just beginning to stir awake. And the first thing you notice, is that you're waking up on a soft bed of pine needles, on the ground, surrounded by ancient fir trees. It's just before dawn, and the air is quite cool, the light is dim, and there's a foggy mist in the air. You can smell the scent of pine, and the damp coolness of the earth. It's quiet, and any sound is blanketed by the mist. Everything is a palette of soft greens, browns, and grays.

Standing up, you begin to walk along a path through the trees, and you can feel the spongy ground beneath your feet. Perhaps you still feel a bit foggy from your sleep, but soon you come to a little spring, cup your hands to get a drink, and splash some of the cool, clear water on your face. Now you're beginning to wake up a bit, and see the trees and plants that surround you more clearly.

As you continue along this path, you feel embraced and comforted by the forest, and encouraged that today you can let go of the past, see yourself more clearly, and begin to move forward with your life.

Walking further, you begin to feel ready to release artificial ideas about beauty, and discover what is truly beautiful about yourself. It's time to stop judging yourself, and gain true perspective, and this feels like the place to do just that.

Soon your path leads to a clearing, a grassy meadow, with a small rustic wooden building in the center, surrounded by wildflowers. Taking off your shoes, you walk easily across the grass, still wet with the morning dew, and feel a clearing and cleansing sensation move up from your feet, all through your body. It's time to make a shift, and you're ready.

Coming up to the little building, you open the door, step through the entryway, and find yourself in a simple room, paneled in rosy colored oak, furnished only with a three sided full length mirror, and a comfortable chair. There's a warm, welcoming feeling here, and it makes you feel very safe, relaxed, and quite at home.

Certain that you are alone, you remove all of your clothing, and place it on the chair. Soon you find yourself standing naked in front of the mirror, able to see your body reflected quite clearly on all sides. Take a full, deep breath, and release it, as you slowly turn in front of the mirror, and look.

As you take in your image, you view your body, perhaps for the first time, with objectivity and neutrality. This is your body, as it is today. It's neither right nor wrong. It simply is. No matter how it may appear, it is in fact a miracle of nature. Just for now, forget about how you're supposed to look, and don't think about your shape as wrong in any way. Take in your image, and simply say to yourself:

This is my body, it's neither good or bad, it's OK just as it is, and I'm OK, just as I am.

Take some time to set aside any judgment, view your image with neutrality, and allow that message to sink in.

As you continue to view your image, consider all the times you may have thought badly of your body, been disappointed by it, or told yourself you were not good enough. Imagine a column of light descending from the highest heavens, straight through this room, through you, and deep into the earth. And feel all the accumulated negativity you've held against yourself begin to dissolve and release into this light. Take some time to experience this, as you release the past, and accept your body, just as it is.

Take a while longer here, as you begin to view yourself and your body with appreciation and compassion. It's not easy being here on Earth. Life presents many, many challenges, and you've always done the best you could, given your circumstances and what you've had to work with at the time. Can you find tenderness toward yourself now, for the person you are? If this is difficult, imagine that standing just behind you is someone who you know to be full of care, compassion and love for others, and for you. This could be someone you know personally, a friend, spiritual figure, angel, or even an historical figure. As you look in the mirror, see and feel that person standing behind you, pouring love, appreciation, and compassion into you, and receive it now.

There's still more for you here, so have a seat in the chair, perhaps first putting your clothing back on if you wish.

Your body has an extraordinary intelligence all its own, and if you listen to it in a spirit of cooperation, it will tell you how to best work with it, to help you be healthy and enjoy life as fully as possible. You may have an interest in changing your body in some way, perhaps in terms of your weight, your appearance, your health, and so on. Some things may be very possible to change, and other things may be more difficult. But you will gain the most benefit by changing your body in a gentle, respectful, and cooperative way.

Take some time to communicate directly with your body now. Ask it any questions you may have about how to change, and listen carefully. Allow your body to tell you what it needs, and the best way to work with it. Be open to hearing whatever it may have to say about your desire to change, as well as any suggestions it may have for you. It may communicate to you inwardly with words, images, sounds, or feelings.

Listen, look, feel, and know.

Listen to the following affirmations, and allow them to resonate deeply within.

I love and appreciate my body, just as it is.

My body is my most valuable and precious possession, and deserves my appreciation and respect.

My body is my operating vehicle here on Earth, and makes my time here possible.

My body allows me to experience pleasure and enjoy life, and I am grateful for it.

My body is uniquely beautiful.

I accept my body as is, and leave self-judgment behind.

I listen to my body, respect its wisdom, and cooperate with it.

I am gentle and patient with my body, and enjoy healthy, gradual change.

I let go of things I can not change about my body, and patiently work on those things I can.

I am becoming comfortable and happy in my own skin.

It's almost time to bring this inner journey to a close. But first, take a moment to thank your body for being with you all these years, and for being your faithful servant and vehicle, here on Earth.

Gradually bring your awareness back into your body, and your physical surroundings.

Take your time, and when you're ready, open your eyes, and feel awake, alert, and refreshed.

WEIGHT LOSS: TRANSFORM FROM WITHIN

INTRODUCTION

The many small choices we make every day determine our future. This program is about helping you connect inside to the place where good decisions and positive choices are made; small choices that over time produce big results.

Because we're separated from consequences by time, it's easy to delude ourselves into thinking what we eat in this moment isn't so important. We think, "Enjoy this now, and the future will take care of itself." Denial comes easily when faced with immediate gratification, so we continue eat the wrong foods, or eat too much, often immediately followed by feelings of shame, failure, and frustration.

Fortunately, we're each equipped with powerful inner resources that can be drawn upon to overcome difficult habits. Using the following guided meditation, you'll learn to tap those resources, override negative eating habits and establish new, healthy ones. When we change from the inside out, we have a much greater chance of success, and that's what makes this program so effective.

This guided meditation is about learning to become more fully present whenever food choices are being made. Bringing more awareness to eating is not really hard to do. It just takes a little effort at the times we'd normally be on autopilot. By working with this guided meditation, you'll cultivate the habit of conscious, healthy eating. Then you'll be able to enjoy the results you're looking for; more good quality, steady energy, and a slimmer, healthier body.

Listen to the guided meditation at least once a day for a full week or more, to help establish your positive eating habits while you transform from within. Use the meditation less frequently only once your new eating habits are well established. At various points in the meditation you'll be asked to envision certain things. Bring your energy into the program by making those things as real within you as possible.

MEDITATION

Make yourself comfortable, and close your eyes. Take a slow deep breath, and let go of any tension in your body, as you feel yourself sinking into the surface you're resting on, becoming still more comfortable and relaxed. Take another slow, deep breath, and feel a sense of calm and peace begin to fill you, as you relax further. And take another slow, deep breath, and let your thinking begin wind down and smooth out, as you become still comfortable, and relaxed.

Imagine you've been sleeping a deep, sound sleep for many hours, and you're just beginning to stir awake. And the first thing you notice, is that you're waking up on a soft bed of pine needles, on the ground, surrounded by ancient fir trees. It's just before dawn, and the air is quite cool, the light is dim, and there's a foggy mist in the air. You can smell the scent of pine, and the damp coolness of the earth. It's quiet, and any sound is blanketed by the mist. Everything is a palette of soft greens, browns, and grays.

Standing up, you begin to walk along a path through the trees, and you can feel the spongy ground beneath your feet. Perhaps you still feel a bit foggy from your sleep, but soon you come to a little spring, cup your hands to get a drink, and splash some of the cool, clear water on your face. Now you're beginning to wake up a bit, and see the trees and plants that surround you more clearly.

Walking further along, you come to a small wooden building, beautifully set into a little hillside in the forest, surrounded by wildflowers. There's a little sign on the door, and looking more closely, you see that the sign has your name written upon it in a beautiful script, followed by the words, *Transforming from Within*.

Open the door, and step inside, and you'll find yourself in a small movie theater for an audience of one, with a comfortable chair, thick carpet, sloping walls with speakers set into them and a sleek movie screen at the front. Have a seat in the chair and make yourself at home, as the house lights dim, and the screen fills with your name, and just below it, the words, *Transforming From Within*.

Consider something about yourself that you value and appreciate, and as you do, you'll see that the screen before you begins forming an image that represents it. Get more fully in touch with that aspect of yourself now, and get a strong sense of how it feels, as you see it represented on the screen as completely as possible. And as your connection to this feeling and this image reaches its peak, the screen changes to display one word: *Choices*.

Your life is precious, and you are entirely worth being supported and sustained, from the inside out, and the outside in. And so there is a need for the many small choices you make from now on to come into alignment with supporting and sustaining your life, your health, and your happiness.

The word "Choices" fades, and the screen displays a table laden with all the foods you currently eat. Some may be good for you, but others are contributing to poor health, extra weight, and emotional instability.

Now the picture changes to display only those foods that are not good for you. In general, those would include highly processed foods and beverages, things made with sugar or artificial sweeteners, deep fried and fatty foods, refined starches like white bread, and anything you know you're allergic or sensitive to. Take a moment to notice how your body feels as you look at those foods. Eating them may give you a temporary lift, but in the long run they make you feel heavy, tired, and depressed, and may eventually contribute to serious illness.

Now the screen changes to display foods that are good for you. In general, those include fresh fruits, fresh vegetables both raw and lightly cooked, water and fresh juices, whole grains and vegetable proteins like legumes and tofu, healthy animal proteins like chicken, eggs, fish, and lean cuts of beef, and certain dairy products like low fat yogurt and cottage cheese.

Consider how your body would feel with this as your day to day way of eating. Over time, you'd loose your craving for unhealthy fatty, sugary foods, and come to only desire this clean, healthy way of eating. You'd have more sustained, even energy, you'd feel lighter, you'd be happier, and you'd live a longer, healthier life. Take a moment to imagine this, see the image on the screen, and feel what that might be like.

Listen to the following affirmation, as you watch the words fill the screen:

By eating a clean, healthy diet, I treat myself very, very well.

Listen to that affirmation again, and let it resonate deeply within you.

By eating a clean, healthy diet, I treat myself very, very well.

And listen to that affirmation once more, and feel it connect to the place deep inside, where your many small choices come from every day.

By eating a clean, healthy diet, I treat myself very, very well.

Now see yourself on screen sitting down to a meal with the amount of food on your plate you'd normally eat. Look at a close-up of your plate. This is the volume of food your stomach is used to receiving, and it feels normal. But your stomach is able to stretch, and it's able to shrink. If you were to begin eating a little less, in a short period of time your stomach would adjust, and that amount would feel normal. Your body would have less work to do with less food to process, so you'd have more energy.

Imagine the amount of food on your plate shrinking to something a bit smaller than what you've been used to. Look at that amount of food, and listen to the following affirmation:

It feels more natural for me to eat less, and I'm more comfortable with smaller meals.

Listen to that affirmation again, as you watch it fill the screen, and resonate deeply within you.

It feels more natural for me to eat less, and I'm more comfortable with smaller meals.

And listen to that affirmation once more, and feel it connect to the place deep inside, where your many small choices come from every day.

It feels more natural for me to eat less, and I'm more comfortable with smaller meals.

Now the screen shows you going about your day, and focus on a time within an hour or so before you'd normally have something to eat. Notice yourself experiencing hunger, your body's natural urge to eat, and watch your emotional reaction to that physical urge. Do you become agitated, excited, or notice a slight sense of panic coming on? Connecting anxiety to hunger often stems from early childhood, and if that's a habit you have, you can let it go now. Take a moment to watch yourself waiting longer before you eat, and letting your hunger build.

Listen to the following affirmation:

It's healthy to be hungry for a before I eat, and it feels OK to wait a while.

Listen to that affirmation again, as you watch it fill the screen, and resonate deeply within you.

It's healthy to be hungry for a before I eat, and it feels OK to wait a while.

And listen to that affirmation once more, and feel it connect to the place deep inside, where your many small choices come from every day.

It's healthy to be hungry for a before I eat, and it feels good to wait a while.

The screen changes again, and you observe yourself facing the opportunity to eat something you know isn't good for you. Perhaps it's sweets, or empty calorie snack food, or something you're allergic to.

Instead, take a moment to watch yourself avoid the bad food, and reach for a healthy replacement, or wait for your next meal.

Listen to the following affirmation:

Since eating bad food leads to unhappiness, it feels better to avoid it and be healthy, as I truly deserve.

Listen to that affirmation again, as you watch it fill the screen, and resonate deeply within you.

Since eating bad food leads to unhappiness, it feels better to avoid it and be healthy, as I truly deserve.

And listen to that affirmation once more, and feel it connect to the place deep inside, where your many small choices come from every day.

Since eating bad food leads to unhappiness, it feels better to avoid it and be healthy, as I truly deserve.

The scene changes once more, and you see yourself, the way your body would look in six months, if you made positive choices 95% of the time you eat. Take a moment to see yourself, not as an unrealistic superstar image, but a healthier, more fit version of where you are now.

Notice that you'd feel lighter, happier, and younger, and have more energy. Joy would come more naturally, and you'd naturally want to exercise more.

Listen to the following affirmation:

When it comes to eating, I make grounded, healthy choices that support my happiness and wellbeing.

Listen to that affirmation again, as you watch it fill the screen, and resonate deeply within you.

When it comes to eating, I make grounded, healthy choices that support my happiness and wellbeing.

And listen to that affirmation once more, and feel it connect to the place deep inside, where your many small choices come from every day.

When it comes to eating, I make grounded, healthy choices that support my happiness and wellbeing.

The picture on the screen fades, and in its place once again are your name, and just below it, the words, *Transforming From Within*. Your life is precious, and you are entirely worth being supported and sustained, from the inside out, and the outside in. All the many small choices you make from now on can come into alignment with your health and happiness, on all levels.

It's almost time to bring this inner journey to a close. So take a moment to thank yourself for giving yourself this nurturing gift.

Gradually bring your awareness back into your body, and your physical surroundings.

Take your time, and when you're ready, open your eyes, and feel awake, alert, and refreshed.

IMMUNE SUPPORT: ENVISIONING GOOD HEALTH

INTRODUCTION

Consider your attitude toward your own body, and the way you think of yourself when it comes to health, wellbeing and vitality.

The body-mind component of health is all about the way your thoughts and feelings influence your body's ability to ward off and recover from illness. The way you think and feel about yourself can effect immune response, digestion, reproductive functioning, and more.

For example, beliefs like "My body is strong and resilient," and "I have the energy to overcome any obstacle when I need to," have a very different tone than, "I always seem to get sick," or "There's something wrong with me."

You can see how one way of thinking would keep things moving in a positive direction, and the other would tend to set up a kind of negative or sluggish response in our system.

So in this program you'll have the opportunity to focus on your body and your health in a very positive way, adjust your thinking, and help your entire system to become brighter and stronger. Working with a program like this one can make a positive difference, so let's get started.

MEDITATION

Make yourself comfortable, and close your eyes. Take a slow deep breath, and let go of any tension, as you feel yourself sinking into the surface you're resting on, becoming still more comfortable and relaxed. Take another slow, deep breath, and release your thoughts, letting them drift far away. And take another slow, deep breath, and know that in this moment, all is well.

Imagine you're surrounded by a bubble of light, clear and perfect, and within this bubble you're becoming lighter, and lighter. Soon you're so light that you begin to float up, into the air, though the ceiling, and into a clear blue sky.

Safe within your bubble you float and drift across lush forests, mountain meadows, and peaceful lakes and streams that mirror the sky above.

Nestled in the countryside below is a weathered old house with an expansive, rambling garden, and you find yourself drifting gently down toward it.

Soon you softly come to rest in the middle of the garden, by a bubbling fountain. Have a seat at the edge of the fountain, and enjoy this lovely setting, landscaped with hedges, colorful flower beds, and a few leafy old shade trees. The sound of the fountain's splashing water makes a soothing background to the day. Take a few moments to enjoy the feeling of peace and comfort here.

Although at first it seemed as if you were the only person here today, soon you begin to notice a few others walking along the paths, or seated on benches, quietly enjoying the garden.

Someone comes and sits beside you, and their company feels most welcome. And as if it were the most natural thing in the world, they offer you their hand. As soon as you take their hand in yours, you feel a flood of positive energy, as if you were receiving a transfusion of love, filling you from head to foot. Take time to receive this loving energy, as it continues to flow into you, clearing away any darkness, and leaving you fully alive.

Now listen more closely to the fountain, and you'll notice that its gentle splashing sound seems to resonate within your body. The sound is creating a healing resonance, clearing, brightening, and strengthening your system. And as this occurs, it also clears your mind of any thoughts of weakness, hardship, or struggle concerning your health, giving you a clean mental slate. Take a few moments to experience this, and simply enjoy the feelings it brings.

The water itself has still more healing for you to experience. So if you wish, remove your shoes, turn around on the comfortable edge of the fountain and place your feet in the water, which you'll find is the perfect temperature, and very refreshing.

Experience the healing energy as it flows into your feet and ankles, and gently flows up into your calves and knees.

And now it flows into your upper legs, hips, and reproductive organs.

This positive energy finds its way into your abdomen and lower back.

And it flows into your upper back and chest.

The healing energy of the fountain finds its way into all your internal organs, going wherever needed.

Now feel it flowing into your shoulders and arms, into your hands and out your fingertips. And finally, it makes its way into your head and face, filling your eyes, ears, nose, mouth and brain.

Now healing energy is circulating throughout your entire system, bringing strength and support wherever needed.

Your body, mind and emotions are adjusting to this higher vibration, letting go of old patterns and programs, and stepping up to a new level of wellness.

As you continue to enjoy this positive transformation, listen to the following affirmations, and allow them to find their way deep within.

My mind is at peace, and my body is relaxed.

Light fills my body, mind and emotions, and I'm flooded with good health.

My body is a miraculous instrument, working in perfect harmony.

I am healthy and strong, and receive everything I need.

I enjoy a healthy mental diet of good, positive thoughts

I easily adjust to life's challenges with flexibility, and bounce back better than ever.

Life naturally flows throughout my system, feeding my body and mind with vibrant energy.

My body is naturally in tune with nature and the world around me, and operates in perfect harmony.

It will soon be time to bring this journey to a close. But first, take a moment to thank yourself for giving yourself this gift.

Bring your awareness gently back to your physical surroundings. Take your time, and when you're ready, open your eyes, and feel awake, alert, and refreshed.

YOUR SUCCESSFUL SURGERY

INTRODUCTION

In the modern era, millions of dedicated men and women have been researching, studying, and practicing medicine in universities, hospitals and clinics all over the world. And thousands of talented engineers and inventors have developed and perfected leading edge technology, to help those highly skilled medical professionals do amazing work, and produce miraculous results.

All of this sophisticated training, skill, and technology has been passed forward, year after year, decade upon decade, into in the hands of the capable doctors and assistants who'll soon be serving your needs.

The best way to optimize your surgery, and take full advantage of all the medical advances of the last century, is to put your mind at ease, rest easy, and anticipate a successful outcome. The following guided meditation will help you do exactly that.

MEDITATION

Make yourself comfortable, and close your eyes. Take a slow deep breath, and let go of any tension, as you feel yourself sinking into the surface you're resting on, becoming still more comfortable and relaxed. Take another slow, deep breath, and release your thoughts, letting them drift far away. And take another slow, deep breath, and know that in this moment, all is well.

We'll be using color to help you go deeper, so consider your favorite colors, and choose the color you'd like to use to represent the successful outcome of your surgery, the most successful outcome possible. Focus on that color for a moment, and see and feel it all around you.

Imagine the setting in which your operation will occur, a well lit room containing the best staff and equipment available. Take a moment to envision the whole setting; the room, the doctors, the assistants, and you, all encompassed by that color you just chose.

Imagine your body surrounded by your successful surgery color, to help prepare for your procedure. Experience your body taking in that color now, as it opens, cell by cell, allowing your favorite color to penetrate everywhere within. And as your body receives this color of healing, you can feel it relax deeply, all over. Your body is getting ready to let go of the problem it carries, receive the healing it needs, and transform toward greater health.

Send your healing color into the part of your body where the surgery will be take place. Imagine it flowing there, giving notice to all the cells that good support is coming, and that change for the better is about to occur. Help is on its way, and your body now understands that the stress it's been under will soon be alleviated, bringing greater ease to every day life. Take a few moments to be with your body now, and experience this realization.

Imagine the time for your surgery has come, everything is in place, and you're entirely ready. Your successful surgery color surrounds the day. You arrive at the hospital on time, all the doctors and assistants are there, ready for you, as you enter the setting for your operation.

If you wish, envision a beautiful light from a higher source all around you and everyone present, guiding and watching over your procedure, helping to insure that everything is going just as it should. You may also imagine your friends and loved ones, either nearby or with you in spirit, as well as angels, spiritual figures, and anyone else who helps you feel safe, supported, and loved. You are cared for, loved, and supported on all levels. Take a few moments to allow this positive scene to fill your imagination, and be with it peacefully, now.

Your procedure takes place, and everything goes smoothly and perfectly from beginning to end. Everyone does their job exactly as they should, and your body receives the surgery easily. Take a moment to simply enjoy the fact that the work is done, you're safe and secure, and all is well.

Now imagine that with your successful surgery accomplished and behind you, your body is recovering, and adjusting smoothly and quickly. Your body loves the new changes, and is learning to adapt and perform beautifully as a result. If a period of follow-up therapy is part of the process, you have expert support to assist you, and you're doing everything necessary to treat yourself well. You're well on track for a full and complete recovery. Take a moment to envision yourself becoming healthier, and healthier, until you're at your optimum level.

Imagine yourself using your body to happily do the things you most love to do, and the things you need to do, moving gracefully and easily. Your successful surgery is well behind you now, and you're going ahead with life. Take a few moments for this, now.

Listen carefully to the following affirmations, and allow them to resonate deeply within.

Everything is in place to support my successful surgery, and I'm in good hands.

I'm in the right place at the right time to receive my procedure, and I am ready.

My body is looking forward to this positive intervention, welcomes the changes to come, and anticipates all the benefits.

All the cells in my body are ready for my surgery to occur.

My body is learning how to relax and receive help in the most ideal way, to make the most of my procedure.

I am loved, supported, and protected from on high.

I'm looking forward to completing my successful surgery, and enjoying life more than ever.

I'm careful to follow directions and take the proper care before surgery, to optimize the results and speed my recovery.

I am well on track for a successful surgery, and a full, and rapid recovery.

It will soon be time to bring this journey to a close. But first, take some time to simply be grateful for all the love, assistance, and support you are about to experience.

And take a moment to thank yourself for giving yourself this gift.

Gradually bring your awareness gently back to your physical surroundings.

Take your time, and when you're ready, open your eyes, and feel awake, alert, and refreshed.

CLEARING CANCER, PART ONE: CLEARING YOUR CELLS WITH LOVE

Make yourself comfortable, and close your eyes. Take a slow deep breath, and let go of any tension in your body, as you feel yourself sinking into the surface you're resting on, becoming still more comfortable and relaxed. Take another slow, deep breath, and relax your mind, letting your thoughts drift far away. And take another slow, deep breath, and know that for now, all is well, you're safe, and you can devote the next little while all to yourself, for healing, and deep inner peace.

Imagine that all of the energy you've sent out into the world lately is coming gently back home to you, helping you to feel more whole, and complete, as if pieces of a puzzle were coming together.

As your energy continues to return to you, it's followed by a feeling of love, collecting within you, warm, and comforting. Allow yourself to soften and let go, and you can feel more of this love, as it gently gathers within you, easing everything.

Bring your awareness into your heart center, in the center of your chest, and notice a softness there. When you center in your heart, you can more easily access your deepest inner resources, and receive guidance and input from above, for healing and direction in life. And right now, your heart is the perfect place to be.

Imagine your heart's beginning to expand with love, becoming larger and larger, until it's big enough to gently envelop you. Your heart has become a cozy room, with a comfortable reclining chair, a beautiful old rug on the wooden floor, perhaps a softly crackling fire in the fireplace, a bookshelf filled with books, and lovely wall hangings. It feels like the perfect place for you to visit and relax.

As you settle into the recliner, you realize it's possibly the most comfortable and supportive chair you've ever experienced. And as you relax a bit more, you notice it has a wonderful, loving energy that seems to totally envelop you.

The arms of the recliner include a pair of high-tech controllers, and your hands rest comfortably over them, with your fingertips positioned perfectly on the buttons. The buttons aren't activated yet, but you can press them and feel how nicely they work, with just the right kind of satisfying, springy feel.

This recliner, with its wonderful energy and the button controllers at your fingertips, has been designed to help you receive very high levels of love, focus it into healing rays, and point the rays wherever cancer cells may be. In fact, it's designed so the rays of love will automatically seek out every single cancer cell, and dematerialize each and every last one of them! The whole process is entirely automated, and all you need to do is sit back, give the go ahead, press the buttons, and let love do the rest.

It's time to get started, and you must be ready, or you wouldn't be here, in your heart center, in this healing recliner. To activate the program, inwardly say the words:

May the healing power of love guide my life.

Immediately an upsurge of loving energy begins flowing into your heart, and distributing all through your body. The system is activating and building energy, preparing you to operate the controllers. It's almost ready, give it just a bit longer to build...

Now! Begin pressing the buttons on the controllers, and rays of healing love will start to seek out and eliminate cancer cells. Love knows everything, including the exact location of every cell. And if you watch, you can see very fine rays of light going from your heart center to any areas within your body that need help. These rays work very quickly and efficiently, finding one cell, then another, and another. And each time, all they need to do is come into contact with a cancer cell, and it instantly realizes it doesn't belong there, and dematerializes of its own accord.

The whole process is very easy, efficient, and automatic. You may find it works best by pressing and holding the buttons, by repeatedly pressing them very lightly, or by pressing them in a slow rhythmical pattern. Take a few minutes to continue, as you simply let love flow in, and watch it go out in ray after ray, eliminating cancer cells wherever needed.

As more an more cancer cells dematerialize, any and all cancer within you begins to get the message, "I don't belong here," and becomes weaker, and weaker, loosing its hold. Help it get the message even more by inwardly repeating the following affirmations, allowing them to resonate everywhere within you.

I am full of life, and life is good.

Love guides my thoughts, feelings, and actions.

Light and love flow through my entire body, mind, and spirit, bringing healing everywhere.

My body knows love, and love is clearing and releasing anything that is not love.

Love flows through my entire system, affirming life within me.

Life is unfolding perfectly within me, and I am safe and whole.

Perhaps there are other important affirmations for you to say within you, or messages for you to receive. Take a few moments to listen, and know whatever you might need to know just now.

It's almost time to bring this inner journey to a close. But first, ask for a sphere of light to be placed all around you, and this experience, so that all the positive benefits will stay with you, and anything that you've released can be left behind. Envision that perfect sphere of light surrounding and filling you, or simply know that it's in place.

Thank yourself for giving yourself this gift.

Gradually bring your awareness gently back to your physical surroundings.

Take your time, and when you're ready, open your eyes, and feel awake, alert, and refreshed.

CLEARING CANCER, PART TWO: PREPARING TO RECEIVE TREATMENT

Make yourself comfortable, and close your eyes. Take a slow deep breath, and let go of any tension in your body, as you feel yourself sinking into the surface you're resting on, becoming still more comfortable and relaxed. Take another slow, deep breath, and relax your mind, letting your thoughts drift far away. And take another slow, deep breath, and know that for now, all is well, you're safe, and you can devote the next little while all to yourself, for healing, and deep inner peace.

Imagine that all of the energy you've sent out into the world lately is coming gently back home to you, helping you to feel more whole, and complete, as if pieces of a puzzle were coming together.

As your energy continues to return to you, it's followed by a feeling of love, collecting within you, warm, and comforting. Allow yourself to soften and let go, and you can feel more of this love, as it gently gathers within you, easing everything.

Bring your awareness into your heart center, in the center of your chest, and notice a softness there. When you center in your heart, you can more easily access your deepest inner resources, and receive guidance and input from above, for healing and direction in life. And right now, your heart is the perfect place to be.

As part of your healing process, your body has been receiving or is about to receive treatment that will help your body heal. To maximize the benefit of this treatment, and make it as easy as possible to assimilate, you'll want your body to become very open and receptive, flexible and resilient. That way it can metabolize and take full advantage of the treatment, in the easiest, most comfortable way possible.

Imagine there's a gateway to your body, much like the gate house of a fancy home. And in the gate house is a friendly but powerful gatekeeper who oversees everyone who approaches. Imagine the treatment you're about to receive is approaching the gate to your body, and your gatekeeper is ready. He looks at it carefully, checks his notes, finds that this is what you want, and lets it through the gate. Notice the treatment yourself, and choosing a color you like, imagine what color it is, because we'll be using that color in just a bit.

Now imagine all the cells in your body, alive with light, turning toward the incoming treatment, welcoming it, surrounding it, and openly receiving it. Even though the treatment may be foreign to your body, all your cells are friendly, and do everything they can to help the treatment find its way around. A special welcoming committee of cells is even assigned to make sure the treatment has everything it needs, and introduces it to other cells. Now the treatment is going where the cancer is, so it can do its job, and it goes to work.

This treatment is efficient, fast, and effective, and you can see it surrounding cancer cells, and eliminating them, all very quickly and easily. As you watch, you can see the treatment, which is one color, working on the cancer, which is another color, until the treatment color is the only thing left. Take a few moments to watch and imagine it working, in with your body in total support and cooperation.

Now, because your body is assigning some of its energy reserves to help the treatment function effectively, it would be good to receive some additional energy to help your body with its normal operations. Imagine you're lying on a comfortable table inside a pyramid that's made of golden light. And imagine that powerful light energies are flowing into the pyramid from the Universe, God, angels, master healers, or whatever source you prefer.

The pyramid is collecting this powerful light, and stepping it down in frequency, so it's a perfect match for your own energy. And this light, in a perfectly refined state, is flowing easily into your body, entering through your feet, hands, the top of your head, and all energy centers along the front and back of your torso.

Take some time to experience this golden light energy filling you, going wherever needed, and helping your body prepare for or take care of any special needs it has during the duration of your healing process.

As you continue to receive the golden light within your pyramid, inwardly repeat the following affirmations, and allow them to resonate deeply within:

My body is strong and resilient, and ready for change.

My body is ready to receive treatment, welcomes the help it brings, and makes the most of this opportunity to heal.

All of the cells in my body are flexible and capable of change, and can easily adjust to support the healing process.

My body easily adapts to treatment, and recovers quickly, becoming better than ever.

My body is made of light, and can heal from the inside out, and the outside in.

Take a few moments to listen within, receive any other affirmations that might be helpful to your recovery, and know whatever you might need to know just now.

It's almost time to bring this inner journey to a close. But first, ask for a sphere of light to be placed all around you, and this experience, so that all the positive benefits will stay with you, and anything that you've released can be left behind. Envision that perfect sphere of light surrounding and filling you, or simply know that it is in place.

Thank yourself for giving yourself this gift.

Gradually bring your awareness gently back to your physical surroundings.

Take your time, and when you're ready, open your eyes, and feel awake, alert, and refreshed.

CLEARING CANCER, PART THREE: EMOTIONAL SUPPORT WHILE HEALING

Make yourself comfortable, and close your eyes. Take a slow deep breath, and let go of any tension in your body, as you feel yourself sinking into the surface you're resting on, becoming still more comfortable and relaxed. Take another slow, deep breath, and relax your mind, letting your thoughts drift far away. And take another slow, deep breath, and know that for now, all is well, you're safe, and you can devote the next little while all to yourself, for healing, and deep inner peace.

Imagine that all of the energy you've sent out into the world lately is coming gently back home to you, helping you to feel more whole, and complete, as if pieces of a puzzle were coming together. As your energy continues to return to you, it's followed by a feeling of love, collecting within you, warm, and comforting. Allow yourself to soften and let go, and you can feel more of this love, as it gently gathers within you, easing everything.

Bring your awareness into your heart center, in the center of your chest, and notice a softness there. When you center in your heart, you can more easily access your deepest inner resources, and receive guidance and input from above, for healing and direction in life. And right now, your heart is the perfect place to be.

Imagine your heart's beginning to expand with love, becoming larger and larger, until it's big enough to gently envelop you. Your heart has become a cozy room, with a comfortable armchair, a beautiful old rug on the wooden floor, perhaps a softly crackling fire in the fireplace, a bookshelf filled with books, and lovely wall hangings. It feels like the perfect place for you to visit and relax, and soon you find yourself sitting in the comfy chair, feeling quite content. This is a lovely place to be, and it occurs to you that it would be just perfect, if there was someone to share it with. And the next thing you know, a small child is seated in your lap, looking up at you. This is your own inner child, you as a little one, between two and six years old, come to visit.

Your inner child is here today to help you better understand your feelings, and release anything within you that might be in the way of your healing. And, your inner child has come to and receive comfort, love, and support from you.

If you're experiencing illness, your inner child may be sad or frightened by the situation, angry at your body for not being well, or even ashamed or guilty that you've done something wrong. That's quite a lot for any small child to manage, so it's time to find out how your inner child feels, to give them some relief. Ask your inner child to talk with you now about his or her feelings, and be sure to listen very patiently and carefully. Sometimes children are shy, so you may need to encourage them at first, or even bend your head down so they can whisper in your ear. Take some time now to learn what's going on inside, understand what your feelings really are.

No matter what's going on inside with your inner child, you can reassure them that you're safe, so they can relax. Take a moment to tell your inner child that even though things may seem mixed up right now, what you're going through is all part of a much bigger plan, and everything is working the way it's supposed to.

Imagine you're showing your inner child a picture of some woven material, very close up, under a microscope. As the two of you look at this, you have no way of making out where the material comes from or what it's for, and all you can see are some fuzzy threads, crisscrossing over each other. But as you take the material out from the magnifier, and unfold it, you can both see that it's actually a wonderful giant tapestry with landscapes, houses, people, and animals all living out their lives, growing, learning, and sharing together. Put the tapestry up on the wall of your heart room, so you can both admire how beautiful it is.

This moment in your life is one that may be hard to make sense of, like looking at the tapestry under a microscope, because you're so close to it. But seen in perspective, it's just one part of a much larger story. A good story, about you and your inner child. And even though it may seem like you're in a rough patch at the moment, all is unfolding according to plan, and all is well.

Take a moment to let your inner child know that you love and appreciate them, that you're being well taken care of, and that they don't have to worry.

You need all your energy right now to heal, but emotional stress keeps some of your energy tied up. The more you're able to let go of anything that's been bothering you, the more of your energy you can reclaim. Ask your inner child to tell you if there's anything you've been holding against yourself, perhaps about something you did or didn't do.

If there is anything at all, this is the time to release it and let it go. So make an agreement with your inner child that the both of you forgive yourself right here and now, and put it forever in the past. Take some time to handle this now.

Now ask your inner child to tell you if there is anything you've been holding against someone else, about something they did or didn't do. No matter who it is, and what it was, you need the energy back that you've been hold against that person, and you need it back now, for your own healing. If there is anything at all, this is the time to release it and let it go. Make an agreement with your inner child that the both of you forgive that person right here and now, and put it forever in the past.

It's almost time to bring this inner journey to a close. But first, ask for a sphere of light to be placed all around you and your inner child, so that all the positive benefits will stay with you, and anything that you've released can be left behind. Envision that perfect sphere of light surrounding and filling you, or simply know that it is in place.

Thank your inner child for working so well with you today, and give them a big hug.

And thank yourself for giving yourself this gift.

Gradually bring your awareness gently back to your physical surroundings.

Take your time, and when you're ready, open your eyes, and feel awake, alert, and refreshed.

PART THREE

EMOTIONAL WELL-BEING & HAPPINESS

FEELING LOVE INSTEAD OF FEAR

Make yourself comfortable, and close your eyes. Take a slow deep breath, and let go of any tension, as you feel yourself sinking into the surface you're resting on, becoming still more comfortable and relaxed. Take another slow, deep breath, and release your thoughts, letting them drift far away. And take another slow, deep breath, and know that in this moment, all is well.

Bring your awareness into your heart, in the center of your chest, and notice a softness there, a feeling of peace. Take a moment to enjoy this feeling, as you quietly focus in your heart, and follow your breath, in, and out.

Imagine you're seated on a comfortable couch, in the middle of a large living room accompanied by several dozen people who are very kind, friendly, and loving. Some of the people you may know, some of them seem familiar, and some you've never seen before.

There is little conversation, the lighting is soft, and quiet music is playing in the background. Everyone has gathered here to honor, appreciate, and meditate on universal love. It's the love that stands behind all of creation, weaves it's way through everything, and supports all life, including your own.

Soon everyone becomes silent, and a deep feeling of peace settles over the room. Love is filling the room, being welcomed in by the open hearts and the kind thoughts of everyone here. Some of the ones closest to you are first to notice it, but soon, everyone, including yourself, is feeling the warm, comforting feeling of love.

You may first notice it as a gentle warmth around your chest, delicate and sweet, and soon you can feel it surrounding and filling your entire body. Take a few moments to allow love to fill you, and enjoy its presence, and the feeling of safety and support that it brings.

To experience love even more deeply, follow your breath. As you breathe in, inwardly say the word, "love." And as you breathe out, inwardly say the word "peace."

Continue to follow your breath, and as you breathe in, inwardly say the word, "love." And now as you breathe out, inwardly say the words "I am safe."

Imagine that the warm, gentle feeling of love flowing over and expanding throughout your life, supporting you 24/7, every day, from now on. Envision yourself as you go about your day, filled and surrounded by the support and protection that love offers, banishing fear and negativity of any kind. You may choose to see it as a beautiful golden glow, surrounding you in every situation, and even while you're sleeping. Take a few moments to do this now.

Listen to the following affirmations, and allow them to resonate, deep within.

Love supports me every moment of the day and night.

No matter what happens, I am safe, and comforted by love.

I am surrounded and filled by love, from head to toe.

Everything in my life is held by love, and unfolding according to plan.

Take a moment to project your mind forward in the future, to a time where you might normally experience fear. Send your future self the feeling of love and safety you're experiencing now. Imagine your future self receiving this, and becoming peaceful.

It will soon be time to begin your return home. But first, take a moment to thank yourself for giving yourself this opportunity to get quiet, rest, and connect within.

Bring all the benefits of this experience with you, as gently bring your awareness gently back to your physical body.

Take your time, and when you're ready, open your eyes, and feel awake, alert, and refreshed.

HEALING TRAUMATIC MEMORY: GUIDED IMAGERY FOR PTSD

INTRODUCTION

Whenever we experience events that are overwhelmingly painful, part of our inner self is left with a kind of wound. That part of us is unresolved, almost in a kind of suspended animation, until such time as we're able to heal and release the pain.

Carrying the memory of a traumatic event is a bit like living in a house with a room that's closed off. We never want to enter that room because of the painful feelings it holds, but we can't clean it up and begin using it again without going through the door.

So in this program you'll have the opportunity to heal painful memories without reliving them. You'll visit the past through a protective filter that will allow you to clear out negativity, without stepping into it again. You'll be able to do this in a way that's safe, comfortable, and effective. Let's get started.

GUIDED MEDITATION

Make yourself comfortable, and close your eyes. Take a slow deep breath, and let go of any tension, as you feel yourself sinking into the surface you're resting on, becoming still more comfortable and relaxed. Take another slow, deep breath, and release your thoughts, letting them drift far away. And take another slow, deep breath, and know that in this moment, all is well.

Imagine you're walking in a peaceful mountain meadow, on a warm summer morning. The air is fresh and clear, and you can smell the scent of wildflowers on the gentle breeze. It's quiet here, and you're greeted by the soft sound of a stream close by, the rustle of the leaves in the trees, and a bird song. All around you are soft green colors of the plants, grasses and trees, dotted here and there with blossoms of purple, white, and cornflower blue. And as you walk along you can feel the soft ground beneath your feet, and the warm sun on your face.

There's a little stone cottage up ahead, one that looks as if it's been here for ages, with a small garden in front, a stone chimney, painted shutters by the windows, and an old wooden front door. Coming closer, you see there's a paper note pinned to the door, and as you step up to it you'll see your own name on the paper, followed by the words, "Come In."

Just to be sure, you knock, and from within the cottage, you hear someone say "It's open." As you step inside you're greeted by someone who's known and cared about you a long time. This may be a relative who's alive today or passed on, an old friend, or a spiritual figure who's meaningful to you. But most important, this is an ally —someone you trust deeply, who helps you know that you're safe, and that all is well. You may see this person, hear them, feel them as a presence in the room with you, or simply just know that they're there. Take a moment to connect with them now, and feel the love and support they bring you.

Your ally is about to help you as you step back in time, not to relive your past, but to release it. Together, with complete protection and safety, you'll touch very lightly into past events, in order to resolve and let go of any pain you experienced.

Checking to be sure you're ready, your ally looks at you, gets the go-ahead, and opens the back door of the cottage. The doorway is immediately flooded with light of whatever color you choose. There's so much light that it's impossible to see beyond the doorway. And as you and your ally step through the door together, you arrive at a scene where you experienced trauma in the past, touching down just before the event is about to take place. But this time, the whole scene is surrounded by that same color light as the doorway you just stepped through. And this time, you and your ally begin changing that scene. Together, you're doing whatever necessary to insure that nothing disturbing happens. That may involve putting up a barrier between you and any danger, creating a protective force-field, or neutralizing the danger in some way. Or it may involve removing yourself and anyone else in danger from that scene. Take some time to re-envision this scene, surrounded by that color of light, so it unfolds in a new way that keeps you and anyone you care about from harm. Continue to imagine this, until you come to a point where any danger or harm is completely neutralized.

Now, together with your ally, and surrounded by that same color of light, travel to another point in time when you experienced trauma, just before the event is about to take place. This time, let that scene represent all the painful experiences you've ever had, so that today they can all be neutralized and released. As before, you and your ally begin changing that scene, doing anything necessary to insure that no harm comes to you or anyone you care about. Change the sequence of events, put up barriers, create a force field, or remove yourself and others from the situation, as needed. Take some time to re-envision this scene, surrounded by the light, and continue until you come to a point where all the danger is completely gone.

Now you find yourself back in the cottage with your ally, sitting comfortably, safe and sound. There's still a protective light all around you, bringing you a feeling of peace, and wholeness. Your ally comes around behind your chair, and places their hands on your shoulders. And as they do, you feel a warm, healing energy traveling all through your body, mind and emotions. This energy is sweeping through you from head to foot, clearing away any remaining threads of darkness within you, helping you trust that the past is now truly past, and all is well. Take a few moments to experience this clearing process.

If you've been holding anything against yourself, any feelings of remorse, guilt, or thoughts that you should have done something different, now's the time to let that go as well. You're a human being, and a good person, and did your best given the circumstances and what was known to you at the time.

As you continue to sit here, in the presence of your ally, in safety and comfort, place your hand on your heart, and give yourself the gift of love, forgiveness and healing. Do this now, and let nothing stand in the way.

It will soon be time to bring this journey to a close. So take a moment to thank your ally for their love and support, and to thank yourself for giving yourself the opportunity to be open to receive it.

Bring your awareness gently back to your physical surroundings. Take your time, and when you're ready, open your eyes, and feel awake, alert, and refreshed.

LOVE & FORGIVE YOURSELF

Make yourself comfortable, and close your eyes. Take a slow deep breath, and let go of any tension in your body, as you feel yourself sinking into the surface you're resting on, becoming still more comfortable and relaxed. Take another slow, deep breath, and relax your mind, letting your thoughts drift far away. And take another slow, deep breath, and know that all is well, and you can devote the next little while all to yourself, for healing, and deep inner peace.

Imagine you're walking barefoot along a secluded beach, close to where the surf thins out onto the sand, and then recedes again. It's early in the morning, and you seem to have the world all to yourself. Perhaps you'd enjoy letting the water softly lap up to your ankles, or prefer to make your way just out of its reach. It's a beautiful, warm day, with just the right amount of cloud cover, and as you walk along, you can feel the packed sand beneath your feet, as you sink in a little with each step. A light breeze brings a touch of ocean mist to your face, and you can smell the clean scent of the sea. The rhythmic sounds of the waves and the sea birds soothe and comfort you, and all the sights, sounds, and feelings convey a deep sense of peace, and harmony with nature.

As you cast your gaze down the beach, you notice someone coming toward you, and as they draw closer, you can see them waving, as if they recognize you. And although you may not at first recognize them, they certainly seem to know you. They're smiling as if you were a very close friend or relation, radiating love and good feelings toward you.

This may be someone from your past, an old friend, parent or teacher, a spiritual guide, or even an historical figure. But whomever it is, this is a person who knows you very well, and thinks of you as completely good, and totally lovable. When they look at you, they see someone whom they love, dearly and completely.

As they greet you, you feel a deep understanding between the two of you, and you'd like to receive more of their love. Well, it's a beautiful day, and you could certainly use a hug, so take a moment to feel their embrace, and let in all the love you can.

As they continue to hold you and pour love into you, allow yourself to open your heart, your whole body, and your soul, and take some time to experience this deep, healing connection.

As the two of you walk together along the shore, you seem to be surrounded by the glow of this love between you, and you begin to realize you've had misunderstandings within yourself for quite some time: mistaken beliefs that you were not good, didn't measure up in some way, and didn't deserve to be loved and be happy just as you are. And as you spend more time in the presence of this old friend, love is surrounding and dissolving all of those misunderstandings, leaving a deep sense of peace in their place, and making much more room inside. Your friend has made you OK, and now, you feel you can begin to make yourself OK as well. Take some time to let this unfold now.

You decide to sit on the sand for a while with your friend, and watch the waves. And before long there's a small child sitting in your lap, watching along with you. It's you, when you weren't more than 5 years old, come to visit and spend some time with you here on the beach. Perhaps the openness and love you're starting to feel toward yourself makes it safe for your inner child to appear now. And perhaps they've come because now there's an opening for healing.

With all the love you've been receiving, you find it easy to love this little one, who only needs to know he or she is good, and worthy of being happy and safe. As you wrap your arms around them, take some time to let love pour out of your heart, surround and fill your inner child.

As you continue to watch the waves coming into shore, and feel waves of love coming from your heart, consider the one thing you've most held against yourself. It's time now to find a way to forgive yourself, and let this go. After all, you're just a human being like all of us, learning as you grow. Every one of us is given challenges to overcome, and we all fall short in some way. So no matter what you did or didn't do that you've made wrong inside, find a way, right now, to have compassion toward yourself, and forgive yourself. Take a few moments to do this, now.

Now consider a situation in the days ahead, where you might typically tend to be cross with yourself, ill at ease, or not as kind to yourself as you could be. And imagine that instead of reacting negatively, you remember this time on the beach with your loving friend, and your inner child. Take some time to send the love you feel now to your future self, and ask your future self to remember to relax, let go of your hard feelings, and feel love and compassion inside. Do this now, as a gift of love from you to your future self.

It's almost time to bring this inner journey to a close. But first, thank your friend and your inner child for their love.

And thank yourself for giving yourself this gift.

Ask for a sphere of light to be placed all around you, and this experience, so that all the positive benefits will stay with you, and anything that you've released can be left behind.

Gradually bring your awareness gently back to your physical surroundings.

Take your time, and when you're ready, open your eyes, and feel awake, alert, and refreshed.

SAYING GOODBYE: HEALING THE LOSS OF A LOVED ONE

INTRODUCTION

When we loose someone important to us, that loss is painful, and deeply felt. Although we can try to avoid feeling the pain for a time, eventually we must allow it to pass through us, so we can fully regain ourselves. This grieving process—allowing the sadness, anger, and other feelings to surface and release—is the natural, human response to loss, and it's the only way for us to come fully back to life.

There are some who say, "Why grieve for your loved one, when their soul has moved on to a better place, and their suffering has ended?" Well, we're not grieving for them, we're grieving for our own loss. To best honor the one who's passed, we must allow ourselves to feel the loss, the love we have for them, and all the feelings in between that arise within us, so we also can move on.

It's common to feel as though we have unfinished communication with the one we've lost, either because we've lost them suddenly, or because there wasn't a good flow of communication with them when they were alive. But we can accomplish a sense of closure, completion, and healing, by having a kind of purposeful inner conversation with our loved one, at any time after they've gone. And in some cases that can be the beginning of a whole new dialog that unfolds over time. Not as a way to hang on to the one you miss, but to acknowledge that you're both moving on in different ways.

The following guided meditation provides an opportunity to visit with the one you've lost in a very real way, within your own heart, to let go of painful feelings, and move through the grieving process in perfect timing for you.

GUIDED MEDITATION

Make yourself comfortable, and close your eyes. Take a slow deep breath, and let go of any tension, as you feel yourself sinking into the surface you're resting on, becoming still more comfortable and relaxed. Take another slow, deep breath, and release your thoughts, letting them drift far away. And take another slow, deep breath, and know that in this moment, all is well.

Bring your awareness into your heart center, in the center of your chest, and notice a softness there. Imagine all of the energy you've sent out into the world lately coming gently back home to your heart, helping you to feel more whole, and more complete. Quietly receive this energy, and know that for now, it's OK to simply be here, relax, and receive.

Bring yourself more fully into your heart, as if you were standing there now, inside a cozy room. Soon, you'll notice a doorway, and as you walk through it, you'll find yourself in a setting that might be a very good place to visit with the one you've lost. This may be a place you both knew, or perhaps it's a beautiful place in nature you would both enjoy, like a quiet beach, or a mountain meadow. Take a moment to look around, and let your surroundings become more real to you, as you notice the colors, shapes, and sounds here.

Begin to call to mind things you and the one you've lost may have done together, or things you talked about. And before long, he or she will come more fully into your awareness, as you begin to see them, hear their voice, or simply feel their presence. Take a few moments to just be with them, together once again.

As you continue to spend time here with the one you've lost, take this opportunity to say whatever you wish . This can be as simple as telling them what it's been like for you since they left; it might be things you've wanted to get off your chest for some time; or you may just want to express your love by telling them what they've meant to you. Take some time for this now.

Now it's time to hear what they have to say to you. All you need do is quietly listen, feel, and receive. You may experience their words, thoughts, or felt communication, or there may simply be a quiet feeling of peace. Take some time for this now. If there is anything you would like to know or hear from your loved one now, this would be a good time to ask. Take a few moments to ask, listen, and receive.

Imagine that the two of you now stand facing one another, as you look into each others eyes, and open your hearts. Take some time now, as best as you can, to be together, and give and receive love.

Although it's not easy to loose a loved one, you can and will go on with life. And although you will never see them again physically, your love for them will live on. In your own perfect timing you'll adjust to life in a new way. "Goodbye" can mean different things at different times, so say the goodbye that's right for you, just now. And if you can, let your loved one know that they are free to go on with their journey into love. Ask for a sphere of light to be placed around them, to help guide them on their way.

Now, ask for a sphere of light to be placed all around you, and this experience, so that all the positive benefits will stay with you, and anything that you've released can be left behind.

Take a moment to thank yourself for giving yourself this gift.

It's time to bring your awareness gently back to your physical surroundings.

Take your time, and when you're ready, open your eyes, and feel awake, alert, and refreshed.

YOUR INNER CHILD'S STORY

Make yourself comfortable, and close your eyes. Take a slow deep breath, and let go of any tension in your body, as you feel yourself sinking into the surface you're resting on, becoming still more comfortable and relaxed.

Bring your awareness into your spiritual heart, in the center of your chest, and notice a softness there. Your spiritual heart resides within you, always ready to give and receive love. Here, you may receive guidance from above, and counsel from the deepest part of your being.

Imagine that all of the energy you've sent out into the world lately is coming gently back home to your heart, helping you to feel more whole, and complete. Quietly receive this energy in your heart, and know there's nothing else you need to do right now. You can simply be here, relax, and receive.

As your energy continues to return to you, it's followed by a feeling of love, coming toward you, and collecting within you, warm, and comforting. Allow yourself to soften and let go, and you can feel more of this love, as it gently gathers within your heart, easing everything, and helping you to know that all is well.

Imagine your heart's beginning to expand with love, becoming larger and larger, until it's big enough to gently envelop you. Your heart has become a cozy room, with a comfortable armchair, a beautiful old rug on the wooden floor, perhaps a softly crackling fire in the fireplace, a bookshelf filled with books, and lovely wall hangings. It feels like the perfect place for you to visit and relax, and soon you find yourself sitting in the comfy chair, feeling quite cozy. This is a lovely place to be, and it occurs to you that it would be just perfect, if there was someone to share it with. And the next thing you know, a small child is seated in your lap, looking up at you. This is your own inner child—you as a little one, between two and six years old, come to visit.

Look back at your inner child with love, as you both enjoy the feeling of peace, comfort, and warmth that surrounds you, and give him or her a hug. Inner children love hugs. Notice that your inner child has brought with them one of the books from the bookshelf, and wants you to see, and the title on the cover says, "My life in pictures." Open the book to page one, as you and your child look at the first picture together. Perhaps it's a picture of your mother holding you as a newborn baby, or both of your parents with you together. How does your inner child feel about the picture you're seeing? What does your inner child need to hear from you?

Turn the page, and look with your inner child at the next picture in the book of your life. What feelings does this image bring up, and what needs to be said about it between you? Take the time to tenderly talk to your inner child to help him or her understand that everything is all right, and you're safe and secure. Your child needs to hear these things, and know that you're there listening, and taking care.

Take some time with your inner child to look at the pictures, one by one, as the story of your life unfolds. Allow your child to ask any questions, or talk about anything he or she needs to. Patiently listen, and answer with love.

Ask your inner child if there is anything he or she needs from you today, or in the coming days and weeks, in order to feel comfortable, and loved. Listen carefully.

Your inner child holds a sacred place within your spiritual heart, representing you at your most open, and vulnerable. By helping your inner child feel safe and loved, your heart will grow, and blossom.

It's time to bring this journey to a close for now. So take a moment to give your inner child a hug and a kiss, tell him or her that you'll be back soon, and to gather anything you'd like to bring with your from this experience.

Bring your awareness gently back to your physical surroundings. Take your time, and when you're ready, open your eyes, and feel awake, alert, and refreshed.

TRUSTING YOURSELF

Make yourself comfortable, and close your eyes. Take a slow deep breath, and release any tension, as you feel yourself sinking into the surface you're resting on, becoming still more comfortable and relaxed. Take another slow deep breath, and release your thoughts, letting them drift far away. And take another slow deep breath, and know that in this moment, all is well.

Bring your awareness to your heart, in the center of your chest, and notice a softness there, a feeling of peace. Take a moment to enjoy this feeling, as you quietly focus in your heart, and follow your breath, in and out.

Bring your focus more deeply into your heart, as if you were standing there now, inside a cozy room. And image that there, deep in your heart room, you find a beautiful cord, woven of golden threads. But as you look more carefully at the cord, you see that it has become severed, broken in half.

One side of this cord leads up to your mind, and the other side connects into your heart. This cord, when whole and properly in place, allows you to know, with certainty, that you have the answers you need within you. It allows you to tap into your inner wisdom, receive direction that's good and true, and know that you can trust and use your own inner direction in your daily life. In short, it allows you to trust yourself.

In order to mend and restore this cord, you will envision yourself in three scenarios in your life, knowing, following, and trusting your own inner guidance.

To begin, consider a situation in your life where you have uncertainty, and need to know what to do. You might normally ask someone else's advice, but not this time.

Imagine yourself going within, into your own heart. Feel the presence and power of your own inner knowing, your own wisdom. Your own wisdom is rich and powerful, and comes from all the experiences you've ever had. Imagine you're plugging into all that accumulated wisdom, and becoming filled with inner certainty. Any stress you may have experience about what to do is dissolving, as a feeling of calm, quiet assurance comes over you.

Take another look at that golden cord in your heart, and you'll see that now it's partially mended. Some of the threads are still unconnected, but it's definitely better than it was before.

Consider another situation where you might be faced with the need for advice or direction. Imagine yourself going within, into your own heart. Feel the presence and power of your own inner knowing, your own wisdom. Again, your own wisdom is rich and powerful, and very deep. Imagine you're plugging into all your accumulated wisdom, and becoming filled with inner certainty. Any stress you may have experience about what to do is dissolving, as a feeling of calm, quiet assurance comes over you.

Take another look at that cord in your heart, and you'll see that now it's almost entirely mended. There are still a few threads that need to be healed, but it's well on its way now. And you definitely feel stronger inside.

Consider one more situation where you might be faced with the need for advice or direction. Imagine yourself going within, into your own heart. Feel the presence and power of your own inner knowing, your own wisdom, and imagine plugging into it, and becoming filled with inner certainty. Any stress you may have experience about what to do is dissolving, as a feeling of calm, quiet assurance comes over you.

Now look at that beautiful, golden cord in your heart. It's completely mended, with no sign that it was ever broken. In fact, it's radiating with light. Your heart and mind are connected now, and you have full confidence in your own inner wisdom.

Listen to the following affirmations, and allow them to resonate deep within.

I am learning to trust myself, and to rely on my own good inner wisdom.

I am taking the time to listen within, and following my own inner guidance.

I have a deep reservoir of inner wisdom and strength, and am calling upon it whenever I need to.

My heart's wisdom is solid and dependable, and I am valuing and appreciating it.

I am keeping my own council, and following my heart.

It will soon be time to bring this inner journey to a close. But first, take a moment to thank yourself for giving yourself this gift.

You have the ability, deep within, to know whatever you need to know, in any given situation. And you can trust yourself. Don't ever give that away, by seeking advice outside of yourself when it's not necessary.

Allow all the benefits of this experience to stay with you, as gently bring your awareness gently back to your physical body.

Take your time, and when you're ready, open your eyes, and feel awake, alert, and refreshed.

FORGIVING YOUR FATHER: HEALING INNER CONFLICT ABOUT YOUR DAD

INTRODUCTION

(This introduction applies also to the program, *Forgiving Your Mother*.)

As infants, we're entirely open to our environment, with no emotional boundaries. Like sponges, we pick up on our parents' energy as if it were our own, and absorb the vibration of all their emotional patterns. As we learn to walk and talk we begin to emulate their quirks, habits, communication styles, and beliefs. By the time we hit puberty, we've inevitably become like our parents to a large extent, albeit with our own unique spin.

Once we reach our twenties and begin to make our way in the world, we start to find out how the traits we've adopted work out for us. Specifically, we learn whether the emotional patterns we've picked up from our parents lead to good relationships or cause us problems.

That's the way things work on the unconscious level: We absorb patterns early on, find out which ones get in our way when we become adults, and then typically have to work hard to change them, sometimes for the rest of our lives. Meanwhile, we try not to pass the negative parts down the line to our children, often with mixed results. It can take several generations or more for a negative pattern to get ironed out. When we're in the middle of the process it can seem like we're not getting anywhere, but when viewed over time, we are getting better. Evolution of consciousness tends to be a long term, group effort. This program is a way to speed that up.

Grown up and far from the nest, it's not at all uncommon to find ourselves with unresolved feelings of anger, sadness, and even fear toward our parents. These emotional patterns play out in our relationships with everyone else in our lives, as we unconsciously try to resolve our father and mother issues with each new person we meet, often leading to frustration and disappointment.

A much better approach is to deal directly with the way we feel about our parents, and clear up those issues at the source. And by the source, I don't mean our parents, because it's the feelings within us we need to change, not them. Forgiveness is all about healing the forgiver. It doesn't matter whether our parents are still alive. By letting go of negativity toward them, we can move on and finally live our own lives. As with all personal growth, it's an inside job.

The following two guided meditations will help you forgive your father or mother, release stored negativity, and open up a clear space inside for you. If you were raised by someone other than your birth father or mother, you can use the meditation for whomever stood in as the most prominent father or mother figure for you. You'll probably notice an immediate effect from the first time you listen, though using this program repeatedly over a period of time will produce the best results.

GUIDED MEDITATION

Make yourself comfortable, and close your eyes. Take a slow deep breath, and let go of any tension, as you feel yourself sinking into the surface you're resting on, becoming still more comfortable and relaxed. Take another slow, deep breath, and release your thoughts, letting them drift far away. And take another slow, deep breath, and know that in this moment, all is well.

Imagine you're walking down the street in a friendly city, carrying an umbrella on a rainy weekday afternoon. You have some time on your hands, and when you spot a movie theater, you decide to see what's playing. It's an old theater, with ornate, colored scrollwork and a big marquee overhead, though the marquee is blank. There's a ticket booth in front, and as you walk up, you find it empty, but there's a note taped to the window. The note has your name on it, followed by the words, "Come in."

Puzzled, but anxious to get out of the rain, you enter the lobby, find it empty also, and approach the swinging doors into the theater. You step into a beautiful old movie room with ornate wall decorations, thickly upholstered seats, carpet with swirling patterns, and maroon velvet curtains covering a large screen. You're the only person here, so find a seat wherever you wish, and get comfortable.

The curtains part, the houselights dim, and the screen fills with your father's name, followed by the subtitle, *The Early Years*.

As the film begins, you can see it's a home movie, the print a bit scratchy and worn, possibly even in black and white. There your dad is as an infant, being held by his mother. Notice whether his father is in the scene, and what he's doing. How does his father seem to behave, and what is his attitude toward your father, as a baby. Does it seem like your father is being well cared for by both his parents?

The scene changes, and now your father is a toddler, just as vulnerable as you were at that age. You can see him looking up at his parents, for love and reassurance, perhaps unsure of receiving it. His parents may be attentive, or they may be busy with other things. Watch for a moment, and see how it goes.

Now he's a young boy, and perhaps he's picking up his own father's traits. Or, maybe his dad isn't in the picture. He may not have much exposure to his father, and what he has may or may not be positive. But you can see that as he grows into his teenage years, he's got challenges. Things are not always easy, and his life isn't perfect. Take a moment to watch things unfold.

Now your father's become a young adult, learning to make his way in the world, with faults and fears, strengths and weaknesses like everyone else. He's a human being, shaped by his family and the events that happen to him, doing the best he can. Watch him move through life for a bit, and see if you can get a feel for what it's like to be in his shoes.

The scene fades at this point, and the movie stops for a moment. As you sit in the theater, you may notice that you're feeling a little differently about your father, with a new perspective. He was your dad, but also, he was a man, in some ways ordinary, perhaps in some ways unique, but with a life full of his own challenges and concerns. Of course he fell short of being the perfect father, but really, there is no perfect father, and he did the best he could do under the circumstances that shaped him as a person. Take a moment and do your best to feel empathy for him, and his struggle in life.

The movie begins again, but this time it's not a home movie, but more of a Hollywood production, in full color. This is a movie about what your dad would have liked your life to be together, if it could have been.

You're about to enter the picture, and he's there with your mother when you're born. He's holding you in his arms, totally focused on you, gently rocking you and speaking quietly, and telling you how glad he is to see you.

There you are together a little later, when you're learning how to walk, as he's holding your hands, catching you or helping you up when you fall down. He talks with you, encourages you, hugs you, and lets you know how much he loves you by his actions and his words. He's your dad, and he makes you feel safe, and good.

Now you're seven years old, sitting with your family at the dinner table, next to your dad. He's happy, and he looks at you, and smiles. The two of you are talking about something, maybe joking around a little, and there's an easy, comfortable feeling between you. But he's still your dad, and you know that whatever happens, he'll be there for you. He lets you know where the boundaries are, and you know how he expects you to behave. And because of all that, you admire and respect him, just as he loves and appreciates you.

You're a teen now, and you and your father are doing something together that you both enjoy, perhaps something he taught you or introduced you to. That easy feeling and good connection is still there between you. You're having a conversation now, and he's listening to what you have to say, taking it in. He says something back that lets you know he understands, and supports you, and perhaps has a suggestion you feel good about.

The movie ends at this point, and as the house lights come up a little, you feel someone sit down next to you. You turn and find your father there with you, in the theater, on this rainy afternoon. He's not perfect, but he's real, and he's your father. Take some time to be with your him now, and let your time together unfold peacefully. Say whatever you need to say to your father now, as he listens, hears, and understands you, perhaps as never before.

Now give your father a chance to speak to you, to perhaps say things he was never able to say, that would be most important for you to hear.

As you sit here in the theater, on this rainy afternoon, you may notice that your feelings toward your father have softened, lightened, and become more neutral. Your father will always remain a part of you, but you are a very different person than he, and you're free to be yourself, and live your life, as the unique individual you are. If your father had the freedom of spirit to allow it, he would surely want it that way.

It will soon be time to bring this journey to a close. But first, take a moment to thank your father, for bringing you into the world, and passing down to you all the good things that he did.

And take time to thank yourself for giving yourself this gift.

Bring your awareness gently back to your physical surroundings.

Take your time, and when you're ready, open your eyes, and feel awake, alert, and refreshed.

FORGIVING YOUR MOTHER: HEALING INNER CONFLICT ABOUT YOUR MOM

INTRODUCTION

See the previous program introduction for *Forgiving Your Father*.

MEDITATION

[This is the identical guided meditation to *Forgiving Your Father*, with the wording changed for "mother."]

Make yourself comfortable, and close your eyes. Take a slow deep breath, and let go of any tension, as you feel yourself sinking into the surface you're resting on, becoming still more comfortable and relaxed. Take another slow, deep breath, and release your thoughts, letting them drift far away. And take another slow, deep breath, and know that in this moment, all is well.

Imagine you're walking down the street in a friendly city, carrying an umbrella on a rainy weekday afternoon. You have some time on your hands, and when you spot a movie theater, you decide to see what's playing. It's an old theater, with ornate, colored scrollwork and a big marquee overhead, though the marquee is blank. There's a ticket booth in front, and as you walk up, you find it empty, but there's a note taped to the window. The note has your name on it, followed by the words, "Come In."

Puzzled, but anxious to get out of the rain, you enter the lobby, find it empty also, and approach the swinging doors into the theater. You step into a beautiful old movie room with ornate wall decorations, thickly upholstered seats, carpet with swirling patterns, and maroon velvet curtains covering a large screen. You're the only one there, so find a seat where ever you wish, and get comfortable.

The curtains part, the houselights dim, and the screen fills with your mother's name, followed by the subtitle, The Early Years.

As the film begins, you can see it's a home movie, the print a bit scratchy and worn, possibly even in black and white. There your mom is as an infant, being held by her mother. How does her mother seem to behave, and what is her attitude toward your mother, as a baby. Does it seem like your mother is being well cared for by both her parents?

The scene changes, and now your mother is a toddler, just as vulnerable as you were at that age. You can see her looking up at her parents, for love and reassurance, perhaps unsure of receiving it. His parents may be attentive, or they may be busy with other things. Watch for a moment, and see how it goes.

Now she's a young girl, and perhaps she's picking up her own mother's traits. Or, maybe her Mom isn't in the picture very much. She may not have much exposure to her mother, and what she has may or may not be positive. But you can see that as she grows into her teenage years, she's got challenges. Things are not always easy, and her life isn't perfect. Take a moment to watch things unfold.

Now your mother's become a young adult, learning to make her way in the world, with faults and fears, strengths and weaknesses like everyone else. She's a human being, shaped by her family and the events that happen to her, doing the best she can. Watch her move through life for a bit, and see if you can get a feel for what it's like to be in her shoes.

The scene fades at this point, and the movie stops for a moment. As you sit in the theater, you may notice that you're feeling a little differently about your mother, with a new perspective. She was your Mom, but also, she was a woman, in some ways ordinary, perhaps in some ways unique, but with a life full of her own challenges and concerns. Of course she fell short of being the perfect mother, but really, there is no perfect mother, and she did the best she could do under the circumstances that shaped her as a person. Take a moment and do your best to feel empathy for her, and her struggle in life.

The movie begins again, but this time it's not a home movie, but more of a Hollywood production, in full color. This is a movie about what your Mom would have liked your life to be together, if it could have been.

You're about to enter the picture, and soon she's holding you in her arms, totally focused on you, gently rocking you and speaking quietly, and telling you how glad she is to see you.

There you are together a little later, when you're learning how to walk, as she's holding your hands, catching you or helping you up when you fall down. She talks with you, encourages you, hugs you, and lets you know how much she loves you by her actions and her words. She's your Mom, and she makes you feel loved, and comforted.

Now you're seven years old, sitting with your family at the dinner table, next to your Mom. She's happy, and she looks at you, and smiles. The two of you are talking about something, maybe joking around a little, and there's an easy, comfortable feeling between you. But she's still your Mom, and you know that whatever happens, she'll be there for you. She lets you know where the boundaries are, and you know how she expects you to behave. And because of all that, you admire and respect her, just as she loves and appreciates you.

You're a teen now, and you and your mother are doing something together that you both enjoy, perhaps something she taught you or introduced you to. That easy feeling and good connection is still there between you. You're having a conversation now, and she's listening to what you have to say, taking it in. She says something back that lets you know she understands, and supports you, and perhaps has a suggestion you feel good about.

The movie ends at this point, and as the house lights come up a little, you feel someone sit down next to you. You turn and find your mother there with you, in the theater, on this rainy afternoon. She's not perfect, but she's real, and she's your mother. Take some time to be with your her now, and let your time together unfold peacefully. Say whatever you need to say to your mother now, as she listens, hears, and understands you, perhaps as never before.

Now give your mother a chance to speak to you, to perhaps say things she was never able to say, that would be most important for you to hear.

As you sit here in the theater, on this rainy afternoon, you may notice that your feelings toward your mother have softened, lightened, and become more neutral. Your mother will always remain a part of you, but you are a very different person than she, and you're free to be yourself, and live your life, as the unique individual you are. If your mother had the freedom of spirit to allow it, she would surely want it that way.

It will soon be time to bring this journey to a close. But first, take a moment to thank your mother, for bringing you into the world, and passing down to you all the good things that she did.

And take time to thank yourself for giving yourself this gift.

Bring your awareness gently back to your physical surroundings.

Take your time, and when you're ready, open your eyes, and feel awake, alert, and refreshed.

GOOD BOUNDARIES

INTRODUCTION

Living without healthy boundaries deprives us of our dignity, is destructive to relationships, and keeps us from fulfilling ourselves physically, emotionally, and spiritually.

Like a broken fence, there are two sides to unhealthy personal boundaries. On one side is the pattern of disrespecting personal space, taking advantage of others, and being abusive. On the other is allowing oneself to be disrespected, taken advantage of or abused; and deliberately doing things for others that are the other person's responsibility to do for themselves.

This program focuses on the second side of the issue, and can be helpful for those who tend to be abused or taken unfair advantage of, who tend to give too much, and who in general tend to be a doormat for others.

Developing healthy boundaries may require some "personal space housekeeping." It may be time to change who you allow into your life, or stop giving others all the time or attention they've come to expect from you. Use this guided meditation to learn what changes you need to make. Then, if you're willing to put forth the effort, you can make a shift, establish good healthy boundaries, and enjoy the freedom in life they make possible.

MEDITATION

Make yourself comfortable, and close your eyes. Take a slow deep breath, and let go of any tension in your body, as you feel yourself sinking into the surface you're resting on, becoming still more comfortable and relaxed.

Take another slow, deep breath, and feel a sense of calm and peace begin to fill you, as you relax further. And take another slow, deep breath, and let your thinking begin to wind down and smooth out.

Imagine you've been sleeping a deep, sound sleep for many hours, and you're just beginning to stir awake. And the first thing you notice, is that you're waking up on a soft bed of pine needles, on the ground, surrounded by ancient fir trees.

It's just before dawn, and the air is quite cool, the light is dim, and there's a foggy mist in the air. You can smell the scent of pine, and the damp coolness of the earth. It's quiet, and any sound is blanketed by the mist. Everything is a palette of soft greens, browns, and grays.

Standing up, you begin to walk along a path through the trees, and you can feel the spongy ground beneath your feet. Perhaps you still feel a bit foggy from your sleep, but soon you come to a little spring, cup your hands to get a drink, and splash some of the cool, clear water on your face. Now you're beginning to see the trees and plants that surround you more clearly.

Walking further along, you come to a small bunker with what appears to be a cellar door folded down into it. There's a little sign on the door, and looking more closely, you see that the sign has your name written upon it, followed by the words, "Enter To Wise Up."

Before you do enter, consider that you're about to gain clarity on a pattern that has controlled and limited you, probably for many years. With this new clarity, you'll have the opportunity to make a change. But the choice to change your behavior will remain in your hands. Are you ready? It's time to find out.

Open the door. Before you are five stairs down to a landing, and you can see a soft light coming from the other side of the landing, at the bottom of the stairs.

As you step down onto the first step, take a moment to consider the following question: *What do I do for others that should be their responsibility to do themselves?*

As you step down to the second step, take a moment to consider this question: *In what situations do I give away my time, energy, or money, to gain acceptance, love or appreciation?*

As you step down to the third step, consider this question: *In what ways do I leave my own center and ignore my own truth to try and get my physical or emotional needs met?*

As you step down to the fourth step, take a moment to consider this question: *What do I feel or believe about myself, that makes me willing to leave my center and ignore my own truth?*

And as you step down to the fifth step, take a moment to consider this question: *What situations do I allow to occur, or not take precautions to prevent, that result in my being abused, hurt or taken unfair advantage of?*

Step down to the landing, look through the doorway, and you'll see you've come to a small movie theater for an audience of one, with a comfortable chair, thick carpet, sloping walls with speakers set into them and a sleek movie screen at the front. Have a seat in the chair and make yourself at home. The house lights dim, and the screen fills with your name, and just below it, the words, "Time To Wise Up."

The movie begins with a recent scene from your life, in which you were either taken advantage of or abused, or in which you took it upon yourself to do something for someone else that was not appropriate or healthy for you to be doing for them. Watch that scene unfold, and notice how your energy is effected in the movie, and how you feel.

Watch that scene again, and see, hear, and feel it with as much clarity as possible, as everything comes into sharper focus.

Watch that scene one more time, and this time notice the point at which you either made the decision to do what you did, or chose not to take action to stop it from happening. Notice whether you were conscious of the decision or choice, or if it seemed to happen without you even being aware of it.

The next scene is one that's not quite so recent, and again it's one in which you were either taken advantage of or abused, or in which you took it upon yourself to do something for someone else that was not appropriate or healthy for you to be doing for them. Watch that scene unfold, and notice how your energy is effected in the movie, and how you feel.

Watch that scene again, and see, hear, and feel it with as much clarity as possible, as everything comes into sharper focus.

Watch that scene one more time, and this time notice the point at which you either made the decision to do what you did, or chose not to take action to stop it from happening. Notice whether you were conscious of the decision or choice, or if it seemed to happen without you even being aware of it.

The movie changes now, and goes back to a point in time to where the theme of your story seems to have its beginnings, probably in childhood. As you watch this part of the movie, remember that you are now all grown up, are safe and protected in this moment, and have all the resources of a fully grown adult to take good care of yourself. You're only watching this movie to gather information, and there's no need to re-experience your emotions from the past.

What were the circumstances that made you leave your center, take on responsibilities that shouldn't have been yours, do something for someone else that wasn't good for you to do, or become the object of abuse or being taken advantage of?

Watch this scene just one more time, but this time, see your adult self come into the scene to guide and protect your childhood self, either by helping you make a better decision, by physically protecting you, or by completely removing yourself from that situation, taking your childhood self to a safe place.

See yourself safe and protected, and take a deep breath. See and feel that situation completely surrounded and filled with healing light, of whatever color you and your childhood self would like. Take another deep breath, and allow all feelings of fear, anger, or sadness to be released into the healing light, as you recognize that this happened long ago, and it's past and finished. Today you're all grown up, and can take good care of yourself, just as you've just taken care of your childhood self, and today you have many more choices and opportunities to shape your life.

The next part of the movie will show you how to let go of old patterns from the past, and establish a more positive, healthier way of being.

See yourself standing alone in a favorite setting, a place of your choice that feels safe and comfortable, and you feel relaxed and free to be yourself. As you stand there, become aware of a column of light extending from the highest heavens, straight through you and deep into the earth, all the way to earth's core. As the light passes through you, it resonates especially in your heart center, merging with your own energy, and expanding outward. Focus in your heart, and you can feel a deep sense of connection and strength.

As the light continues to pass through you, you feel more and more centered, grounded, and whole. You are fully self-contained and content, complete unto yourself. A circular zone of protection seems to project out all around you, and you can see it expanding out from your feet, your heart and your head. This zone, and the column of light passing through you, represent your healthy boundary. It's both an energetic boundary and a physical one, and it comes from the center of your own being. As you continue to stay centered, heart focused, and grounded, your energy becomes stronger, healthier, and more self-contained than ever.

Take some time to experience this inner connection, as you listen to the following affirmations, and allow them to resonate deep within.

I am centered, grounded, and connected inside, and know who I am.

I allow into my circle only those who are supportive of me and my life.

I take care of myself first, not selfishly, but as my healthy responsibility to myself.

I do things for others only when appropriate and supportive for everyone involved, including myself.

When I find myself faced with any person or situation that would threaten my safety, dignity, or well being, I physically remove myself from that situation without delay, and go somewhere safe.

I look out for myself, and plan so that my needs are covered, and I always have somewhere safe to be.

I choose to be only with those who respect my healthy boundaries, and insist that all others go their own way.

I am worthy of love, respect, and appreciation, and find that within myself.

Watch yourself on the screen, centered within your zone of protection, and notice how vital and strong your own energy is. Notice that when you reach out to someone else while centered, your energy stays strong, and your light stays bright. But when you reach for someone from sadness or a sense of lack, you move out of your circle, and your energy drops, and darkens. As soon as you leave your center to try to gain satisfaction, you can not be truly satisfied. But when you remain centered, you have the opportunity to find the love, acceptance, and support you're looking for within yourself. At that point you can begin to attract people to you who will honor, appreciate, and respect who you are.

Take some time to watch yourself on screen, as you experiment staying in your center and connecting with yourself and others in a healthy way; as well as seeing what happens when you do the opposite, and leave your center to try to gain someone else's approval or sympathy. Notice how your energy changes, what leaves you feeling drained, and what supports you.

Now take a few moments to consider what changes you might need to make in your life, to create the opportunity to develop good healthy boundaries. What situations would you need to avoid, and what would you need to cultivate? What relationships would you need to change or diminish, and how would you change them?

It's almost time to bring this inner journey to a close. So gather together anything you have learned, and plan to write about your experience and any changes you'll need to make, after the meditation.

Gradually bring your awareness back into your body, and your physical surroundings.

Take your time, and when you're ready, open your eyes, and feel awake, alert, and refreshed.

Pick up your pen and paper, and write about your experience now, while it's still fresh in your mind.

LETTING GO OF THE PAST, EMBRACING THE PRESENT

Make yourself comfortable, and close your eyes. Take a slow deep breath, and release any tension, as you feel yourself sinking into the surface you're resting on, becoming still more comfortable and relaxed. Take another slow deep breath, and release your thoughts, letting them drift far away. And take another slow deep breath, and know that in this moment, all is well.

Bring your awareness to your heart, in the center of your chest, and notice a softness there, a feeling of peace. Take a moment to enjoy this feeling, as you quietly focus in your heart, and follow your breath, in and out.

Imagine you've come to a point in your life where you need to pull up roots, and set off for a new home. It could be that an opportunity is calling to you. Or it might be that something is pushing you, forcing you to leave.

And imagine you're walking backwards toward your destination, so that you're facing the home you're leaving, not the one you're moving toward. It feels quite difficult to walk backward for a long time, and it's hard to see where you're going. But on you go, always looking backwards. Imagine looking at a globe, and tracing your movement as you travel half way around the world—as far as you can get from home, and still looking backward.

When you finally arrive, everything feels off, not quite right, and you miss your previous home. Nothing about this new place pleases you, and you sink into a depression. And so you go to sleep, and dream about your old home, and all the things you enjoyed.

Then, your dream changes, and you're looking at the outside of your new home, and you notice that honeysuckle vines have grown around your front door. The vines are blooming, and have the sweetest, most intoxicating scent, and you become filled with a bright, happy feeling.

You walk inside, and in your dream a tree begins to sprout, right in the middle of your living room floor. Its roots go deeper and deeper, and it grows taller and taller, forcing its way through your ceiling, and branching out in all directions. Then the tree flowers, and then bears beautiful fruit. You taste the fruit, and it's the most delicious thing you've ever tasted; juicy, sweet, and complex. And then you awaken from your dream.

There you are in your new home. It's not your old home, but it doesn't feel quite like your own home yet. But now you have a desire to make it yours. It may take time to put down roots. And it may take time for your life here to blossom, and bear fruit. But you can still smell that sweet honeysuckle scent, taste the delicious flavor of the fruit. And you feel magically connected to your new home.

Consider one thing you could do to become engaged in your new setting, in a positive way; a way that could help you put down roots, and bear fruit. Take a moment to imagine yourself doing that one thing, or perhaps ever more than one thing, now.

It will soon be time to bring this inner journey to a close. But first, take a moment to thank yourself for giving yourself this gift.

Allow all the benefits of this experience to stay with you, as gently bring your awareness gently back to your physical body.

Take your time, and when you're ready, open your eyes, and feel awake, alert, and refreshed.

PART FOUR

ELEVATE YOUR
ATTITUDE

CONTENTMENT: PEACEFUL & SELF-CONTAINED

Make yourself comfortable, and close your eyes. Take a slow deep breath, and let go of any tension, as you feel yourself sinking into the surface you're resting on, becoming still more comfortable and relaxed. Take another slow, deep breath, and release your thoughts, letting them drift far away. And take another slow, deep breath, and know that in this moment, all is well.

Imagine you're the center of a little tornado, and all of your own problems are the dirt and debris swirling around you. There is so much going on, so many things to worry about and sort out, that you feel compelled to talk about it all with someone you know, someone who will listen and understand.

So imagine you find a friend, perhaps someone you often talk to, and as you begin speaking to them, they get pulled into your tornado, and become covered with your own dirt and debris, until they feel just as bad as you do.

Now imagine that your friend somehow manages to pull free. Suddenly you're left alone again, with that same swirling tornado of problems, looking for another person to share them with. But no one is available. The tornado is getting stronger, more powerful, and it seems as if you might not be able to survive. But just when it seems the strongest, you begin to turn inward, in order to avoid the intense stress of all that bad weather.

And as you turn inward, focusing away from the tornado and the problems that surround you, you become more peaceful. And it feels better. And you notice that the more you focus within, and the further inside you go, the more calm you become, and the better you feel.

Going deeper still, you come to a lake, serene and perfect, at your very center. It's a beautiful lake, surrounded by high mountains and pine trees, reflecting the sun. Birds are flying overhead, and now and then a fish will break the surface of this placid lake, making ripples out from the center.

There's a large smooth outcropping of rock by the edge of the water, a fine place to sit and contemplate the lake. As you sit, a deep feeling of calm gathers within you. All the problems you so desperately wanted to talk about with others seem rather insignificant and distant now. Instead, you feel quite settled, and at peace.

A journal appears in your hands, and you find yourself writing down a few things that you might have normally sought other people's attention for. And as you write, a dialog begins, between you, and your own higher guidance. It's as if the lake, that part deep within you, were listening, really hearing you, and gently guiding you toward the comfort, and answers you've been seeking. Take a few moments here, as you imagine connecting within, to this deep source of comfort, and wisdom.

Now that you know about this source within, you have a choice. You can either focus outwardly, exaggerate your problems, and pull others into your drama. Or you can cultivate the habit of going within, settling down, and connecting with the peace that's already inside of you.

Are you afraid to be alone? Do you worry that if you don't rope people into your drama, that no one will come for you? The amazing thing is that people are more attracted to you when you're calm, and interested in listening to them, rather than telling them about yourself.

Imagine you're with someone who you normally enjoy being around, someone you might normally tell all your problems to. And imagine that this time, instead of the usual, you're asking about them, and listening to what they have to say about their own life.

Notice how engaged they become with you. Notice how they warm up to you, and seem to light up. And notice that they're not trying to get away from you, as they might normally do. This is the payoff for being interested and listening to others. They tend to like you, and want to be around you. Take a few moments to imagine yourself in this kind of relationship, with several other individuals, now.

Listen to the following affirmations, and allow them to resonate, deep within.

I am interested in other people, especially those closest to me, and am making it a point to ask about their lives.

I am carefully listening to what others have to say, and finding deep fulfillment in quietly hearing about them.

I am enjoying helping other people, and forgetting my own problems as I do.

I understand that my problems are only as big as I make them, so I am seeing things in proportion, and focusing on the good things in my life.

I am happy to let others get the attention they need and am quietly listening and supporting them.

It will soon be time to bring this inner journey to a close. But first, take a moment to thank yourself for giving yourself this gift.

Bring your awareness gently back to your physical surroundings.

Take your time, and when you're ready, open your eyes, and feel awake, alert, and refreshed.

While it's still fresh in your mind, take time to write down anything you may have heard, felt, or learned in this exercise.

PAYING ATTENTION: ABSORBING EVERY LESSON THE FIRST TIME

Make yourself comfortable, and close your eyes. Take a slow deep breath, and let go of any tension, as you feel yourself sinking into the surface you're resting on, becoming still more comfortable and relaxed. Take another slow, deep breath, and release your thoughts, letting them drift far away. And take another slow, deep breath, and know that in this moment, all is well.

Imagine that all the energy you've sent out into the world over the last few days is coming gently back to you, like the last parts of a puzzle coming into place. And as your energy returns, you begin to feel more whole, more like yourself.

Bring your awareness to your heart, in the center of your chest, and notice a softness there, a feeling of peace. Take a moment to enjoy this feeling, as you quietly focus in your heart, and follow your breath, in, and out.

Imagine you're walking along a quiet path through the woods, on a warm summer day. The trees are tall and majestic. The path is lined with mushrooms, moss, and tiny flowers of all colors. And the sky is showing through the tree tops in a deep, dazzling blue. Birds are singing. And squirrels and chipmunks are scampering here and there, collecting acorns and seeds.

But for some reason, your mind is elsewhere, and you're not noticing the beauty around you. It feels as if you were walking a few inches off the ground, missing life. And that's too bad, because if you were paying attention, you could enjoy this walk so much more.

There's a large boulder by the path, just up ahead. Climb up, and have a seat, and rest for a while. Imagine that while you're resting here, on this boulder, by the side of this path, that you're closing your eyes, and going deep within. And as you do, you notice an elevator, directly in front of you. The door slides open, you enter, and the elevator begins to take you up. It goes from the first floor... to the second floor... to the third floor... to the fourth floor... to the fifth floor... to the sixth floor... and finally comes to rest on the seventh floor.

The door opens, and you step out on the seventh floor, and find yourself in a room full of computer equipment. All kinds of very sophisticated machines are here, humming along. But over in one corner of the room is a computer that's blinking on and off, with the word "restart" on the screen. Looks like this one has a glitch.

Look at the keyboard, and you'll see a restart key. Go ahead and press that key now, and watch that computer come back online. Now it's humming away and doing what it's supposed to do. But take another look at the monitor, and you'll see that it's showing a movie of you, walking along that very same forest path. But this time you're walking with your feet firmly on the ground, and taking in all the scenery. You're quite enjoying the walk too.

Go ahead and take that elevator back down to the first floor, and step outside again. It feels good to be here now. Sit down on that boulder for a moment, because you have one more thing to do.

Imagine yourself in a situation, one that might normally cause you a bit of trouble. Perhaps this is a situation in which you struggle to focus and pay attention to what you're doing. Perhaps you might normally have to go through something like this situation many times, without learning what you need to learn.

But this time, imagine yourself with your feet on the ground, and your mind fully switched on and connected. Notice yourself being very observant, focused, and awake. Take a few moments to imagine and build this new image for yourself, now.

Listen to the following affirmations, and allow them to resonate, deep within.

I'm becoming relaxed and present, noticing all that's important, and fully absorbing my experiences.

I'm allowing myself to receive all the input that is relevant to my life, and processing it fully.

I learn quickly and completely, whenever I am exposed to new information.

I'm am open to life's lessons, and am easily gaining wisdom through experience.

My mind is fully engaged with life, and I am learning easily as I go.

It's almost time to bring this inner journey to a close. But first, take a moment to thank yourself for giving yourself this gift.

Bring your awareness gently back to your physical surroundings.

Take your time, and when you're ready, open your eyes, and feel awake, alert, and refreshed.

APPRECIATION: MESSAGES FROM A DEER

Make yourself comfortable, and close your eyes. Take a slow deep breath, and let go of any tension, as you feel yourself sinking into the surface you're resting on, becoming still more comfortable and relaxed. Take another slow, deep breath, and release your thoughts, letting them drift far away. And take another slow, deep breath, and know that in this moment, all is well.

Bring your awareness into your heart center, the energy center, in the middle of your chest, and notice a softness there. Imagine all of the energy you've sent out into the world lately coming gently back home to your heart, helping you to feel more whole, and more complete. Quietly receive this energy, and know that all is well, and you can simply be here, relax, and receive.

Bring yourself more fully into your heart, as if you were standing there now, inside a cozy room. Soon, you'll notice a doorway, and as you walk through it, you'll find yourself at the edge of a forest, looking down a long, winding trail. It's late afternoon, and the light is soft. The air is warm, and as a breeze finds you, you can smell pine, the sweet scent of the forest floor, and the yellow buttercups and bluebonnets along the trail before you. The path beckons, and it feels like the perfect day for a walk, so you set off on your way.

The forest is quiet, and your steps are soft on the spongey ground. And as you walk along you're soon enveloped by a peaceful feeling of enchantment, slowing everything down, taking you deeper and deeper within.

Soon it feels as if you've entered another world, like a dream where the shapes and colors of the forest glow from within, coming gently alive.

Your path leads to a little stream, one you can easily step across, and you stop to look in at the clear water, the bright copper colored stones, and the little fish darting here and there in the current.

Your path winds its way through ancient firs and oaks tangled with vines, until you come upon a huge boulder in the shape of a human heart. Standing before this boulder, you take it in for a moment, and feel your own heart begin to open and expand in response, preparing for what's to come.

Stepping quietly around the boulder, you discover a small clearing, a meadow filled with wild flowers and waving grass.

Entering the clearing, you come upon a solitary deer, who immediately senses your presence, and looks up to face you. As your eyes meet, you're flooded with a sense of awe and wonder at the beauty of this creature. The deer is totally at home in this setting, as if he were an extension of the plants, trees, and even the air you're sharing. And in the deer's eyes, you don't see fear, but recognition, as if he were expecting you. You're here to make a discovery, and the deer is here to help you.

Standing very still, you feel the unspoken connection between the two of you, and soon the deer begins speaking to you telepathically, as you hear his words resonate within your mind.

"Reality is upside down. Although this may seem like a dream, I am very real. But in your life, what you think of as your problems are imaginary. Look: All around me are gifts—the trees, the moss on the rocks, the air, the water. You have gifts all around you also. Do you see them?"

Take a moment to consider one situation in your life, and let the gifts surrounding it come into focus.

The deer continues:

"In winter, snow covers most of the ground, but I find a few leaves to eat, or I become very quiet and rest to conserve energy. I am humble and cooperative, and therefore can live and appreciate this world; a world that offers me everything."

Take a moment to consider another situation in your life, and open to the awareness of how you might come into greater cooperation, to better support yourself, appreciate your life, and enjoy what you've been given.

Again you hear the deer speak, saying,

"Do not worry. Do not fear. Everything comes as you need it, and all is in perfect order. Life is in motion behind every leaf and blade of grass, creating the scenery. Observe."

Take another moment to view your life through the eyes of this simple, beautiful animal, see what you've not before seen, and know what you have not known.

Sensing you have just a bit more time in this encounter, listen now for any other messages the deer, and the forest itself, may have to share with you.

It will soon be time to bring this journey to a close. But first, ask for a sphere of light to be placed all around you, and this experience, so that all the positive benefits will stay with you, and anything that you've released can be left behind. Take a moment to thank yourself for giving yourself this gift.

Bring your awareness gently back to your physical surroundings.

Take your time, and when you're ready, open your eyes, and feel awake, alert, and refreshed.

LIGHTEN UP! STOP BEING HARD ON YOURSELF

INTRODUCTION

We've all heard the expression, "stop being so hard on yourself," but what does it really mean? What are we actually doing when we're being hard on ourselves? Being hard on oneself is a state of mind that triggers an emotional response, resulting in a feeling of pressure. It's stressful being hard on ourselves, and if we're not careful, that kind of stress can also contribute to physical illness.

The "hard on yourself" state of mind begins with thinking "I'm not good," "I'm not good enough," "I'm not doing well enough," "I'm terrible at this," "I'm taking too long," and so on. In response to this line of thought, we create corresponding feelings of bitterness, frustration and anger toward ourselves. If we repeatedly do this, we become accustomed to these thoughts and emotions, and eventually they become normal for us. Then the whole pattern goes unconscious, and we find ourselves in a persistent state of gloom.

Why would we do such a thing to ourselves? Well, it starts out innocently enough, in childhood, when we pick up disapproval from our parents and the other adults around us. We adopt disapproval as a way of being, in part because it makes us seem more like the grown-ups, and in part because if we're disapproving of ourselves, we won't feel their disapproval. It's a kind of inoculation against criticism. We carry that pattern forward, and eventually we're disapproving, mopey adults, walking around being hard on ourselves. What a party, huh?

So, you're probably wondering, "How do I get myself to stop doing this?" Well, it's tricky, because you can't stop doing something you're not aware you're doing. And like most negative patterns, this one is unconscious most of the time. But, don't worry, we're going to get you out of this!

The first thing you'll need to do is start looking for the places where this tendency kicks in, and catch yourself in the act. In other words, start developing some awareness about it. You can do that, with practice, simply by paying attention. The guided meditation will help you with this, and pretty soon you'll begin to catch yourself being hard on yourself in all kinds of surprising and colorful ways.

You'll also need to start initiating a new behavior that interrupts the old one. So for example, say you catch yourself in a typical hard on yourself situation, like say you made a mistake; anything from buying the wrong kind of bread at the market, to forgetting to pay the mortgage, to making a social faux pas. When you find yourself in that situation, instead of going "Damn, I'm so stupid," you tell yourself it's OK. As in, "I just forgot something really important, and I do that sometimes, but it's OK." Or, "I just got angry, said some things I shouldn't have and made a total ass of myself, but it's OK."

When I said that, did you think, No! It's not OK! Well, that's just because you're used to being hard on yourself! Of course it's not a good idea to say bad things to people and make an ass of yourself, but you already know that. Hitting yourself over the head with an emotional hammer will not make you be a better person. It hasn't yet!

Punishing yourself never works. But what does work is tolerance, compassion, love, and understanding. Giving yourself a space for those things allows you to soften inside and change. So, you begin by giving yourself a break, and telling yourself "it's OK." Trust me, the world won't fall apart if you start being nice to yourself.

Now, if just saying "it's OK" doesn't sound like much to you, that's probably because you're hard on yourself, and you think you need to do incredibly hard, difficult things to be good enough. You don't! You start by doing the simplest, easiest thing, which is telling yourself it's OK. If you get into the habit of doing that, it's going to drive a wedge into that whole negative pattern. You know how a wedge works; it gets in with the smallest edge, and then keeps expanding. That "OK" is the smallest thing. It's being nice your yourself, and if you practice, it will slip in and bust the whole hard-on-yourself thing wide open.

Now, telling yourself it's OK is the first part. The second part is you *lean into the feeling* that it is OK. Just a little bit. Don't strain yourself, but try feeling OK about things, just to see what it feels like. Hey, if you don't like it, you can always go back to beating yourself up!

Am I making fun of this serious problem? Just a little. If we can laugh at ourselves, it loosens everything up inside, and makes it a lot easier to let this pattern go. And it's hard to be hard on yourself when you're laughing at yourself.

So that's the basic overview of how this pattern works, and how you can start to change it. The guided meditation will give you a lot more leverage to work with this from a deeper level. Use it on a regular basis for a while, to get the most out of it.

MEDITATION

Make yourself comfortable, and close your eyes. Take a slow deep breath, and let go of any tension, as you feel yourself sinking into the surface you're resting on, becoming still more comfortable and relaxed. Take another slow, deep breath, and release your thoughts, letting them drift far away. And take another slow, deep breath, and know that in this moment, all is well.

Imagine you're walking along a quiet path through the woods, on a beautiful, spring day. The trees form a canopy of bright new leaves, making lacy patterns against the sky. And the ground beneath your feet is layered with old brown leaves and twigs from years before, sweet wildflowers, and little mushrooms popping up here and there. All is calm, and you're taking your time to walk along, observe nature, and spot squirrels and chip monks running by, commuting from tree to tree.

Up ahead you can see an old stone wall winding its way along the path, all shades of brown and gold, covered here and there with soft green moss. A few small birds are flying in and out of the trees nearby, or hopping about on top of the wall. There's an enchanting feeling in the air, and you have the uncanny sense that you're not quite alone here.

Out of the corner of your eye you begin to catch a glimpse of two or three small people sitting on the wall by the path up ahead, but as you look toward them they disappear. As you start to look away, you can almost see them again, or *feel* them. And as you come closer you start to hear bits of conversation. They're talking about someone… saying

"So worried all the time. That dark cloud has to go. 'I'm bad, I'm bad, I'm so bad'. So sad! What can we do?"

"Tickling? Would that work?"

"No, too unpredictable."

"Oh, I know," one of them says, "Hugs. We'll use hugs."

"No, that won't work," another one says, "You know we can't actually touch a human. Maybe a distraction. We could use butterflies!"

"Too flighty," another one says. "We should use buttercups."

"Hey, how about we just say 'Lighten up, Buttercup'."

And they all burst out laughing.

And at that point you realize two things. One, you've just come upon some kind of wood elves, fairies or odd little angels, and two, they're talking about *you*. They seem to think that phrase, "Lighten up Buttercup" is hilarious, and soon they start saying it to each other, and making up songs about it.

"Lighten up buttercup".

"No, you lighten up. Ha ha!"

But as you come up along side them they all become very quiet. You try not to look directly at them, because it makes them harder to see. And they're looking all around too, trying not to look at you, as if they didn't want you to know they were just talking about you. But as soon as you pass by, one of them giggles, and then the others start laughing, and soon they're all singing again... "Lighten up, buttercup, lighten up."

There's a fallen log a little way up the path, and that looks like a good place to rest for a while, and as you sit down you notice a little spring just behind it, with water falling down over rocks into a tiny pool, making a sweet, trickling sound. You can still hear the wood fairies singing "Lighten Up Buttercup" down the way, but it's in the background now, and it's actually kind of enjoyable. You do feel a little lighter, as a matter of fact.

As you sit and relax, consider something in your life that you're not happy about, that you tend to get down on yourself for. Summarize the situation to yourself in one sentence. For example, "I lost my temper today at work."

Now say that same sentence to yourself, and end with, "but it's OK," as in "I lost my temper today at work, but it's OK."

Take a slow, deep breath, and as you exhale, allow in the idea that whatever happened in that particular situation, it's OK.

Now allow yourself to relax into the feeling that it's OK.

Consider another situation in you tend to give yourself a hard time about. Summarize the situation to yourself in one sentence, and end with, "but it's OK."

Take a slow, deep breath, and as you exhale, allow in the idea that whatever happened, it's OK.

Allow yourself to relax into the feeling that it's OK.

Now review one or two other things you generally give yourself a hard time over. With each one, summarize the situation in one sentence, end the sentence with "but it's OK," take a deep breath, and let in the idea and the feeling that it's OK. Take some time to do this, now.

Imagine yourself floating, it could be in a pool on a rubber raft, in the ocean, or in the air. All around you are feelings, thoughts, words, sights and sounds that reflect the idea that you're OK, and all is well. Spend some time here, just being, just floating, as you feel all the stress you've accumulated over time beginning to soften, and melt away.

Take some time to listen to the following affirmations, and allow them to resonate deeply within.

Today I'm being kind to myself.

I'm easy on myself when I make a mistake, and make it OK.

When things don't go my way, I breathe, relax, and treat myself with dignity.

I'm doing my best, and respect myself not matter the outcome.

I do what I can to take pressure off myself, and live in peace.

I work in harmony with myself, gracefully accept my faults, and celebrate my successes.

I will always be a work in progress, and can relax about my growth.

I'm a good person, doing my best, and I'm OK.

Look into the future, at a situation you may find challenging, where you'd normally give yourself a hard time. Imagine yourself giving yourself a break instead, and making it OK. Take a moment to do this now, with one or more possible situations.

As you walk back along the path, approaching the forest elves on the wall you can hear them talking again, this time saying things like,

"Look how much better!"

"Wow, what happened?"

"See, it worked, we did it!"

And after you pass by, on the way out of the woods, you can hear one of them call after you, "Hey Buttercup! Remember to lighten up," and they all crack up laughing and talking again.

It will soon be time to bring this journey to a close. But first, take a moment to thank yourself for giving yourself this gift.

Bring your awareness gently back to your physical surroundings.

Take your time, and when you're ready, open your eyes, and feel awake, alert, and refreshed.

RELEASING JUDGMENT &
EMBRACING LIFE

INTRODUCTION

Being in judgment makes us feel a little more secure about ourselves, momentarily. Here's what else it does:

- Creates a false sense of separation between ourselves and others.
- Puts us squarely in the ego and the intellect, and takes us out of our heart.
- Causes a   fixed attitude that cuts off the flow of love.
- Sends a message to the universe that we're not ready to move forward spiritually.
- Makes it impossible to o ffer genuine compassion to others.
- Makes it impossible to receive love and compassion.
- It can lead to depression, and ultimately to physical illness.

Judgment is not about seeing clearly, recognizing fault, or knowing something special. It's about holding a negative focus, and shutting out life. It's a kind of "against-ness" that puts up walls. Our judgment of others and the world around us has little effect outwardly, because it happens inside our own system. But it poisons us where we live, and causes everything within to go sour.

Why do we judge? It's an unconscious pattern connected to insecurity that often originates when we feel marginalized, belittled, oppressed, overlooked, unseen, or hurt in some way. When we feel disadvantaged or insecure, judgment creates a temporary feeling of superiority. Judgment can also be triggered by seeing things in others we find repugnant in ourselves. When confronted with such a mirror, judgment gives us a sense of distance from how we fear being seen by others.

The worst part about judgment is that when we have this pattern, we tend to focus it on ourselves most of all, and we can be very harsh in the process.

If you have an interest in real spiritual growth, connecting with your higher self and God, and sharing love with others in a genuine way, judgment has to go. That includes judgment about yourself, others, God, the world, politics, religion, and everything that happens here on Earth that you might currently consider to be bad.

This doesn't mean we have to like everyone and everything, it means coming to an attitude of neutrality and acceptance of what is.

To release judgment, we have to first be willing to become aware we're doing it, and acknowledge it within us. This isn't so easy, because the habit is so ingrained within us it happens automatically. It takes serious conscious motivation and effort to become an observer at this level. And then there's the ego factor that tries to keep us from admitting that we're doing it. Self honesty is some of the most difficult inner work we can do.

But if you've come to the point where living a heart-centered life, and having a conscious connection to your own higher self and God is your goal, then this is for you. The following guided meditation will provide the structure and focus to help you get started.

MEDITATION

Make yourself comfortable, and close your eyes. Take a slow deep breath, and let go of any tension, as you feel yourself sinking into the surface you're resting on, becoming still more comfortable and relaxed. Take another slow, deep breath, and release your thoughts, letting them drift far away. And take another slow, deep breath, and know that in this moment, all is well.

Imagine that all the energy you've sent out into the world over the last few days is coming gently back to you, like the last parts of a puzzle coming into place. And as your energy returns, you begin to feel more whole, more like yourself.

Now, send some of your energy down into your feet, and from your feet, straight through the ground and deep into the earth, all the way to Earth's core. Your body and Mother Earth are connected energetically, and you can feel her support.

Bring your focus into your spiritual heart, in the center of your chest. Your heart is a great place to connect deeply within, find peace, and receive guidance, and it's the ideal place for you to be right now. Imagine you're standing within your heart space, as if it were a cozy room.

There's a wonderful, welcoming feeling of warmth, peace, and comfort here, and as you continue to spend time in your heart, you can feel love gathering all around you. It's a feeling of total acceptance of you, just as you are, and a feeling of support, for your desire to let go of negativity, and embrace life.

You've come to your heart today to uncover and release judgment patterns within you, that have limited your flow of love, and it's time to make this shift, now. So, concentrate your energy on your intention to release judgment, and repeat the words, "Please help me see, know, and let go."

A doorway opens in your heart, and as you step through, you find yourself in a circular chamber, like a cave. The walls and ceiling are completely covered with beautiful crystals of purple, gold, and white, all radiating a profound, healing energy.

This chamber was created to help amplify and bring to light all the thoughts, feelings, and subconscious patterns within you that you're ready to release. There is a soft mat on the floor, and you lie down face up, looking at the crystals surrounding you now.

The work is about to begin, and you relax even more deeply, opening to the powerful energies that are here for you. Call to mind someone you don't like, and let any feelings of judgment come up from within you, as you allow the unconscious to become conscious.

Take some time to bring that person more and more present into your awareness, as you uncover judgment, release it, and find neutrality, then acceptance, and finally, compassion for that person.

Call to mind a situation you think is wrong, or even unforgivable. This could be something happening out in the world you have little contact with, or something much closer to home.

Let your feelings of judgment toward this situation come up from within you, as you allow the unconscious to become conscious. Take some time to bring that situation more and more present into your awareness, as you uncover judgment, release it, and find neutrality, then acceptance, and finally, compassion for the situation and the people involved.

Consider something about yourself, or something you've done, that you hold judgment toward.

Let your feelings of judgment toward this come up, as you allow the unconscious to become conscious.

Take some time to bring that situation more and more present into your awareness, as you uncover judgment, release it and find neutrality, then acceptance, and finally, compassion for yourself.

Ask your higher consciousness to bring to mind someone, or something that you haven't considered so far, that brings up judgment within you.

Let your feelings of judgment toward this come up from within you, as you allow the unconscious to become conscious.

Take some time to bring that situation more and more present into your awareness, as you uncover judgment, release it, and find neutral-ity, then acceptance, and finally, compassion for the situation and the people involved.

As you continue to lie within this crystal chamber, purged as you have been of some of the judgment within you, experience the energies here beginning to intensify, pouring love into you, powerfully, and steadily. Take some time to simply open and receive, allowing any negativity within you to release.

Listen to the following affirmations, and allow them to resonate deeply within:

I am opening my awareness to uncover judgment within me, so I can release it.

As soon as I become aware of judgment, I quickly let it go.

As an aspiring person of peace, I am making a shift, and releasing judgment within me.

I look past the surface, set aside judgment, and open my heart.

As I release judgment, I accept myself and others. I drop down from my judging intellect to my compassionate heart.

I am giving myself a break, stepping off of judgment about myself, and making myself OK.

Perhaps there are other affirmations for you to hear, and know. Take a moment now to listen within, and receive.

Imagine yourself going forward into life in the coming days and weeks, and becoming more aware of judgment within you than ever before.

Make a firm agreement with yourself now, that from now on you will become more sensitive to your inner climate, and as judgment comes up, you'll recognize it, and quickly let it go.

See and feel your future self establishing a new pattern of awareness, neutrality, and freedom.

It will soon be time to bring this journey to a close. But first, take a moment to thank yourself for giving yourself this gift.

Bring your awareness gently back to your physical surroundings.

Take your time, and when you're ready, open your eyes, and feel awake, alert, and refreshed.

ENCOURAGEMENT: RECONNECTING TO LIFE

Make yourself comfortable, and close your eyes. Take a slow deep breath, and let go of any tension, as you feel yourself sinking into the surface you're resting on, becoming still more comfortable and relaxed. Take another slow, deep breath, and release your thoughts, letting them drift far away. And take another slow, deep breath, and know that in this moment, all is well.

Imagine you've been scuba diving in just off the coast of a tropical island, looking for a rare fish you've heard about, but only seen in pictures so far. You've heard from the locals that you can find this fish here, right in this spot. So you've come to dive here every day, but without success. You've seen a few fish, some of them very pretty, but not the one you're looking for.

Day after day you come and dive, and day after day you've had no luck. On the fifth day, you're diving, and feeling pretty discouraged. And as that discouragement comes over you, you also begin to doubt you'll ever find what you're looking for. All the other times you've tried things and failed begin to play in your memory. And before long, you're feeling quite hopeless, and depressed.

So you drift all the way down to the ocean floor, and lay down there, in your scuba gear. You've got plenty of air, but the longer you lay there, the less you feel like getting up. You're stuck, and something needs to change. So, you inwardly say the word, "help."

Suddenly, a push of warm water begins to bubble up beneath you, coming right out the sea bed, like a deep sea Jacuzzi. The bubbles feel good, and are kind of tickling you, so you begin to move a little, on the ocean floor. Then the bubbles increase, and they begin to push up, up off the sea bed, up through the depths, and up toward the surface.

It feels as if the sea itself has decided you've been down there long enough, and is giving you a hand back up. Take a moment to feel yourself floating, up, up, and up, toward the surface, but not quite to the top.

Just as you're nearing the surface of the water, you suddenly see the fish you've been looking for. There it is, absolutely beautiful, even more striking than the pictures you've seen, and full of color. And there's another. And more still. You're now swimming in the center of a school of those fish—hundreds of them! Take a moment to enjoy this thrilling, ecstatic feeling of success and beauty.

Take some of this feeling, and connect it back to your life, and the challenges you may have been facing recently. Know that you have the power, the energy, and the will within you to reengage with life, pursue your dreams, and do whatever it is you need to do. Take a moment with this, now.

Now take a moment to visualize yourself taking your next step, and doing whatever needs to be done. See and feel yourself taking action, engaging, and having the good feeling of being connected to life, once again.

It will soon be time to bring this inner journey to a close. But first, take a moment to thank yourself, for giving yourself this gift.

Let all the benefits of this experience stay with you, and you gently bring your awareness gently back to your physical surroundings. Take your time, and when you're ready, open your eyes, and feel awake, alert, and refreshed.

POSITIVE THINKING: CHANGING YOUR INNER CLIMATE

INTRODUCTION

The idea that our thinking determines our reality goes back thousands of years. It was popularized in the second half of the 20th Century by the self improvement movement, and again more recently by popular authors and spiritual teachers. The notion that we can change our lives by changing our thoughts is a compelling one, and it appeals to multiple levels of our consciousness. On the high end, it inspires hope for a better world; and on a more mundane level, it inspires hope for a bigger TV, nicer car, and better boyfriend or girlfriend, *if only we can think them to us*.

While it's true that our thoughts influence who we are to become, this seemingly simple concept is far more complex. Who we are and who we will be is determined by a combination of factors, including our thoughts, our feelings, our accumulated emotional baggage, our experiences, our heritage, our environment, our higher plan, and most importantly, and most often left out of the "formula," Divine Will.

And actually, when you consider the kinds of things we typically have running through our minds, it's a very good thing we *don't* instantaneously create our reality with our thoughts. Thank God we're not that powerful!

Regardless of how our thoughts influence our reality, the indisputable fact remains that our thinking colors our experience of life in the present moment. If I'm thinking dark thoughts, I'll be living in a dark mental environment. If my thoughts are charitable and appreciative, I'll be living in a much more comfortable and inviting place. And my mental climate will not only effect how I feel, but how others feel about me, and whether they prefer to be near me or keep their distance.

Like moving from a dump into a nice home, once we begin to become aware of our mental environment and consciously feel the difference between positive and negative, we typically become motivated to do some "home improvement."

But changing our thinking is not easy, because the intellect is like a computer, and tends to respond to the way it's been programmed. The messages we absorb in childhood form our programming, and how we respond to life as a result becomes our patterned behavior. Old habits die hard, and patterns are difficult to change.

Difficult, but not impossible! The first step to changing any pattern is to become aware of it. To change our thinking, we must first begin to notice what we're thinking about. Call it "meta-thinking," or "thinking about our thinking from the outside-in." We need to form a new habit of watching ourselves and noticing when our thoughts are turning negative. Not to judge ourselves, because that would only add to the negativity, but to make a shift as soon as we recognize what we're doing.

The following guided meditation can help you establish the habit of watching your thoughts and recognizing when you're in negativity, and provide you with a simple but powerful technique you can use to help make a shift.

MEDITATION

Make yourself comfortable, and close your eyes. Take a slow deep breath, and let go of any tension, as you feel yourself sinking into the surface you're resting on, becoming still more comfortable and relaxed.

Take another slow, deep breath, and release your thoughts, letting them drift far away. And take another slow, deep breath, and know that in this moment, all is well.

Envision a column of light extending down from the highest heavens, around and through you, going deep into the Earth, and experience yourself lifting up on this column of light.

Higher and higher you go, until the Earth is quite far in the distance.

Continuing on, you feel drawn upward higher still, into the heavenly realms, arriving finally at a beautiful sanctuary.

The floor and walls of this sanctuary are made of light, with the ceiling open to the heavens. Created by thought waves from on high, this is a place for transformative work to occur. You're intending to make some changes to your thinking patterns, and have been brought here to receive higher support for your efforts.

In this environment, charged with healing energy, all of your positive efforts can be amplified and accelerated, making it easier for changes within you to occur. Your desire to make your inner climate a more positive and loving one is in alignment with Higher Will, and because of that, assistance and support is being offered. However, much of the work is still up to you, and it's time to get started.

To begin, observe yourself in the world below, in a typical situation in your daily routine, as you're engaged in a neutral or positive line of thought.

Imagine the colors in your energetic field, and you'll see that they're clear, beautiful, and bright.

Imagine the vibrational sound within your field, and you'll notice it's gentle, resonant, and harmonic.

And observe the feeling that seems to permeate your being, and notice that it's warm and uplifting.

Now observe yourself as you're engaged in a negative line of thought.

Imagine the colors in your energetic field, and you'll see that they're dark, muddy, and unappealing.

Imagine the vibrational sound within your field, and you'll notice it's harsh, dissonant, and unpleasant.

And observe the feeling that seems to permeate you, and you'll notice it's abrasive and uncomfortable.

You've just gotten a brief glimpse into the way your thoughts influence your inner climate. Now you're going to do something that will help you make a shift. Call to mind a physical object, and make sure this is something you like, something that has positive associations for you. You'll be using this object as a symbol to help remind you to keep a positive focus. It could be as simple as a candle, a piece of jewelry, or a book.

Envision that object, feel it's presence, and send it right down into your life below, so it rests comfortably somewhere inside your energetic field.

Envision it there within your field, surrounded and glowing with your favorite color of light, and making a sound that you find very pleasing. Take a moment to use your imagination, focus upon this, see it clearly and feel it strongly within you.

Now once again observe yourself, as you're engaged in a line of thought that's negative.

Notice again that your energetic field begins to take on colors that are dark and muddy, sounds that are dissonant and grating, and feelings that are uncomfortable.

But notice the object you've just placed in your energetic field is beginning to glow with that favorite color of light, brighter, and brighter, and gradually making a sound you find very pleasing.

The object continues to brighten and sound louder, almost like an inner alarm clock, until it catches your attention. And as soon as you notice it, you realize you're in the midst of a negative line of thought, and immediately begin to change it.

Take a few moments to use your imagination, and envision yourself in several different situations, as this symbolic object catches your attention, helps you recognize negativity, and begin to make a shift.

Bring your awareness once again to your presence in the sanctuary of light. When you find yourself in negativity, it would help to have some positive thought patterns readily available, so that you can easily make a shift, and that's what we'll work on next. The energy surrounding you now shifts to a higher frequency, as the second stage of this process begins.

Call to mind one scene from your life when you felt comfortable and happy, and imagine you're in that scene.

See, feel, and hear that scene, and make it as real as possible. Hold out your hand with your palm facing upward. At the peak of your experience, curl your first two fingers and press them into the pad of your thumb. Do this physically, so you'll have a tactile sensation. That scene is now programmed into your system, as if you were programming a remote control for a TV set.

Call to mind another scene from your life when you felt comfortable and happy, and imagine you're in that scene.

See, feel, and hear it, and make it as real as you can. Hold out your hand, and at the peak of your experience, press your fingers into the pad of your thumb. The second scene is now programmed into your system.

And call to mind one more scene from your life when you felt comfortable and happy, and imagine you're there. Make it as real within you as possible. Press your fingers and press into the pad of your thumb. The third scene is now programmed into your system.

Now, take a few moments to practice calling forth each of the three scenes by pressing your finger to the pad of your thumb, one after another, switching as you go. Make each scene as real as possible.

Observe yourself once again in the world below, engaged in a negative line of thought. Notice again the dark muddy colors, the dissonant sounds, and the uncomfortable feelings in your energetic field. And see that your symbolic object begins to glow with that favorite color of light, ringing with a pleasing sound until it catches your attention. And as soon as you notice it, you realize that you're in the midst of a negative line of thought, and begin to change it.

This time you access your remote control, press your finger to your thumb pad, and immediately switch to one of the positive scenes you've programmed in. Take a few moments to go through this experience again, and practice, switching from a negative line of thought to a positive scene.

From now on, it will be your responsibility to become more aware of the thoughts you hold, recognize when they're negative, and make a switch. By doing this, you'll enjoy all the benefits of maintaining a positive inner climate, and attracting to yourself all that is positive.

It will soon be time to bring this journey to a close. So take a moment to thank the support that's all around you, and to thank yourself for giving yourself this gift.

Bring your awareness gently back to your physical surroundings.

Take your time, and when you're ready, open your eyes, and feel awake, alert, and refreshed.

DAILY FOCUS

INTRODUCTION

The daily focus process is a way of making a strong connection to any personal quality you wish to adopt. Do this process as you begin your day, and it will help you embody a specific quality, and draw upon it throughout the day.

To prepare for this process, decide upon one quality you'd like to focus on. For example, you might choose to focus on trust, honesty, calm, spontaneity, courage, or love, to name just a few. Pick something you feel might be of particular value to you, or just let any quality come to mind.

MEDITATION

Make yourself comfortable, and close your eyes. Take a deep breath, and let go of any tension in your body, as you settle into a more relaxed posture. Feel yourself dropping down from your mind into your body. Feel the weight of your body sinking into the surface you're resting on, as you become still more comfortable and relaxed.

Consider the quality you've chosen to focus on today. Imagine that the word is floating before you in space, and visualize it clearly spelled out, the letters glowing with light. This quality, and the light that surrounds it, come from the highest source of all creation, from the center of the universe. It is living energy, a message for your heart, mind, and soul, and brings with it tremendous power and support, for you.

Imagine that light from this word, this quality, is flowing into you through the top of your head.

Envision and feel it flowing all through your head, face, and neck.

And let it flow down your shoulders, into your arms, and out your hands.

And experience the light of this quality flowing into your chest and upper back, your abdomen and lower back, and into your hips.

And let it flow down your legs and into your feet, as it connects all the way through your body.

And now hear this word, this quality, as if it were being sung to you now by a heavenly messenger, or perhaps spoken to you by someone you love.

Allow the sound of this quality, its very essence, to resonate throughout your body, touching into every cell, and awakening its meaning and potential everywhere within you.

Allow it expand throughout your energetic field—the aura surrounding your body—as it radiates all around you. Take a few moments to experience this.

Perhaps there's an even higher aspect of this quality, an even deeper meaning you can discover. Allow your higher consciousness, the guiding force in your life, to reveal the highest aspect or deepest meaning that this quality might hold for you, especially today. Take a few moments to receive any new information your guidance system may have for you at this time.

Now let's use your creative imagination to project this quality forward with you into your day. Envision yourself doing the things you might normally do, enhanced and supported by this quality. Be sure to include your relationships and meetings with other people, perhaps at work, or with family, or friends, and see them responding to you in positive ways. Take a few moments to visit one scene and then the next, spending time where you'll gain the most benefit.

As you bring this quality into your life, more and more opportunities present themselves, and you experience each event, and every encounter, in richer, deeper, and more meaningful ways. With this quality, a whole series of positive changes continues to unfold within and around you.

Now gather together all the positive energy you've created though this process, and bring it to a gentle focus within your heart.

Feel, see, and hear this energy collecting itself into a small point of light in the center of your chest, and experience it gently pulsing there, steadily and softly.

Know that the positive energy of this quality is available to you any time during the day, by simply reconnecting in your heart center.

It's almost time to bring this process to a close for now, and so gradually direct your focus back to your physical surroundings.

Take your time, and when you're ready, open your eyes, and feel awake, alert, and refreshed.

FINDING HOPE

Make yourself comfortable, and close your eyes. Take a slow deep breath, and let go of any tension, as you feel yourself sinking into the surface you're resting on, becoming still more comfortable and relaxed. Take another slow, deep breath, and release your thoughts, letting them drift far away. And take another slow, deep breath, and know that in this moment, all is well.

Imagine you've been searching for a dear friend of yours, someone you've known and loved for many years, named Hope. You and Hope had some wonderful times together, and when you're with her, you always feel uplifted, and willing to try new things. But lately you've been separated, and you've had trouble finding your friend Hope, and you've become quite sad.

You thought you might find Hope in the north central United States, in Minnesota, because there's a city there called New Hope. And so you travel by airplane, and train, and then bus, and finally arrive in New Hope.

You have no idea where to begin, so you simply start going door to door, asking for your friend, Hope. And at each house you're told "No, there's no Hope here, no Hope at all," and "No, they don't know where to find your friend Hope."

And so you decide to rest. You find a park, with a grassy lawn, and some comfy old benches, and you settle down, close your eyes and take a snooze for a while. Soon you're dreaming about going door to door, and finding no Hope. And in the dream you're sitting on the curb, and you see a car go by. And for just a moment, just before the car passes out of sight you think you see Hope riding along in the front seat.

That's when you wake up. And who do you suppose is sitting right next to you, on that park bench, in New Hope Minnesota? It's Hope of course, just like you remember her. She's looking at you, and smiling, just as lovely and friendly as ever. Take a moment to catch up with her, find out where she's been, and get reacquainted. You might want to tell her how you've been looking for her, all the things you've tried, and how hard it's been. She'll listen, understand, and help you to lighten up. Do this for a moment now.

Now that you've found hope, consider one thing you can do, perhaps something you can look into, someone you can talk to, or something you can try, to help your situation. Imagine yourself doing that, and visualize yourself doing it, as soon as this meditation is over. Take a moment to do this visualization, now.

Listen to the following affirmations, and allow them to resonate, deep within.

I am opening to new possibilities, and allowing life to fill me with enthusiasm.

I am allowing life to breathe new energy into me, and am being lifted.

I am hoping for the best possible outcome, and am embracing all that is good.

I am taking charge of my attitude, looking forward, and turning toward the light.

I am finding hope and encouragement at the core of my being, and making a choice to feel optimistic.

It will soon be time to bring this inner journey to a close. But first, take a moment to thank yourself, for giving yourself this gift.

Let all the benefits of this experience stay with you, and you gently bring your awareness gently back to your physical surroundings. Take your time, and when you're ready, open your eyes, and feel awake, alert, and refreshed.

NO MORE GUILT

Make yourself comfortable, and close your eyes. Take a slow deep breath, and let go of any tension, as you feel yourself sinking into the surface you're resting on, becoming still more comfortable and relaxed. Take another slow, deep breath, and release your thoughts, letting them drift far away. And take another slow, deep breath, and know that in this moment, all is well.

Imagine you're walking across a desert landscape, dragging a ball and chain behind your left foot. You have the feeling you know where the key is, to unlock the cuff around your ankle, and yet you don't look for it. Somehow you feel as though you deserve this, because of something you said or did. A lingering feeling of guilt follows you along with the ball, and weighs heavily on your mind.

Perhaps you've been dragging this behind you for quite a long time, and you don't even remember what you did to deserve it; or perhaps something happened recently. Either way, you're tied to your fate, and you feel as if you'll never be free of this terrible weight, one that you drag along with you, across the desert, hour after hour, day after day.

One spring day you see something green on the far horizon. At first it's too far away to make out clearly. But eventually you can see that it's a hilly landscape, covered with pine trees. As you draw nearer, the scene takes shape, and you can see the majestic tall pines, standing out against the blue sky. And as you come closer still, you can begin to smell the scent of pine.

Finally, you come to the pine covered hills, and follow a path into the woods. There's a wonderful, refreshing feeling in the air here, with the pine trees blooming, birds singing, and little streams bisecting your path. It would be fun to enjoy this world, and explore a bit more, if it weren't for that ball and chain strapped to your ankle, and the lingering feeling of guilt weighing on your mind.

You've walked a long way today, so you sit by a stream, listen to the water, have a drink, and take a little nap. You're soon dreaming, and find yourself in an old courtroom, all paneled in knotty pine wood, with pine benches, and a judge on his great dais, robed in black. You're standing before the judge now, and he looks at you fiercely, asking your name.

You tell him your name, and he says, "Why, you're not even on the docket. Why are you here?" And you say, "Excuse me Your Honor, but I believe I'm guilty. I've done something awful, and deserve to be punished."

The judge confers with his attendant, looks over some material on his desk and sternly says, "Listen carefully, because I'm only going to say this once. You have accused yourself falsely, and entirely without merit. You have imprisoned yourself with a self-imposed sentence that is invalid, null, and void. With all the authority invested in me by the great state of (and here he mentions the name of your location) I hereby order you to release yourself forthwith from any further burden, punishment, or obligation. You are not only not guilty and free to go, but you are to forgive yourself immediately, and stop being so hard on yourself. It's a crime against nature to punish yourself. Do you understand what I've just said to you?"

To which you reply, "Yes, Your Honor."

"Is there any part of what I've said that is not clear?"

"No, Your Honor."

"Then leave my courtroom. We have important work to do here, and you're taking up our valuable time."

And as you're about to say "Thank you, Your Honor," you find yourself stirring awake, listening once again to the sound of the stream, smelling the scent of pine, and feeling the fresh air on your skin.

And before you have time to give it a thought, you reach in your pocket, find a little metal key, unlock the cuff around your ankle, and release the ball and chain, and with it, the heavy burden of guilt, that's never been yours to carry, and was a crime against nature for you to do so.

You stand up, and begin to dance, right there on the path, in the stream, and on the rocks, on the path again, holding your arms up to the heavens, breathing deeply, and feeling the love of the universe embracing you, allowing it in all the way, for the first time in too long. Take a moment now, to enjoy your freedom.

It will soon be time to bring this inner journey to a close. But first, take a moment to thank yourself, for giving yourself this gift.

Let all the benefits of this experience stay with you, and you gently bring your awareness gently back to your physical surroundings.

Take your time, and when you're ready, open your eyes, and feel awake, alert, and refreshed.

PART FIVE

VISUALIZATION FOR
SUCCESS

OPENING TO WEALTH

Make yourself comfortable, and close your eyes. Take a slow deep breath, and let go of any tension, as you feel yourself sinking into the surface you're resting on, becoming still more comfortable and relaxed. Take another slow, deep breath, and release your thoughts, letting them drift far away. And take another slow, deep breath, and know that in this moment, all is well.

Bring your awareness into your heart center, the energy center, in the middle of your chest, and notice a softness there. Imagine all of the energy you've sent out into the world lately coming gently back home to your heart, helping you to feel more whole, and more complete. Quietly receive this energy, and know that for now, it's OK to simply be here, relax, and receive.

Bring yourself more fully into your heart, as if you were standing there now, inside a cozy room. Soon, you'll notice a doorway, and as you walk through it, you'll find yourself in a corporate meeting room, with beautifully paneled walls, a polished conference table with a flower arrangement in the center, swivel executive chairs, and in the front of the room, a sleek media system with a large screen.

And seated around the conference table are the world's most powerful business giants, financial advisors, and success coaches, all gathered for a meeting with you. Some are dressed in formal business attire, with laptops and briefcases by their side, and others may be dressed in exotic clothing from other cultures. Some may be media personalities, famous for their great wealth and successful business ventures. And some may be historical figures, such as Ben Franklin or FW Woolworth. And depending upon your wish, there may also be certain spiritual figures present, as part of this group.

The chair at the head of the table is open, and waiting for you. As soon as you sit down, you feel yourself plugging into an incredible source of power—the combined energy of all of those present. All the information, power, and support you'd ever need is here, just waiting for you to take it in.

As you sit at this table, you can feel the powerful energy here beginning to flow into you from the bottom of your feet, up through your legs, through your hips, into your abdomen and lower back, into your chest and upper back, through your shoulders, arms, and hands, and into your neck, head, and face, and right out the top of your head.

Whatever inner limitations you may have held regarding wealth are now being dissolved by the powerful energy flowing through you now, and will be cleared out during the remainder of this process.

You're about to receive some very keen, focused insight into your situation, along with highly personalized information about how you can change. So begin to feel yourself opening up, and preparing to hear what you've not heard before, and see what you've yet to see. Prepare to change your beliefs about you, and what is possible for you, as you allow in new insight, information, and energy as never before.

As you continue to open, you form a telepathic bond with all the experts here, so that what they know, you will soon know. In order to receive the information that will best serve you, you'll be led through several series of questions, each designed to open up a different part of your consciousness. To make sure you're not unconsciously blocking something that might help you, be open to all of them, and stay open until the process is complete.

You're about to begin. Each question will be followed by a period of quiet, so you can search your heart and mind, and find the answers you need. And after each series you'll have time to work more directly with the information you receive.

The first series of questions is about what you could be doing to become more wealthy, but have been unwilling to do. Here we go:

What have you been unwilling to do because you tell yourself it's too hard, though it really isn't?

What have you been unwilling to do because it would push you beyond your comfort zone?

What could you do that you've been unwilling to do, because you feel it's beneath you, though it really isn't?

What have you been unwilling to do because you're afraid you might fail?

What have you been unwilling to do because even though it would be all right to do, it might embarrass you?

What have you been unwilling to do because you tell yourself it's immoral, when deep inside you know that it really isn't?

What if anything else have you been unwilling to do that could help you move forward?

Consider the answers that stood out most prominently from this first series. The media screen at the front of your conference room now activates, and the lights dim. A movie begins playing that portrays you doing the very things you've been unwilling to do, successfully, with a positive attitude, and appreciation for the wealth it brings you. Take some time to watch this unfold, and envision yourself in action.

The next series of questions concerns resources you have available, either within you, or on the outside, that you've not been using, that could add to your wealth and success. Here we go.

What good advice from others have you been ignoring, not listening to, or not following, that could help you?

What inner messages have you been hearing within yourself, and ignoring?

What skills, talents and abilities do you have that you do not use?

Who could help you that you avoid asking for help?

What latent talents and abilities do you have that you could tap into, that you have not developed or utilized?

What other help, resources, or support have you not taken advantage of or utilized?

Consider the answers that stood out most prominently from this series. The media screen at the front of your conference room again activates, and the lights dim. A movie begins playing that portrays you accessing and using all your resources to help your situation, with gratitude for the opportunity they provide, and appreciation for the wealth they bring you. Take some time to watch this scene unfold, and envision yourself in action.

The next series of questions is about deep feelings and beliefs within you that block your success. Here we go:

Do you feel, somewhere within you, that you are not worthy of being wealthy?

Do you feel, somewhere within you, that you don't deserve more than you already have?

Do you feel, somewhere within you, that you are not ready to be wealthy?

Do you feel, somewhere within you, that wealthy people are not as good as people who struggle?

Do you feel, somewhere within you, that being wealthy would make you lazy, unkind, uncaring, irresponsible, or bring out some other negative character trait in you?

Do you have any other negative feelings or beliefs about being wealthy that block your success?

Consider the answers that stood out most prominently from this series, about deep feelings and beliefs within you that block your success. As you sit at the head of the conference table, the consultant to your immediate left pushes a button that automatically folds the entire table in half, opens the floor, and hides the table under the floor, which closes up again.

You now stand in the middle of the room, surrounded by all of your consultants. They each extend their hands toward you, and begin to energetically send clearing energy into your system, directly toward the deep feelings and limiting beliefs you recognized, as well as any you did not. Take a few moments to receive their energy, as these feelings and beliefs are cleared and dissolved.

As you continue to receive the supportive energy of your team of consultants, listen to the following affirmations, and allow them each to resonate deeply within.

I am willing to do whatever necessary, from the smallest job to the biggest, in order to succeed.

I am willing to step beyond my comfort zone and grow as a person, for the success and abundance it brings.

I follow my own inner compass toward greater wealth and happiness, unswayed by outside opinion, staying true to my own course.

I know, deep inside, what's right, and follow my heart.

I take in and follow good advice and wise council, and ignore that which does not apply.

I take good advantage of every opportunity to succeed.

I wisely utilize all my natural talents, gifts and abilities.

I wisely seek out and utilize all the resources available.

I gratefully accept the help of others, and allow them to contribute to my growth.

I am a good person, fully worthy of having everything I need, and more.

I am inherently kind and compassionate, and will continue to be so even as I become more wealthy.

It will soon be time to bring this inner journey to a close. But first, take a moment to envision yourself finishing this exercise, writing notes about what you have learned, and taking any steps you need to take, to put your new learning into action.

Take a moment to thank your team of consultants for their energy and support.

And take a moment to thank yourself for giving yourself this gift.

Bring your awareness gently back to your physical surroundings.

Take your time, and when you're ready, open your eyes, and feel awake, alert, and refreshed.

BRINGING CLIENTS TO YOUR DOOR

Make yourself comfortable, and close your eyes. Take a slow deep breath, and let go of any tension, as you feel yourself sinking into the surface you're resting on, becoming still more comfortable and relaxed. Take another slow, deep breath, and release your thoughts, letting them drift far away. And take another slow, deep breath, and know that in this moment, all is well.

Imagine you're walking through the door of your place of business, but as you step across the threshold, instead of the usual setting, you immediately find yourself in a beautiful mountain meadow of waving grass, surrounded by tall evergreen trees. It's a crisp summer day, and an alpine breeze carries the scent of pine, and wildflowers. You can hear the sound of a bird song, and the gentle current of a nearby stream. Everything here is calm and peaceful, a place and time created just for you.

In the center of the meadow is a wide staircase of stone, with seven steps, each of a different color, leading up to a stage made of rock. And upon the stage rests a large searchlight, the kind you might see at the opening of a special event, not yet turned on.

As you come closer, you'll see that each step has something written upon it. The first step is red, and as you step upon the red step its words come into focus, and you read, "I Am Qualified."

As you stand on the red step, consider all the groundwork you've done to make your work professional. Your education, training, and any equipment or furnishings related to your work fully qualifies you to offer your services to the world. Take a moment to reflect on the foundation you've laid, and feel the solid strength it brings you, as you're flooded by the red color of this step, and the words, "I Am Qualified."

The second step is orange, and as you step upon the orange step its words come into focus, and you read, "I Offer Value." As you stand on the orange step, you know that with all you have to offer, your new clients will gain a great deal of value, and be very satisfied. Everyone who walks through your door will receive what they need and more. Take a moment to reflect on value you offer, and feel the sense of quiet assurance it brings you, as you're flooded by the orange color of this step, and the words, "I Offer Value."

The third step is yellow, and as you step upon the orange step its words come into focus, and you read, "I Am Confident I Can Help." As you stand on this step, you know because of all your training and experience, that when people come to you for help, you'll help them. Take a moment to reflect on how you're able to help people, and feel the satisfaction it brings you, as you're flooded by the yellow color of this step, and the words, "I Am Confident I Can Help."

The fourth step is green, and as you step upon the green step its words come into focus, and you read, "I Am Likable." As you stand on this step, know that simply because of who you are, and your good feelings toward others, that people like you. You are a pleasure to know, and a pleasure to work with. Take a moment to reflect upon how people are drawn to you and like you, and feel the happiness this brings, as you're flooded by the green color of this step, and the words, "I Am Likable."

The fifth step is blue, and as you step upon the blue step its words come into focus, and you read, "I Am Fair." As you stand on this step, know that the price you charge is fair for the value you supply, and a good rate for the work you offer. Take a moment to reflect on the fairness of your prices, and feel the sense of balance and calm it brings you, as you're flooded by the blue color of this step, and the words, "I Am Fair."

The sixth step is purple, and as you step upon the purple step its words come into focus, and you read, "I Appreciate People." As you stand on this step, recognize that you like meeting people, and getting to know them. You feel a natural kinship with others, and are grateful they find you and choose to do business with you. Take a moment to reflect on your appreciation of others, and the feeling of inner warmth it brings you that they choose to interact with you, as you're flooded by the purple color of this step, and the words, "I Appreciate People."

The seventh step is violet, and as you step upon the violet step its words come into focus, and you read, "I Deserve Success." As you stand on this step, know that you're a good person, and deserve to be successful, deserve to have material wealth, and deserve to be happy. And if there's anything within you that speaks contrary to this fact, you are letting it go now. Take a moment to know that you're deserving, and feel the peace this awareness brings, as you're flooded by the violet color of this step, and the words, "I Deserve Success."

Stepping up to the rock stage where the spotlight rests, you feel more clarity than ever before. You're clear that the time has come for you to step forward in life, reach out to people with your work, receive as many new clients and customers as you desire, and fully share your gifts with the world. As you stand on this rock stage, in this mountain meadow, you know it's time, and the universe knows it's time as well. All that remains to let your future clients know.

Look at the spotlight, and you'll see a lever, currently set to the "off" position. Once you turn the spotlight on, you'll be setting in motion a chain of events that will bring clients to you, as many as you wish, for as long as you desire. You're ready, and it's time. Pull the lever to the "on" position, and the spotlight will send a powerful beam of light straight up into the cosmos.

This beam of light contains within it the essence of your own personality, and the energy of the work you offer. The beam is networking into the consciousness of everyone on Earth, and will attract people who are right for you. All they will need do is hear or see your name to make the connection, and they will contact you. For that to happen you'll need to first put your name in public, whether that's through word of mouth or media. But once one of your future clients hears about you or learns about your business, they'll instantly know they need to come and see you.

Imagine your future clients as if they were stars in the night sky, each seeing and recognizing your beam of light, and connecting with it energetically. Take a few moments to observe this unfolding, as each client star recognizes and resonates with the energy of your beam of light.

Now imagine that the meadow, the stone staircase, and the spotlight changes back into your place of business, and you're there, welcoming client after new client. Each person has somehow heard about you, knew you were the right person for them to see, and found their way to you. And they're coming from every direction, near and far. Take some time to allow this vision to unfold.

Now fill in your ideal scene further, and imagine yourself enjoying each new client, appreciating them, being grateful for the work and the income they bring.

Envision your ideal balance of work, rest, and recreation time, and imagine yourself enjoying that balance, working as much as you'd like, resting when you need to, and thoroughly loving the free time you have as well.

Envision yourself enjoying the lifestyle, free time activities and material things your new prosperity affords you. Take a few moments with this.

Take a few moments now to consider any next steps you need to take in the world, to bring this vision to reality. This would include any networking, advertising, and marketing you need to do, as well as any other steps regarding your business, so that it's perfectly set up, receptive, and attractive to new clients.

It will soon be time to bring this journey to a close. But first, take some time to simply be grateful for all the new clients you are about to receive, and the prosperity you are about to experience.

And take a moment to thank yourself for giving yourself this gift.

Gradually bring your awareness gently back to your physical surroundings.

Take your time, and when you're ready, open your eyes, and feel awake, alert, and refreshed.

While it's still fresh in your mind, take a few moments to write down any steps you need to take to help bring your vision into reality. Do this now.

ENVISIONING YOUR IDEAL NEXT JOB

INTRODUCTION

Your next job might not be what you expect. Sometimes a new experience is waiting for us, but our limited thinking keeps us from connecting with it.

So in the following guided meditation you'll envision yourself in different scenarios, to review what you already know about yourself, consider new ideas, and see what fits you best. Through this program you'll gain perspective, and gather insight about your ideal job. Let's get started.

GUIDED MEDITATION

Make yourself comfortable, and close your eyes. Take a slow deep breath, and let go of any tension, as you feel yourself sinking into the surface you're resting on, becoming still more comfortable and relaxed. Take another slow, deep breath, and release your thoughts, letting them drift far away. And take another slow, deep breath, and know that in this moment, all is well.

Consider something you enjoy doing. This could be something you're familiar with doing for a living, or it could be something you enjoy, but have never done professionally. Imagine how it would feel to do this activity as part of your new job. Notice whether you feel comfortable, engaged, and fulfilled by doing this activity at work, or otherwise. I'll give you a moment to try this out.

Consider another activity you enjoy, something different than the first, and imagine doing this as part of your job. Notice whether you feel comfortable, engaged, and fulfilled with this activity at work, or otherwise.

Now consider one more activity you enjoy. This time, expand your horizons and make it something you might normally not think of doing for a living, even if it seems like a stretch. Imagine doing this as part of your job. Notice how you feel about doing this activity at work.

Which of the activities you've just imagined seemed most enjoyable to do at work? Which felt most comfortable? Which felt most engaging? Which would be most fulfilling?

Consider something you'd like to learn about. This could be a professional skill, a hobby or personal interest, or something related to your personal growth. Imagine how it would feel to learn about this in the context of your job. Notice whether it feels comfortable, challenging, fulfilling, or otherwise.

Consider something else you might like to learn about, perhaps something you've had in the back of your mind, but haven't really explored. Imagine how it would feel to learn about this in the context of your job. Notice whether it feels comfortable, challenging, fulfilling, or otherwise.

Consider one more thing you might like to learn about, and this time, to stretch your imagination, make it something you'd not normally consider. Imagine how it would feel to learn about this in the context of your job. Notice whether it feels comfortable, challenging, fulfilling, or otherwise.

Which of the areas you've just imagined learning about seemed most enjoyable to be involved in at work? Which felt most comfortable? Which felt most engaging? Which would be most fulfilling?

Consider a way you might like to help other people, or something you'd like to contribute to the world around you. Envision yourself doing this as part of your job, and imagine how it would feel to engage in this way.

Consider another way you'd like to make a difference in the world, perhaps something you've not allowed yourself to really explore before. Envision yourself doing this as part of your job, and imagine how it would feel to help or contribute in this way.

And consider one more way you might like to help people, or contribute to the world. This time, make it something that stretches the boundaries of your imagination, even if it seems like a total fantasy. Envision yourself doing this as part of your job, and imagine how it would feel to help others or contribute to the world in this way.

Which of the ways of helping or contributing to the world you've just reviewed stands out as the most real and fulfilling for you?

Now you'll join together the areas you felt strongest about, and envision yourself doing something you most enjoy, learning something you'd most like to learn, and helping in the way you'd most like, all as part of the same job. Take some time let your imagination freely assemble this image, and allow it to unfold for the time being without concern for how realistic or possible this may be. Imagine yourself doing, learning, and contributing in this job setting.

Now we'll focus on some of the more specific preferences you might have about your job. I'll ask a series of questions, and give you time to consider each one. Let your imagination fill in the picture as freely and completely as possible.

In your ideal job, you might work for a single person, a huge corporation, or any size establishment in between. How many people do you imagine being around in your work? One or two, a small group, or a large number?

What type of setting do you see yourself in; an office, a retail outlet, someplace outdoors… Imagine your ideal work environment.

How much will you interact with other people in your work? Will you be working with other employees or staff, interacting with the public, or spend most of your time on your own?

Will you have a lot of supervision in your work, with very specific tasks to perform, and few decisions of your own to make, or will you have freedom to get things done your own way?

What kind of pay and benefits would you like to receive for your work? Consider receiving that level of income, and imagine what sort of changes it might bring to your life.

Now, join together these aspects and envision a job with that size, setting, level of interaction, supervision, and pay. Imagine yourself in that situation, and notice how you feel working there. Notice whether it feels comfortable, engaging, and fulfilling, or otherwise.

Now you'll imagine three possible job scenarios, with three different levels of satisfaction.

First imagine you've found a job that fulfills some of the ideals you've thought about, though it falls far short of fulfilling all of them. Perhaps the work is good, but the pay isn't enough, or the people and the environment is great, but the work isn't fulfilling. This is a job you'd be willing to settle for, if you can't find anything better.

Envision yourself doing this job, going in to work, beginning, and working throughout your shift. What is your day like? How are you feeling as you work at this job? How do you feel about your work at the end of the day, at the end of the week?

Now, imagine you've found a job that fulfills every one of your ideals, and offers you even more. This is a dream job, and in some ways, it's hard to believe you've even landed it. Envision yourself doing this job, going in to work, beginning, and working throughout your shift. What is your day like? How are you feeling as you work at this job? How do you feel about your work at the end of the day, at the end of the week?

Now, imagine you've found a job that fulfills most of your ideals, and seems to fit you quite well, even though there are some surprises you had not foreseen. Perhaps there are things that could be better, but maybe there's also potential for improvement, as you go along. There are lots of positives in this job, and some challenges too. Envision yourself doing this job, going in to work, beginning, and working throughout your shift. What is your day like? How are you feeling as you work at this job? How do you feel about your work at the end of the day, at the end of the week? I'll give you extra time here, so use your imagination to fill in as much detail as possible.

In this meditation you've given your imagination and your unconscious mind a chance to expand, open to new possibilities, and hone in on what you want. This process will likely continue to unfold within you over the coming days, both in your dreams and your waking hours. Return to this meditation again several times, to gain clarity as you continue to envision your ideal job.

It will soon be time to bring this journey to a close. But first, take a moment to thank yourself for giving yourself this time and space to prepare for your next step.

Bring your awareness gently back to your physical surroundings.

Take your time, and when you're ready, open your eyes, and feel awake, alert, and refreshed.

Begin taking the steps you envisioned in this program, now.

FINDING YOUR IDEAL JOB

Have you envisioned the kind of job you want? If so, this guided meditation will help you find it.

GUIDED MEDITATION

Make yourself comfortable, and close your eyes. Take a slow deep breath, and let go of any tension, as you feel yourself sinking into the surface you're resting on, becoming still more comfortable and relaxed. Take another slow, deep breath, and release your thoughts, letting them drift far away. And take another slow, deep breath, and know that in this moment, all is well.

Imagine you've been sleeping a deep, sound sleep, for many hours, and you're just beginning to stir awake. And the first thing you notice, is that you're waking on a soft camp-side air mattress, high on a mountain top. It's a clear night, and the sky is filled with more stars than you've ever seen, a breathtaking view. You've been dreaming about the next step in your career, and it occurs to you that perhaps the millions upon millions of stars before you each symbolize a job for someone on this planet.

There are so many, it would seem impossible to know which one might be right for you, and even more difficult to connect with any, as they all appear so distant. And so faced with that thought, you find yourself getting up from your cozy bed, and lighting your campfire, for the comfort and warmth it offers.

Settling back down to rest again, you look back up at the stars and see that now there are far fewer. In fact, as you continue to watch the sky, all disappear but just a handful of the brightest, and clearest. And as you begin to drift back off to sleep, you imagine that if those were your potential jobs, now it would be much easier to choose the right one. And falling into a dream, you imagine your campfire has sent out a beam of light, all the way into the heavens, branching out to each of those big, bright stars.

When morning comes, you stir awake, and consider your dream. With the beam of light from your campfire to the stars, you symbolically connected to your ideal job prospects. Now it won't be hard to recognize those jobs when you see them out in the world. You'll know them intuitively, because you've already visited them in the dream state. Now it's just a matter of bringing them into view, in life. Let's work on that, next.

Consider the people you know—family, friends, and professional connections, for the time being excluding any social media connections. Later on you'll have the opportunity to write them all down, but for now, simply bring the people you know to mind. Imagine them gathering together into one group in front of you, as if you were on stage in a small theater, and they made up the audience. Perhaps you have some friends you've not spoken to in quite some time, and would like to visit again. Put them in the audience, too. Take a moment to visualize the theater filling up, and imagine everyone there is glad to see you, and happy to help you in any way they can.

Now consider that everyone in your audience probably knows about as many people as you do. So imagine all of them have also invited their friends, and since word about your meeting has spread quickly, many times the number of people are now pouring in. In fact, you're going to need a much bigger auditorium now, so imagine it expanding, and filling with more and more people, all of whom are interested in receiving a message from you.

Imagine that you walk out on stage, and begin to talk to your audience, telling them about the job you're looking for. Be sure to fill in all the details, the kind of place you want to work, what you want to do, the hours, and so on. Someone in your audience knows about the kind of job you want, and it's often the smallest thing that triggers a person's memory. So take some time to describe your ideal job now, and envision your words setting off lights in the minds of your audience.

Now allow that scene to fade, and imagine yourself out in the world, reaching out to everyone you know personally, letting them know about your job search, and asking them to inquire among their connections on your behalf. Imagine your request being well received. Word about you is going out, and connections to your potential jobs are being easily made. Take a moment to envision yourself taking steps to connect with each person in your network, and watch the positive results.

Now we'll envision your job search from another angle. Consider the kinds of employers you'd like to work for, and imagine yourself doing a search for all the employers that fit your criteria, making a list, and narrowing it down to the handful that suit you best. Imagine yourself taking steps to find out everything you can about those five employers. You're learning about their history, their focus, the character and personality of their work, and all you can about the people who work there. You're even researching whether you might have a first, second, or third hand connection with any of the people already at that employer, who might have a lead into the business. Take a moment to imagine yourself doing this research, and making valuable discoveries and connections; the kind that just may lead to your ideal job.

Now consider the other ways of connecting to your ideal job. These might include employment agencies and job websites, social media, online classified ads, and other possibilities. Imagine organizing your approach so that you can explore the best opportunities available, without becoming overwhelmed or discouraged. Take a few moments to envision yourself embracing this task, enjoying the process, and discovering connections to your ideal job.

Your ideal job may be right around the corner, or it may be waiting for you farther down the road. It's important to stay positive and engaged in your job search, and avoid discouragement, for as long as it takes to reach your goal. Envision yourself staying connected with your future job, and taking the action steps necessary, daily, into the future. Send your future self the encouragement you will need to keep going. Take a few moments to do this now.

Listen to the following affirmations, and allow them to resonate deeply within.

My ideal job exists and is waiting for me to connect, in perfect timing.

I am taking necessary actions steps daily to connect with my perfect job.

I am staying engaged with my job finding process, and keeping a positive attitude, for as long as necessary.

I am already connected with my perfect job, and am doing my part to help it manifest in my life.

The value I offer and the need I can fill is drawing my perfect job and I together. Our connection is inevitable.

I am letting others know about my job search so they have the opportunity to help.

People want to help me, and make positive connections on my behalf as needed.

I take advantage of all the available resources for connecting to my perfect job, on a regular basis.

In this meditation you've primed your unconscious mind, and visualized the steps to find your ideal job. Before we finish, let's do one last visualization. Imagine yourself hearing the end of this recording, opening your eyes, and beginning immediately with actions steps. You'll start by organizing lists of people to contact, and jobs to research, and then following through with them over the coming days and weeks. Envision doing this now.

It will soon be time to bring this journey to a close. But first, take a moment to thank yourself for giving yourself this time and space to prepare for your next step.

Bring your awareness gently back to your physical surroundings.

Take your time, and when you're ready, open your eyes, and feel awake, alert, and refreshed.

Begin taking the steps you envisioned in this program, now.

WINNING YOUR IDEAL JOB INTERVIEW OR AUDITION

INTRODUCTION

Once you've determined what you want to do, and where you want to work, the challenge becomes getting hired. Normally that means winning the favor of either your future boss, employer, or gatekeeper in the form of a human resources interviewer. Sometimes you have to pass two or more interviews to win a coveted position.

Your interviewer's job is to find out about your qualifications and your character. He or she may ask you about your skills and experience, may ask personal questions, and may possibly even ask questions that seem odd or off the wall, just to see how you might respond. Your job is to be yourself—your best self. You don't need to figure out the right things to say. You can simply stick to being honest, open, and positive. Share the best of you, just enough, and leave out the rest. This ability improves with practice, so it would be a good idea to do just that.

It would be a very good idea to find a friend or mentor who can stand in as an interviewer. Practice with them, and make it as real as you can. Have them sit behind a desk as your interviewer might. Walk into the room, shake hands, sit down, and have them ask you the sorts of questions you might be asked, and even throw you some curves. Do this repeatedly until you're comfortable with the process. Then, go interview for some jobs you don't necessarily care about getting, to get some practice with the real thing.

You're looking for a professional position, so be businesslike about the way you prepare for your interview. The small amount of time you spend doing this can make the difference in getting your ideal job.

The following guided meditation will help you feel comfortable in your interview, so you can put your best foot forward.

MEDITATION

Make yourself comfortable, and close your eyes. Take a slow deep breath, and let go of any tension, as you feel yourself sinking into the surface you're resting on, becoming still more comfortable and relaxed. Take another slow, deep breath, and release your thoughts, letting them drift far away. And take another slow, deep breath, and know that in this moment, all is well.

Consider your job skills; those you currently possess, as well as any you might be learning on your new job. Take a moment to envision yourself at your new job, applying those skills, and producing a positive outcome. Use your imagination to put yourself there and make it as real as you can.

Now bring to mind some of the key personal qualities you possess, things about you that will make a positive contribution to the business and people you'll be working with. For example, honesty, reliability, and consideration for others are things that create a positive atmosphere, and help get work done easily. Envision yourself at your new job, bringing out your personal qualities with positive results. Take a moment to use your imagination and make it as real as you can.

Take a little longer to imagine yourself at your new job, as if you're already working there. Envision yourself coming to work, doing your job, interacting with others. Experience yourself fitting right in, feeling connected with that workplace and the people there. Make it as real in your imagination as you can, and get a good strong feeling of being a part of that work environment, bringing all your skills and personal qualities with you.

Now use your imagination to carry forward that feeling of connection with your new job directly into your job interview, so that while you're speaking with your interviewer, it feels as if you are already hired and working there. Imagine yourself in the interview session, being yourself, relaxed and comfortable, with all your skills and personal qualities present.

Take a series of slow, deep breaths now, breathing way down into your abdomen. And as you do, imagine you're also breathing deeply and slowly in your interview. Feel your feet on the floor. You're grounded and connected, relaxed and comfortable. Take some time to hold this focus now, simply focusing on being in your interview, comfortable and relaxed, grounded and connected.

Imagine your conversation with your interviewer. You're being yourself, open and honest, not saying too little or too much. Take a moment to project into your interview, speaking about yourself clearly and openly, putting your best foot forward.

Listen to the following affirmations, and allow them to resonate deeply within.

I take all the time necessary to prepare for my interview, so I'm confident and comfortable going in.

I'm likable and easy to relate to.

I connect easily with others.

When people meet me, they like me, and tend to quickly focus on my good qualities.

I have a natural ability to please people, and enjoy helping them get what they want.

I am confident in my abilities, and radiate ease and comfort.

I am honest and open about myself, my skills, and my qualities, saying what's important to put me in the best light possible.

I represent myself well, speak positively about myself, and say just enough.

I already feel I'm a part of my new workplace, and have the job I've been looking for.

I like my interviewer, and he or she likes me.

It will soon be time to bring this journey to a close. But first, take a moment to thank yourself for giving yourself this time and space to prepare for your next step.

Bring your awareness gently back to your physical surroundings.

Take your time, and when you're ready, open your eyes, and feel awake, alert, and refreshed.

FINDING YOUR NEW HOME

Make yourself comfortable, and close your eyes. Take a slow deep breath, and let go of any tension, as you feel yourself sinking into the surface you're resting on, becoming still more comfortable and relaxed. Take another slow, deep breath, and release your thoughts, letting them drift far away. And take another slow, deep breath, and know that in this moment, all is well.

Bring your awareness into your heart, in the center of your chest, and notice a softness there, a feeling of peace. Take a moment to enjoy this feeling, as you quietly focus in your heart, and follow your breath, in, and out.

Consider your current living situation, the one you'll be moving away from. Perhaps you have good feelings about this place, or some not so good feelings about it. Or perhaps it's some combination that's harder to define. But however you feel about your current home, you know that it's soon going to be time to say goodbye and move away. So let's take this opportunity to make peace with the past, so you can freely move on.

Imagine you're outside your current home, looking at it from some distance away. Notice a band of energy between your own body, and your current home. You can feel it connected to you, and envision it extending into your home, and surrounding it.

This energy represents all your feelings about your current living situation, and any thoughts you may have about it, positive or negative. You may notice that the band of energy is made up of multiple colors, some clear and bright, and perhaps some dark and murky.

Take a moment to focus on this band of energy, it's colors, and all that it represents.

Take a slow, deep breath, and imagine yourself, the band of energy, and your current home, being filled with pure white light. Ask that any connections between you and your current home that are no longer good for you be cleared away.

Take a series of slow, deep breaths, and hold your focus on the light surrounding you, your home, and that band of energy. Take some time to do this, while the colors of your band of energy become clearer and clearer.

Perhaps the colors of your band of energy are now all clear and bright, or the band has gone transparent disappeared. But if there is still any murkiness left, that's OK. Before you go to sleep at night, ask that you be helped to clear and release anything negative connecting you to your current home. Then come back and do this process again soon.

Now we'll focus on your new home.

Re-center in your heart, and feel a sense of peace and calm. Your new home is already in life's plan for you, and you'll be moving there in perfect timing, according to your highest good. Life is orchestrating everything, so that all will unfold perfectly, at just the right time. Your job for now is to let go of any feeling of urgency or impatience, and come into the spirit of cooperation with life.

So, take a moment to simply relax into the feeling that everything is unfolding according to plan, and all is well. Do this now.

Imagine that you're encompassed by a transparent sphere of energy, pulsing out from your heart, and expanding in every direction. This sphere represents your connection to all of life.

Everything you need to know is provided through this connection, whenever you need to know it.

Direct your awareness to the outside edges of this sphere, and you may notice shapes and colors forming, representing new ideas and information, entering your system. Some are staying there near the edge, some are coming toward your center, and some are dissolving before they reach you.

New ideas, information, and inspiration are constantly flowing from life, into this sphere, and into your awareness.

Direct your awareness to the pace in this sphere closer to your heart, you'll notice colors and shapes coming out from there as well, moving out toward the edges of this. These represent you reaching outward to life for answers and input.

Where the colors and shapes meet, and merge, questions you're asking are being answered. It's a beautiful, magical, and continual process that takes place throughout your life on earth. And it's all happening in perfect timing, for your own highest good.

While you're enjoying this display, take some time to ask yourself the following questions, and, simply be open to anything that comes into your awareness. Simply ask, be open, and allow it to unfold. If you find yourself thinking too much, just relax, settle back into your heart, and let process to continue.

Do I feel fully ready to find my new home?

Is there anything I need to do, to feel fully ready?

Are there any steps I need to take, that I have not yet taken, to find my new home?

Is there anyone or anything who I feel might stand in the way of my finding my new home.

If there is anyone or anything in the way, what do I need to do, in order to clear things up?

Take a moment to envision yourself taking any steps you need to take.

Come back into your heart, and once again become aware of that sphere of energy surrounding you, and the shapes and colors flowing in toward your heart, and out from your heart. Enjoy watching those shapes and colors meet and merge.

Now imagine you're standing in front of a new home for you, the home you'll be moving into soon.

Notice the architecture of your new home. Notice the shape of the building, the color, and the material it's built from.

Notice the area around your home, the street, and the landscape. What does it look like, feel like, and sound like. Are there any people, adults, children, animals, or birds nearby? What does the weather look and feel like, at your new home, today?

Imagine you're walking into your new home. What does it look like and feel like, when you first step in? Do you notice any scents, smells, or sounds? What does the floor feel like in the entryway? Is it wood, carpet, tile, or some other material?

Take some time now to walk through your new home, and step into every room. Notice the way each room looks and feels. Notice your connection with each room, and how that might change, depending upon what that room is used for.

Now come into one particular room in your new home, perhaps your favorite, or the one where you'll be spending the most time. Notice your personal belongings there, the furniture, and whatever might decorate the walls. Take some time to enjoy being in that room, and imagine doing what you're most likely to do there.

Now simply stand in the center of your favorite room in your new home, and be still. Imagine a column of light is streaming up from the ground, right though your body in that room, through the ceiling, and into the sky. And take a moment to imagine that you, in the very near future, will symbolically see that column of light, recognize it, and allow it to lead you to this new home of yours. Take a moment to do this now, feeling the connection being made.

It's almost time to bring this process to a close. But first, take a moment to thank yourself for giving yourself this gift.

Let all the benefits of this experience stay with you, as you gradually begin to bring your focus back to your physical surroundings.

Take your time, and when you're ready, open your eyes, and feel awake, alert, and refreshed.

While it's still fresh in your mind, take a few minutes to write down anything that occurred to you during this process, that you might need to do, in order to let go of your current home, and find your new home.

TURNING SELF-DOUBT INTO CONFIDENCE

INTRODUCTION

Confidence is not arrogance, bluster, or posing. It's grounded quiet assurance. Usually those with natural self-confidence had the good fortune to have grown up in an environment where trying new things was encouraged, and making mistakes was simply considered a normal part of learning, not a sign of failure. Those who lack self confidence usually didn't have the opportunity early on to receive encouragement, make mistakes, and be encouraged to try again.

Self doubt and fear go hand in hand, and together undercut confidence. When we fear we'll be punished for our mistakes, self doubt comes in to keep us from taking a risk so we won't get into that position. We subconsciously learn the pattern of self doubt as a kind of protection against failure. Together, fear and self doubt keep us immobile, and unfulfilled, and that's the opposite of what we're after.

When we're new at something, it's important to try it under safe conditions, ideally with others who are also new, with the idea that it's OK if you don't get it right immediately. It's called training. For example, if you've never skied before, you wouldn't be well advised to go straight down the highest mountain. You'd take lessons on the bunny hill until you gain experience and confidence. Then, when you've mastered that stage, you'd move on to something more difficult.

Training is an important step to gain confidence. But to carry self doubt beyond the training stage is to let an unconscious pattern from the past keep you from moving forward, in service to fear of failure.

Self doubt often arises when we're faced with a situation in which the best direction to take is uncertain, perhaps because there's not enough information to know for sure what to do. Those with self confidence don't dwell on decisions under those circumstances. They either pick the most likely direction and move forward, or stop and gather more information until it's clear. Either way they continue to learn and make progress. But for those with self doubt, uncertainty can lead to paralysis, because it triggers old fears that we're about to make a mistake and be punished.

Those for whom self doubt is an issue need to spend time in a culture of acceptance, in which making mistakes is considered a normal and accepted part of making progress, and receive the opportunity to experiment, learn, and grow without fear of ridicule or punishment. As we experience success under those circumstances, we're able to release past programming, and learn we don't need to be afraid of trying new things. Without the fear, there's no need for self doubt, and it can drop away.

The following guided meditation can simulate that culture of acceptance, and provide an opportunity to let go of that old programming. To prepare for the meditation, consider something new you'd like to try, or something you currently do and would like to excel at, where you feel self doubt or lack of confidence has been holding you back. You'll be focusing on that area in the process.

GUIDED MEDITATION
Make yourself comfortable, and close your eyes. Take a slow deep breath, and let go of any tension in your body, as you feel yourself sinking into the surface you're resting on, becoming still more comfortable and relaxed.

Imagine all of the energy you've sent out into the world lately coming gently back home to you, like pieces of a puzzle coming into place, helping you to feel more whole, and more complete. Quietly receive this energy, and know there's nothing else you need to do right now. You can simply be here, relax, and receive.

Bring your awareness into your heart, in the center of your chest, and notice a softness there. Your heart is the ideal place to tap into higher guidance, and find peace, stillness, and deep connection within.

Now imagine you're standing in the center of your heart, as if it were a room, and the first thing you notice is what appears to be a doorway. Moving toward it, you see that it is in fact a door, and that light seems to be shining from behind it, glowing out from underneath.

Consider a new endeavor you'd like to try, or something you wish to excel at. Open the door, and you'll find yourself in the perfect setting for your wishes to unfold. For example, if you wanted to be a great athlete, you might be on an athletic field or in a gym. If you wanted to be an actor, you might be on a stage or a movie set, and if you wanted to be a writer you might be in an office with a computer and perhaps some bookshelves. Take a good look at your surroundings, and notice that everything you'd need to succeed is here.

As your scene unfolds further, you'll find that surrounding you is a circle of support; a kind of cheering section of people who have come to offer you love and encouragement. The circle may include friends, relatives, teachers and others you may know, as well as great figures you admire, whom already excel at what you aspire to.

All of the people in your circle believe in you, want to see you succeed, and know that you can. As they stand around you in the circle, open yourself to the powerful positive energy they're sending your way. Give yourself time to take it in, to the point where you're so full of encouragement there's no room within you for fear or doubt.

Now, out of the circle one person steps forward who'll be working with you, a "super-coach" who embodies all the qualities you seek. This person has excelled at what you aspire to, and has coached many others like you to success. He or she may be someone in particular you know and would like to work with, a prominent current or historical figure, or a composite of people and qualities you admire. But most of all, he or she has tremendous empathy, understanding, and confidence in you, and is not above giving you a kick in the butt from time to time, if needed.

Your super coach places his or her hands on your shoulders, and instantly you feel a powerful surge of energy moving through you, energy so strong you practically have no choice but to use, lest it burn you up. Immediately see yourself working with confidence toward what you most want to do. Watch as you take action, try new things, and find out what works and what doesn't. You're fully confident, swept up in the momentum of what you're doing, and mistakes and miscues don't bother you in the least. You simply take note of how to improve, and keep right on going. Take some time to watch this unfold.

Now envision yourself continuing to pursue your dream, two weeks from today. Notice that your super coach is right there with you, and your circle of support is also close by, all of them lending energy and encouragement. You've made some progress toward your goal, but you've also encountered some unexpected challenges. This is the place where self doubt might have previously made you falter. But watch what you do now, with the support of your super coach and circle nearby. If there is any doubt within you, your coach places hands on your shoulders, flooding you with energy and motivation. There's no time or room for doubt, and you simply move forward on the most likely path. If that path doesn't pan out, you take a different one, not judging yourself for your mistake, not second guessing your choices. You simply remain neutral, engage in your process, and move forward.

Envision yourself continuing to move forward toward your goal with confidence, and notice how you're able to set aside doubt and insecurity, whenever it arises. It gets easier as you go, and soon, you take challenges, setbacks, and questions about what to do next as simply a normal part of your process, without becoming upset. Take a few moments to watch yourself making progress, gathering support when needed, and overcoming anything in the way.

Listen to the following affirmations, repeat them inwardly, and allow them to resound deep within:

I'm confident that I will find what I need at every step along my path.

I enjoy taking steps toward my goal, one after another, and know that I can succeed as long as I keep moving forward.

I'm happy to try different things, discard what doesn't work, and use what does.

I know that making mistakes is a normal part of making progress, and when mistakes occur I refocus and keep moving toward my goal.

Whenever I'm uncertain I simply make decisions using the information available, or take time to learn more as needed.

I'm growing more confident each day as I move forward toward my goal.

It's almost time to bring this inner journey to a close. But first, reconnect once again with your circle of support, and your super coach, and ask that they remain close in the coming days and weeks.

Ask for a sphere of light to be placed all around you, and this experience, so that all the positive benefits will stay with you, and anything that you've released can be left behind.

Gradually bring your awareness gently back to your physical surroundings. Take your time, and when you're ready, open your eyes, and feel awake, alert, and refreshed.

HIGH SELF ESTEEM

Make yourself comfortable, and close your eyes. Take a slow deep breath, and let go of any tension, as you feel yourself sinking into the surface you're resting on, becoming still more comfortable and relaxed. Take another slow, deep breath, and release your thoughts, letting them drift far away. And take another slow, deep breath, and know that in this moment, all is well.

Bring your awareness into your heart center, the energy center, in the middle of your chest, and notice a softness there. Imagine all of the energy you've sent out into the world lately coming gently back home to your heart, helping you to feel more whole, and more complete. Quietly receive this energy, and know that for now, it's OK to simply be here, relax, and receive.

Bring yourself more fully into your heart, as if you were standing there now, inside a cozy room. Soon, you'll notice a small child there with you in your heart room. It's you at about 5 years of age, and we'll just call this person your inner child. Your inner child is your most tender, vulnerable, and impressionable self, and knows quite a lot about how you became the person you are today. Take a moment to greet your inner child now, and let them know they are very welcome, loved, and appreciated by you.

Also with you in your heart room is a very wise and loving person who has come to help teach and guide you, and your inner child, through this process, and we'll just call this person your guide. Take a moment to acknowledge and embrace your guide, and welcome them to your heart room.

As you all sit together, your guide begins talking to your inner child, and you just listen in. Your guide begins, saying "I am so glad you're here, little one, because there's much I've wanted to tell you, and you've never been more ready to hear this than you are at this moment. So listen well and receive the information, and the healing that I have for you now.

"It's possible that you grew up in a situation where you were taught that you were less than fully appreciated and precious to other people. But if that was the case, you were misinformed, and it's time to correct this.

"The real truth is that you are a unique, wonderful, and fascinating human being. You have amazing potential to live a creative, satisfying, and love filled life. No one is quite like you. All of the things you currently think of as your shortcomings, are, in the larger scheme of things, marks of character that will eventually blossom into miracles. Every struggle and difficulty brings you a measure of strength, insight, and the ability to love others more fully. And now it's time for you to begin to receive more love for yourself."

In the presence of your guide, embrace your inner child now. Pour love into them. Let them know how much you love and care for them, and let them feel how precious they are. You are loving you. Feel the hurt feelings of not receiving all the love you needed begin to melt away. Notice that where there may have been dark places in your body and mind, they are now being filled with light. Take some time to do this now.

Your guide continues to speak, now addressing you directly. "Because of the way you were raised, perhaps you developed patterns of thinking and behavior that allowed others to treat you as less than the worthy person you are. Perhaps you learned not to speak up when something happened you didn't like. Perhaps you got into the habit of making excuses for others when they didn't honor you as they should have. And perhaps you began to behave in negative ways toward yourself.

"It's time for these negative patterns within you to dissolve and change now, so that you can move on to the next stage of your life; a stage in which you can experience greater freedom, happiness and love. For that to happen, you must decide to make changes, think differently, act differently, and seek out whatever support might be necessary to help you in the transition process."

Consider the behavior pattern or habit that you believe most stands in the way of you loving honoring, and respecting yourself. This may be a negative way of thinking, feeling, or doing something you know doesn't serve your highest good. Imagine that you, your guide, and your inner child are now standing together in a circle of light, holding hands, and sending positive energy into your life, for you to break free of this. Allow that energy to be represented by a specific color of your choosing. Take a moment to do this now.

Envision yourself in a typical situation in which that pattern or habit might come up, and see and feel yourself receiving all of that positive energy, in the form of that colored energy. See and feel yourself filled and surrounded by that color, and experience the support of yourself, your inner child, and your guide with you there.

Now envision yourself altering your behavior, so that instead of doing that negative pattern or habit, you're doing something positive that supports you. You might see yourself engaging with someone you know who would be a positive influence, or a helper, and this could be a friend, or a counselor, teacher, coach, or support group. Or you might see yourself doing an activity that you enjoy and feels up-lifting. Perhaps it's a kind of physical exercise, hobby, or satisfying project. Or you may simply see yourself surrounded and filled with that color, feeling positive, well, and happy. Take some time to envision whatever suits you best, and use all of your energy and imagination to make it as positive, and real as you can. Your change begins here.

Take a moment to listen to the following affirmations, and allow them to resonate deeply within.

An endless supply of life and love flows through me, for myself first, and then out toward others.

I have a great deal to offer, but am careful to share myself only when my gifts can be met with honor, appreciation, and respect.

I'm happy to share my life with others, as long as it's in a balanced, healthy way for both of us.

Although I'm not perfect, and am still working out things in my life, the same is true for everyone. Everyone including myself deserves to be treated with kindness and understanding.

I deserve to be treated with appreciation, affection, and respect, and am not willing to settle for less.

It's almost time to bring this inner journey to a close. But first, take a moment to consider any actions you can take to support bringing what you've learned in this meditation, into reality. What are the steps you can take to make this happen, that you can begin?

Thank your inner child, and your guide, for helping you today.

And take a moment to thank yourself for giving yourself this gift.

Bring your awareness gently back to your physical surroundings. Take your time, and when you're ready, open your eyes, and feel awake, alert, and refreshed.

While it's still fresh in your mind, take time to write down anything you've experienced or learned in this inner process, and be sure to write about any actions you need to take next.

BREAK FREE & FULFILL YOURSELF

INTRODUCTION

When people are feeling unfulfilled in life, usually one or more of the following elements apply:

- Th ey' don't feel connected to an inner sense of purpose.
- Th ey don't believe that who they are matters or makes a difference in the world.
- Th ey've not been taught that it's OK to try things, fail, and try more things until they succeed.
- They're afraid of being seen as struggling or failing at something, so they avoid committing to anything they truly care about.

Any of those patterns, and a variety of others, contribute to a life unfulfilled, where we never give our dreams a chance to blossom, and sabotage our efforts before they come to fruition.

At some point we've had enough of the failure patterns, and are ready to take a serious look at what's been holding us back. At that point, we can take steps to break free, even if those steps feel strange or uncomfortable at first. Of course they *would* feel strange, because moving forward means to strain against those old ties to doubt, confusion, and insecurity, and that's bound to be uncomfortable. But it's also exhilarating to break free, and it's the beginning of new life.

But let's not get ahead of ourselves. Every change in human behavior is hard won, because old patterns do not give up easily. It takes conviction, and usually some kind of support, in order to keep moving until we're out of that inertia phase, out of the old habits gravitational pull, and into a new pattern of growth.

So, the message here is that when you're making a change, and you know its time, no matter what the pattern or habit is you're trying to break free of, *keep going,* even when it feels like it might be a good idea to stop, rest, or go back. Keep going through that no-man's land of neither here or there, until you're well established in new territory. And make it a point use whatever help and support is available, because you'll probably need it. It's not easy taking a risk to break free and fulfill yourself. But it's worth every effort.

GUIDED MEDITATION

Make yourself comfortable, and close your eyes. Take a slow deep breath, and let go of any tension in your body, as you feel yourself sinking into the surface you're resting on, becoming still more comfortable and relaxed.

Bring your awareness into your spiritual heart, heart center, or heart chakra as it's also called, in the center of your chest, and notice a softness there. Your heart is the ideal place to tap into higher guidance, and find peace, stillness, and deep connection within.

Imagine all of the energy you've sent out into the world lately coming gently back home to your heart, helping you to feel more whole, and more complete. Quietly receive this energy, and know there's nothing else you need to do right now. You can simply be here, relax, and receive.

Now imagine you're standing in the center of your heart, as if it were a big comfortable room. As your eyes begin to adjust to the light, the first thing you notice is what appears to be a doorway. Moving toward it, you see that it is in fact a door, and that light seems to be shining from behind it, glowing out from underneath. Something is waiting for you beyond that door, something that holds the keys to questions you've been having about your life recently.

Step forward, open the door and walk through, and you'll immediately find yourself at the base of a beautiful mountain on a warm, sunny day. The air is soft and sweet with the scent of wildflowers, and patchy white clouds in the sky above provide just the right amount of shade.

This mountain is old and wise, and seems to have its own unique personality, a character you resonate with, as if the two of you were somehow connected. There is a spiritual power at this mountain, with secrets to share, if you're willing to listen. Perhaps that's what's drawn you here. You've come to ask about your life. What is it within you that needs to change, in order to open to the true fulfillment you long for?

The answers are waiting for you, and as you begin to make your way up the mountainside, you feel an initial sense of enthusiasm, almost euphoria, at setting out on this adventure, leaving the flatland behind. The mountain has already revealed its first secret: Simply by changing your routine and embarking on something new, you can break out of stagnation, and bring new energy to your life.

As you continue to climb, you settle into a rhythm, and the journey becomes more normal, so to stay interested you begin to pay closer attention to the plants and rocks that surround you. At first it all seems the same, but as you look closer, you find a fascinating world of texture, color, shape, and beauty. Every plant, rock, and crevice seems to have its own story to tell, if you're willing to give it your focus. And so the second secret of the mountain is revealed: By paying closer attention to your surroundings, by being more fully engaged, your world opens and expands.

Climbing further, you begin to tire. It's hard work making your way up the mountainside, so you find a place to sit and rest for a moment, and have a drink from your water supply. Looking up at the peak, you realize it's still quite a way to go, and begin to wonder if it's really worth the effort. There's no way to know for certain. You're tired, and it could all be a waste of time. Then you remember why you came. You're in need of a change, and the mountain has secrets to share. If you quit now, you'll never find out what they are.

By connecting to your purpose, you suddenly feel your energy restored. The time you took to rest and connect inside seems to have made all the difference. So with renewed enthusiasm and sense of commitment, you continue.

Reaching the peak brings you a sense of pride and satisfaction. You've put forth the effort, stepped outside your routine, and done something to help break free. Taking in the incredible view stretching out before you, you feel indescribably light, set free of your habitual patterns.

And so you begin to use this rare occasion of having stepped out of your routine, to take stock of your life, and from your higher perspective, consider what needs to change. Take a moment for this now.

Imagine you're looking at one scene from your current life, from this high vantage point. Notice what you're doing, the people around you, if any, and the circumstances. As you watch yourself, consider these questions:

Do I seem to be in the process of fulfilling myself?

What would I prefer to be doing, that I have been afraid to try?

What fears are holding me back?

What kinds of support would I need to help me take a new step forward?

Where could I find that support, and how could I bring it in?

Am I willing to take a risk, trust myself, the universe, and the world around me, for my greater happiness and fulfillment?

Now envision yourself taking your next step toward fulfillment, doing the next thing you'd need to do, and notice the sense of satisfaction and freedom you feel, having done just a small amount. Imagine how you'd feel after stepping forward a little more, and a little more. Take a moment to make a commitment to your self, right now, to take your next step, and the next, until you've reached a new level of fulfillment.

As you set forth on your path, chances are you'll meet obstacles that seem to stand between you and your goal. Obstacles are there to test your resolve, and make you stronger, so you'll be better able to appreciate and enjoy your rewards. The question is: *What will you do when obstacles appear?*

Envision yourself moving forward along your path, taking steps toward your goal, and facing an obstacle, one that may at first seem insurmountable. Notice your initial reaction. When faced with a sudden challenge, it's not uncommon to experience anger, frustration, disappointment, self doubt, or confusion. Many will simply give up. But true fulfillment is worth fighting for.

Imagine yourself pulling together all your resources, both inner and outer, redoubling your effort, and moving beyond the obstacle. See, hear, and feel yourself doing that now.

Right now, give yourself permission, from the deepest place within, to make the changes that are necessary, to take the steps you need toward your true fulfillment. And ask that you be provided the strength and the courage necessary to follow through. Take a moment to do this now with full conviction.

This is what it takes to change and break free. Become clear about your direction, move past your fears, and persevere beyond obstacles. Your fulfillment is in front of you, waiting for you to take your next step. Don't wait any longer. Do it now.

It's almost time to bring this inner journey to a close. But first, ask for a sphere of light to be placed all around you, and this experience, so that all the positive benefits will stay with you, and anything that you've released can be left behind.

Gradually bring your awareness gently back to your physical surroundings.

Take your time, and when you're ready, open your eyes, and feel awake, alert, and refreshed.

OVERCOMING SHYNESS

INTRODUCTION

Shyness can keep us isolated and alone. The prospect of being with new people seems daunting, and our limited attempts at socializing can be painful, so we decide it's better not to try, and stay with the few people we're comfortable with, or the dog or cat. As we loose the ability to connect with others, and our world becomes smaller and smaller.

Feelings of shyness are based upon deeply held beliefs that others won't like us, won't understand us, that we have little in common, and if we reach out we'll ultimately be rejected and hurt. For shy people, fear of humiliation and shame is often the bottom line.

The cure for shyness begins with knowing that all of us want human contact, because we're innately social beings. We all have something to offer each other, beginning with the simple ability to listen to another person and hear what they have to say. Through dialog we discover our commonalities. It takes some willingness to bypass our fear, and step out. But everyone can learn the simple skills of listening and talking to others, and with a little practice, shy people can learn to reach out and make new friends.

The following guided meditation will help you get over the initial fear of connecting to others by visualizing yourself in social situations, easily meeting people, and enjoying the results. Use this program as the first step to expanding your world.

GUIDED MEDITATION

Make yourself comfortable, and close your eyes. Take a slow deep breath, and let go of any tension, as you feel yourself sinking into the surface you're resting on, becoming still more comfortable and relaxed. Take another slow, deep breath, and release your thoughts, letting them drift far away. And take another slow, deep breath, and know that in this moment, all is well.

Imagine you're standing in front of a doorway, and as you walk through it, you'll find yourself in a cozy restaurant at lunch time, at a table for two, with someone you recently met.

You're very comfortable here, your breathing is calm, and you feel your feet on the ground, and your back against the chair. The sights and sounds of the restaurant fade into the background, as you focus upon the face of your companion. And what you notice most is that you're interested and engaged in what they're saying. You're listening, hearing the sound of their voice, and the meaning of their words registers in your heart. You can feel something as they speak. It's a feeling of connection, a sense that you've had similar experiences. And even if you come from different backgrounds, the two of you are joining together here, over lunch, in a very natural way.

Your companion has asked you something about yourself, and you feel their interest. It feels easy and natural to answer, and talk about yourself—the things you care about, what you do in life, and what has meaning for you. And it feels good to have someone interested in you. After you've answered their question, and talked a little about yourself, you think of something to ask them, and again find yourself interested in what they have to say.

Take a moment to imagine this interaction, listen, watch, and feel it unfold.

The scene changes, and now you're at a small gathering, perhaps and informal dinner with 4 to 8 people, and you know one or two of them a little. Again notice that you're very comfortable here, your breathing is calm, and you feel your feet on the ground. The conversation is easy, and relaxed. It's OK if more than one conversation is going on at once, and it's OK if the room is quiet for a bit. Someone asks what you do for a living, and you talk a little bit about how you spend your time. You ask about them in return.

Take a moment to imagine this interaction, listen, and watch it unfold, as you chat comfortably with one person, and then another, curious to know about them, and happy to talk about yourself.

The scene changes once more, and this time you're at a large gathering of people. Perhaps it's a party, or a business networking event. There are more people than you could connect with in one evening, and they seem to be concentrated in small groups of two or more, with some individuals standing alone. Looking around, you see someone near you by themselves, and without hesitation you immediately go up to them and introduce yourself. It's easy to look at them, extend your hand, and tell them your name, and they in turn tell you theirs. You begin talking about the event, and how you came to be there, and they reply in kind. This "small talk" is our natural way of getting comfortable with each other; a way of hearing someone's voice, and getting a feel for their personality. All it takes is a little effort, and you can break the ice, and connect with another person in this way.

Take a moment to imagine yourself doing something similar with a number of different people at this gathering, getting to know a little about each one, by making small talk.

Now imagine that you've begun talking with someone at the gathering with whom you feel a kinship and rapport, and the conversation has naturally extended into deeper things. Perhaps you're talking more about your job, or your family. And that person opens up to you as well, as you take turns, speaking to each other. You've spoken to many people here, but now most of the room seems to fade into the background, as you concentrate on the conversation at hand. Take a moment to feel this connection, watch, and listen as the conversation unfolds.

Listen now to the following affirmations, and allow each one to resonate, deeply within.

Everyone desires connection, and all people have needs similar to mine.

I have much in common with other people.

In social situations, as I begin listening and talking, I relax and enjoy myself.

I'm a good listener, and find myself interested in other people and what they have to say.

I'm curious about others and want to hear their stories.

I'm willing to reach out to others and break the ice, to form new connections.

I don't mind making small talk about simple things we all have in common.

I can talk easily about myself and the things I know and care about.

I naturally gravitate to those whose company I enjoy, and they to me.

I challenge myself to expand my circle of friends and meet new people.

I take small steps to go beyond my comfort zone, because it makes me feel fully alive and free.

I'm willing to experiment with new ways of being in the world, to find what suits me best.

I'm at my best when I'm being myself, and expressing myself in a positive way.

People like me because I'm genuine, honest, and care about them.

It will soon be time to bring this journey to a close. But first, consider one thing you can do as a next step, toward reaching out to others. It might be calling someone you'd like to know better, and asking them to have coffee with you, or going to an open social or business gathering. Or it might be initiating a conversation with someone you know you'll be running into over the next day or two. Perhaps you could look up social interest groups in your area and pick one to attend. Decide on one thing you will do, and take a moment to imagine yourself doing that now.

Thank yourself for giving yourself the gift of new beginnings.

Bring your awareness gently back to your physical surroundings. Take your time, and when you're ready, open your eyes, and feel awake, alert, and refreshed.

While it's still fresh in your mind, take a moment to initiate or plan out the next step you envisioned a moment ago. Expand your world now.

PART SIX

LEARN TO MEDITATE

MORNING MEDITATION

INTRODUCTION

Many people like the idea of meditation, but find it difficult to maintain a regular mediation practice. We tend to get easily distracted, have a hard time focusing, and don't know quite what focus on in the first place. So we miss the positive benefits of meditation, because it just seems too hard to do. This program solves that problem, and offers a way to easily do a daily morning meditation that will make a positive difference in your day, and your life.

In Morning Meditation you will relax, connect to your higher source, clear negativity within to give you a clean slate for the day, receive higher guidance for your day, open to miracles large and small, and have gratitude for your life. Begin your day with this guided meditation, and fill your days with grace and ease. As you practice, you'll find it easier and easier to do.

GUIDED MEDITATION

Sit comfortably, with both feet flat on the floor, and close your eyes. Take a slow deep breath, and let go of any tension, as you feel yourself sinking into the surface you're resting on, becoming still more comfortable and relaxed. Take another slow, deep breath, and release your thoughts, letting them drift far away. And take another slow, deep breath, and know that in this moment, all is well.

Bring your awareness into your spiritual heart, in the center of your chest, and notice a softness there.

Become aware of the energy flowing into your heart, and as you do, you'll realize that the energy is love. This love is coming to you from your own higher consciousness, from your spiritual guides and angels, all the way to the sacred source of all creation. We'll just call all of this your Higher Support. Take a moment to simply rest in your heart, follow your breath, and receive love from your Higher Support.

Notice how you're feeling inside, and briefly become aware of any negativity or tension. Perhaps you have stress over something that happened before, or concerns about something coming up. Without trying to solve anything right now, simply notice how you're feeling inside.

Now, refocus in your heart, and feel more of the love that's been flowing in. And as you do, send that loving energy all the way down to your feet. And from your feet, send it straight into the ground, all the way to the core of the earth.

Now the energy of love is flowing into you from the top of your head, and into your heart, all through you, and all the way into the ground.

Continue to focus on this flow of love, and allow any negative feelings to release, dissolve, and flow away. You don't have to think about the troubling stuff, or solve any of it right now. All you need to do is let go, focus on the love flowing through you, and relax. If you feel tension or negativity come up, that's perfectly fine. Just take a deep breath, let it go, and refocus on the love flowing into your heart. Take a few moments to do this now.

Refocus in your heart, and on the love that's flowing into you, and through you. Ask your Higher Support to help you project this love forward into your day. Imagine yourself and different times during the day, receiving the light and love that's connecting with you, supporting you, and lightening you up. Take a few moments to do this now.

Take a moment to receive input from your higher support about anything you're working on or concerned with. This may come to you in the form of words, images, sounds, feelings, or just a sense of knowing. No need to do any heavy thinking, or problem solving right now. Simply open to receive whatever life wants you to know for today. Take a few moments with this now.

Take a deep breath, and open wide to miracles large and small coming to you now, and throughout your day. Set your mind free of any preconceptions, and become willing to allow life, and all your Higher Support, to bring you unexpected gifts of love, wellbeing, and fulfillment. Take a few moments with this now.

Take a moment to be grateful for your life, and inwardly give thanks.

If you would like to spend a little more time in meditation, simply focus in your heart, follow your breathing, and be at peace. If distracting thoughts come in, let them go, and drop back into your heart. Remain there as long as you wish.

Whenever you're ready to come out of meditation, gently bring your awareness back to your physical surroundings.

Take your time, and when you're ready, open your eyes, and feel awake, alert, and refreshed.

SANCTUARY OF PEACE

INTRODUCTION

Our mind was designed to receive input, expand, and develop. But today we can easily become over-stimulated and stressed, and life can become unbalanced. We've become so accustomed to over-stimulation that it's often difficult to find our way back to peace.

Within you is a sanctuary of peace, the antidote to an over-stimulated mind. The definition of an antidote is "a substance or remedy given to counteract or neutralize a particular poison, unpleasant feeling, or situation." Spending time in your sanctuary of peace is the antidote to over stimulation and stress. All you need to do to gain its benefit is be there for a while, and you will regain balance.

The way of being in our sanctuary of peace is different than what we've grown accustomed to. Instead of seeking more and more, and looking for what we should do next, it's about simply being in the present moment, without trying to gain anything.

It's worth noting that while "spending time being in the present moment, without trying to gain anything" might seem like an unproductive use of one's time, it actually turns out to be quite the opposite. Much in the same way that a good night's sleep can bring clarity of thinking and resolve all sorts of issues that seemed unsolvable the day before, time spent in your sanctuary of peace can bring relief, answers, and solutions. The solutions that come from there tend to be simple, organic, and honest, rather than complicated and contrived. You may go into your sanctuary full of questions, and come out saying "I know what I need to do." Or perhaps know that the answer is to do nothing.

Use the following guided meditation to help you find your own inner sanctuary of peace, and establish yourself there. After working with this program for a while, you may find you can easily go there on your own.

GUIDED MEDITATION

Sit comfortably upright, so you can relax and go within, without falling asleep. Close your eyes, and take a slow, deep breath.

Adjusting your breathing will allow you to more easily spend time within your sanctuary of peace, so continue to breathe deeply, and slowly, taking comfortably full breaths. Some of us tend to breathe using our chest, and others with our abdomen, but if you can, use your belly, allowing it to expand as you breathe in, and relax as you breathe out.

Bring your focus into your heart center, in the center of your chest. This will help you relax your mind, wind down, un-busy yourself, and begin to enter your sanctuary of peace. For now, take just a minute to simply focus in your heart, and continue to breathe deeply, and slowly.

[Pause 1 minute.]

We can think of life as a current of energy within us, a river of peaceful support that we all share. It connects us to each other, and sustains us. When you tap into your sanctuary of peace, within your heart, you can experience that current of energy, that river of life.

Take a little longer to sit quietly, breathe deeply and slowly, focus in your heart, and simply be attentive to the river of life with you.

[Pause 2 minutes.]

It's not often easy to quiet the mind, especially at the beginning. The mind is like a flywheel, with its own momentum, and takes a while to spin down. To think about relaxing the mind is to stimulate it further. So the best approach is to simply watch it, recognize when its spinning, and bring your focus back to your heart.

Take a little longer to sit quietly, focus in your heart, and simply attend to the river of life within you, within your sanctuary of peace. When you find yourself thinking, refocus in your heart, and breathe.

[Pause 4 minutes.]

Most of the time we're busy, doing something, thinking about something we'll do, or thinking about something we did. In your sanctuary of peace, there is nothing to do. It's like sitting by a peaceful river on a Sunday afternoon, and simply watching the water. Soon the placid scene in front of you begins to reflect inside you, and you feel quiet, calm, and still.

Take some more time to experiment by quietly focusing in your heart, simply being, without the need to do anything.

[Pause 5 minutes.]

We spend so much of our time being active, thinking, doing, influencing, creating. But your sanctuary of peace is a place for receiving. What you receive there can be described as comfort, healing, love, or peace. Receiving these doesn't require any action on your part, or any thought. All you need to do is just be open, relaxed, and receptive, and they will come.

Take a little while to quietly focus in your heart, rest in your sanctuary of peace, relax, open and receive.

[Pause 6 minutes.]

It's almost time for the end of the narrated portion of this experience. If you wish, get ready to bring yourself back to your physical surroundings, and come fully into your outside world. Or if you prefer, take a while longer to visit your sanctuary of peace, rest, and receive.

DEEP LISTENING 1: WHAT IS MY TRUE NATURE?

ABOUT THIS SERIES

Deep Listening includes seven guided meditation exercises designed to help you calm your mind, engage your imagination, and receive input from higher consciousness. Each meditation shares a relaxation sequence at the beginning, leading to a variety of guided inner journeys. Each meditation ends with a question for you to consider.

All the meditations include instructions to follow your breath. Paying close attention to our breath helps us calm the mind, so we can access deep states of awareness. By following our breath we can quickly bypass the chatter of our intellect and the ego, let go of tension and negativity, and become more open to higher guidance.

Although you may hear answers or receive information during the meditations, it's not so important for that to happen, to benefit from the work. It's only necessary that you listen, and practice being as open as you can. This effort will expand your awareness, helping you learn to be open to higher guidance at any time.

You could think of this as something like target practice. The purpose of target practice is not to hit a bull's eye, but to improve the archer's aim. It's the same with this work. The more you practice, the deeper your listening will become.

INTRODUCTION TO DEEP LISTENING 1

Deep listening and meditation are cousins. While meditation brings us peace, deep listening brings meaning and direction. When we're challenged by life, deep listening helps us respond. And when we're in confusion and doubt, it answers our questions, or helps us ask better ones.

Deep listening begins where normal listening leaves off—just beyond the intellect—and takes us into higher consciousness. Our intellect simply replays the information we've accumulated over time; a constant stream of shallow content. And unless we seek a deeper channel, that's all we hear.

But most people find it difficult, especially at first, to hold an inner focus without the intellect intruding with its distracting chatter. If that's your experience, with patience and some effort over time, you can learn to quiet the mind, and gain the results. Let's begin.

GUIDED MEDITATION

Make yourself comfortable, and close your eyes. Take a slow deep breath, and let go of any tension, as you feel yourself sinking into the surface you're resting on, becoming still more comfortable and relaxed. Take another slow, deep breath, and release your thoughts, letting them drift far away. And take another slow, deep breath, and know that in this moment, all is well.

Bring your awareness into your heart center, in the center of your chest, and notice a softness there.

Imagine all the energy you've sent out into the world lately coming gently back to your heart, like the last pieces of a puzzle, making you feel more whole, and complete.

Follow your breathing, in, and out, as you relax and settle in still more. Breathing is your connection to life, and the natural world, and like all of nature, it has a rhythm. Take a few moments to do nothing more than simply follow the rhythm of your breath, and relax.

Imagine you're walking through an ancient forest of tall oaks, on a warm summer morning. It's peaceful here, and you've come to connect with nature, and reflect. The air carries the comforting scent of last night's rain, and the quiet presence of the trees envelopes you, making you feel watched over, and safe.

The soft earth cushions your steps, and the path is paved with a thick layer of oak leaves and acorn husks from years past. Here and there mushrooms and small, bright flowers poke their way through. Squirrels are busy scampering up and down the rough tree bark, and jays are broadcasting from the canopy high above. Take a few moments to enjoy being here, as you walk along, and follow your breathing.

Soon you come upon a clearing, with tall meadow grass, a scattering of rocks, and a few fallen trees, gradually being reclaimed by the earth. One of the downed trees offers a fine place to rest and view the meadow. The log where you sit is covered with patches of lichen, and bordered by sprays of purple flowers coming up from the crumbling silver bark on the ground. A chipmunk peaks at you from behind the log, and then goes back into hiding. Nature is quiet here, though very much alive, and inspires a feeling of peaceful enchantment. Take a little while to enjoy this feeling, as you follow your breathing, and go deeper.

Looking up, you notice a large butterfly, and your gaze follows as it flutters its way across the meadow, sampling the flowers from one spot, and then another. Finally it comes to rest near you on the log, and waits, as if expecting you to respond in some way. Settle deep into your heart, as you prepare to consider the following question.

What is my true nature?

Sit with this question for some time, without trying to analyze or think, and allow any answers to come up from deep within. Take your time to simply let it be, as you ask, "What is my true nature," listen deeply, and receive.

It will soon be time to bring this inner journey to a close. But first, take a moment to thank yourself for giving yourself this gift.

Bring your awareness gently back to your physical surroundings.

Take your time, and when you're ready, open your eyes, and feel awake, alert, and refreshed.

While it's still fresh in your mind, take time to write down anything you may have heard, felt, or learned in this exercise.

DEEP LISTENING 2: WHAT IS MOST IMPORTANT?

INTRODUCTION

What are your priorities in life? Without knowing what we care about most, we're apt to live a life pursuing what we've been told to care about by parents, friends, society, or advertising. Without knowing ourselves, we may spend years going in one direction or another, never finding true fulfillment. Knowing oneself goes beyond the opinions of others, and beneath the noise of our own intellect. It begins by listening within.

For deep listening to occur, it helps to be as relaxed and free inside as possible, without trying to control the outcome. So in these meditations, as you pose a question and listen, allow yourself to enjoy a free flowing stream of consciousness. The answers that come may not be direct, exact, or fit the question perfectly. But that's just fine, because your question is only a starting point, a gentle stimulation for whatever may come.

GUIDED MEDITATION

Make yourself comfortable, and close your eyes. Take a slow deep breath, and let go of any tension, as you feel yourself sinking into the surface you're resting on, becoming still more comfortable and relaxed. Take another slow, deep breath, and release your thoughts, letting them drift far away. And take another slow, deep breath, and know that in this moment, all is well.

Bring your awareness into your heart center, in the center of your chest, and notice a softness there. Imagine all the energy you've sent out into the world lately coming gently back to your heart, like the last pieces of a puzzle, making you feel more whole, and complete.

Follow your breathing, in, and out, as you relax and settle in still more. Breathing is your connection to life, and the natural world, and like all of nature, it has a rhythm. Take a few moments to do nothing more than simply follow the rhythm of your breath, and relax.

Imagine you're walking along a mountain trail in summer, surrounded by pines, on your way to visit your favorite alpine lake. It's morning, and the air is crisp, and as the sun rises through the trees you can see the sky grow brighter, and bluer. You got up early this morning to come and enjoy the fresh air, sunshine, and peace, and now you're here. It feels good to walk along, hear to the ground crunching with your steps, and witness the birds and squirrels making their morning treetop rounds.

Soon the trail opens out onto a clearing, revealing a majestic lake, it's glassy surface reflecting the sky above. Over to one side you can hear a stream that comes from higher up the mountainside, feeding the lake. And on the far shore you spot a small heard of deer, who have come to drink and nibble on the rich grass at the water's edge. Take a few moments to enjoy this peaceful setting, as you listen to the stream, watch the deer, and follow your breathing.

Sitting on the shore to rest, you enjoy the profound stillness of this place. Time seems to both slip by, and stop all together, and you feel embraced by the serene presence of the mountains, the water, and the sky. Looking at the water's surface, there's no way of knowing how far down it goes. But you might imagine that it's a deep, deep bowl, home to fish and other aquatic life.

Every so often you notice rings on the water, popping up here and there, and you begin to watch the lake more intently. Now you see the water dimple quite close to you, and as the rings fan out you realize that fish are feeding, causing this hypnotic display. You watch the lake with still more interest, guessing where the next fish might rise. Take some time to settle in further, enjoy this simple, rhythmic display of nature, and follow your breath.

The peace and quiet of the lake carries you still deeper within, and the scene fades into you, now a part of you, as you focus softly of the gentle rhythm of your breath. Continue to let your breathing carry you inward, as you consider this question:

"What is most important to me?"

Sit with this question for some time, without trying to analyze or think, and allow any answers to come up from deep within. Take your time to simply let it be, as you ask, "What is most important to me," and allow yourself to know whatever you need to know.

It will soon be time to bring this inner journey to a close. But first, take a moment to thank yourself for giving yourself this gift.

Bring your awareness gently back to your physical surroundings.

Take your time, and when you're ready, open your eyes, and feel awake, alert, and rcfreshed.

While it's still fresh in your mind, take time to write down anything you may have heard, felt, or learned in this exercise.

DEEP LISTENING 3: WHAT DO I WANT?

INTRODUCTION

We typically use concentrated intellectual effort to figure things out, solve problems, and find meaning in life. But thinking is a very limited way of knowing, and it's often when we relax our mind that we finally do get our answers.

Have you ever tried to make a decision by writing a list of the pros and cons of two different choices? You probably wrote out your list in a sincere attempt at making the right choice, and then read it over, and still didn't know what you wanted to do. That's because reason doesn't tell us what we want. Most likely, after making the list you eventually chose to do what you knew you wanted to do on some level all along, regardless of which side of the list was longer.

In the art of deep listening, we skip making the list, bypass the intellect, and go directly into the heart, where we know what we want. There our answers are, and they're usually more simple than what our intellect would have us believe.

The heart is a place most of us inhabit from time to time, when we're feeling especially relaxed and open. In these exercises, we cultivate the ability to go into the heart space at will, and receive higher guidance. It's the only place within us where we truly know what we want.

GUIDED MEDITATION

Make yourself comfortable, and close your eyes. Take a slow deep breath, and let go of any tension, as you feel yourself sinking into the surface you're resting on, becoming still more comfortable and relaxed. Take another slow, deep breath, and release your thoughts, letting them drift far away. And take another slow, deep breath, and know that in this moment, all is well.

Bring your awareness into your heart center, in the center of your chest, and notice a softness there. Imagine all the energy you've sent out into the world lately coming gently back to your heart, like the last pieces of a puzzle, making you feel more whole, and complete.

Follow your breathing, in, and out, as you relax and settle in still more. Breathing is your connection to life, and the natural world, and like all of nature, it has a rhythm. Take a few moments to do nothing more than simply follow the rhythm of your breath, and relax.

Imagine you're lying on a chaise lounge, on the sand, at the seashore, on your own private beach. It's a beautiful morning, and you've got the whole day ahead of you to rest, relax, and just be. The temperature is perfect, the cloud cover just so, there's a light breeze now and then, and all is right with your world.

The ocean is calm today, and the waves are gentle. Far down the beach you can make out someone fishing in the surf, and closer by a flock of pelicans soar close to the water, fishing as well. The sand between you and the water is smooth and unmarked, offering only a few shells and bits of seaweed, and you're watching the water come thinning out toward you, recede, and come back again. Take a few moments to enjoy being here, watch the waves lap the shore, and follow your breathing.

As you continue to enjoy your peaceful beach, you find yourself settling in deeper, becoming one with this scene. It's almost as if the air, the water, and the sand were part of your own soul, on display for you to observe. A pod of dolphins swim by, affirming your connection to this ocean setting, and to all life. Take some time to settle down further, appreciate this time of reflection, and follow your breathing.

The peace and quiet carries you still deeper within, and the beach scene fades into you, now a part of you, as you focus softly of the gentle rhythm of your breath. It synchronizes with the ocean waves, as you breathe in, and out, until you and the sea are one. Continue to let your breathing carry you inward, as you consider this question:

"What do I want?"

Sit with this question for some time, without trying to analyze or think, enjoy the waves, and allow any answers to come up from deep within. No need to strain or analyze. Take your time to simply let it be, as you ask, "What do I want," and allow yourself to know whatever you need to know.

It will soon be time to bring this inner journey to a close. But first, take a moment to thank yourself for giving yourself this gift.

Bring your awareness gently back to your physical surroundings.

Take your time, and when you're ready, open your eyes, and feel awake, alert, and refreshed.

While it's still fresh in your mind, take time to write down anything you may have heard, felt, or learned in this exercise.

DEEP LISTENING 4: WHO AM I?

INTRODUCTION

Perhaps since human beings were able to think, we've pondered the meaning of life, and wondered how we came to be. The question, "Who am I," is one that often begins in the intellect, but quickly transports us toward our higher consciousness. Connecting there can be deeply satisfying, and possibly the closest we'll ever come to an answer. As you work with the question, "Who am I," let go of the need to know, become as present as possible, and perhaps allow the answer to find you.

GUIDED MEDITATION

Make yourself comfortable, and close your eyes. Take a slow deep breath, and let go of any tension, as you feel yourself sinking into the surface you're resting on, becoming still more comfortable and relaxed. Take another slow, deep breath, and release your thoughts, letting them drift far away. And take another slow, deep breath, and know that in this moment, all is well.

Bring your awareness into your heart center, in the center of your chest, and notice a softness there. Imagine all the energy you've sent out into the world lately coming gently back to your heart, like the last pieces of a puzzle, making you feel more whole, and complete.

Follow your breathing, in, and out, as you relax and settle in still more. Breathing is your connection to life, and the natural world, and like all of nature, it has a rhythm. Take a few moments to do nothing more than simply follow the rhythm of your breath, and relax.

Imagine you're following a path by a mountain stream, on a fine spring morning. The air is crisp and sweet, and the water makes a soft, soothing sound, splashing over rocks on its way. Your path meanders close to the water, then further away, then closer again, and the sound follows.

Soon you come to a spot where smooth boulders rest by the water's edge, and you find a comfortable place to sit. Here you can enjoy the sounds, observe the stream, and let your gaze fall upon spots in the current that draw your attention. Take a few moments to enjoy being here, watch the water, and follow your breathing.

Walking further along the stream, you find it widens, and the water flattens out and relaxes. Now it's not splashing over rocks so much as braiding around them, and the sounds have evened out and softened. More boulders by the water invite to you sit and enjoy this new setting, and the melody it plays. A pair of ducks come paddling downstream, staying close to the far bank. Take a while to watch as they make their way around the rocks and through the reeds, looking for tasty bites to eat. Follow your breathing, and let it carry you deeper within.

Looking more closely at the water you can make out the small flat rocks on the bottom, all shades of bronze and gold. The current flowing over the stream bed mesmerizes you. And every now and then the shadows of small fish dart in and out of view, enchanting you still further. Continue to let your breathing carry you inward, as you consider this question:

"Who am I?"

Sit with this question for some time, without trying to analyze or think, and let any answers to come up from deep within. Take your time to simply let it be, as you ask, "Who am I?"

It will soon be time to bring this inner journey to a close. But first, take a moment to thank yourself for giving yourself this gift.

Bring your awareness gently back to your physical surroundings.

Take your time, and when you're ready, open your eyes, and feel awake, alert, and refreshed.

While it's still fresh in your mind, take time to write down anything you may have heard, felt, or learned in this exercise.

DEEP LISTENING 5: WHAT AM I HERE FOR?

INTRODUCTION

The question, "What am I here for," or "What is my life purpose," is one that can be answered on many levels. And the answers can certainly change over the course of a lifetime. As you listen more and more deeply, you may find the answers you receive change from being about what you do in the world, to who you are, and the way you move through life.

GUIDED MEDITATION

Make yourself comfortable, and close your eyes. Take a slow deep breath, and let go of any tension, as you feel yourself sinking into the surface you're resting on, becoming still more comfortable and relaxed. Take another slow, deep breath, and release your thoughts, letting them drift far away. And take another slow, deep breath, and know that in this moment, all is well.

Bring your awareness into your heart center, in the center of your chest, and notice a softness there. Imagine all the energy you've sent out into the world lately coming gently back to your heart, like the last pieces of a puzzle, making you feel more whole, and complete.

Follow your breathing, in, and out, as you relax and settle in still more. Breathing is your connection to life, and the natural world, and like all of nature, it has a rhythm. Take a few moments to do nothing more than simply follow the rhythm of your breath, and relax.

Imagine you've planned a quiet vacation at a comfy mountain cabin. Food will be laid in, you'll have plenty of solitude, and your time will be yours to enjoy as you wish.

As your vacation begins, it's a fine fall afternoon, and you find yourself walking through the woods toward your cabin, for the first time. The air is cold and crisp, and you can smell the clean scent of pine. And as you walk, you hear the soft crackle of old leaves beneath your feet.

Stepping through the front door, you feel the toasty warmth of a wood stove, and smell the soup that's been steaming on the stove for you. So you put down your things, take a seat in the old rocker by the window, and settle in to watch the fall foliage outside, from the comfort of your chair. Birds are making their daily rounds, and this simple setting is at once soothing, and engrossing. Take a few moments to enjoy being here, watch the trees and the birds, and follow your breathing.

The sky's been dotted with clouds all day, and as the afternoon progresses, it grows overcast. And from your cozy, warm vantage point, that feels just fine, and even makes you feel more relaxed, as a deep feeling of peace settles over your cabin. Take a little while to enjoy this feeling, and the stillness here, as you follow your breathing, and go deeper.

Soon you notice snowflakes falling outside your window. At first there are just a few, floating here and there, and then gradually more, until there's a steady fall of flakes drifting down, tossing on the breeze, landing softly on the ground. Watch the snow falling, settle deep into your heart, and take some time to consider the following question.

"What am I here for?"

Sit with this question for some time, without trying to analyze or think, watch the snow from your cozy cabin, and allow any answers to come up from deep within. You may find that things are very quiet inside, or that you get lots of inner commentary, or something in between. Take your time to simply let it be, as you ask, "What am I here for," listen deeply, and receive.

It will soon be time to bring this inner journey to a close. But first, take a moment to thank yourself for giving yourself this gift.

Bring your awareness gently back to your physical surroundings.

Take your time, and when you're ready, open your eyes, and feel awake, alert, and refreshed.

While it's still fresh in your mind, take time to write down anything you may have heard, felt, or learned in this exercise.

DEEP LISTENING 6: WHAT DOES LIFE WANT ME TO KNOW?

INTRODUCTION

The wisdom and "higher information" we tap into in deep listening doesn't necessarily come in the form we're used to. Where our intellect is eager to communicate with us in complete sentences, the language of the soul is often more subtle. You may experience it in the form of single words, short phrases, seeds or kernels of ideas, symbolic images, lofty feelings, or simply a sense of peace and tranquility. Taking time to write immediately after your time inward can be especially helpful, allowing you to "unpack" the more condensed input you may have received.

GUIDED MEDITATION

Make yourself comfortable, and close your eyes. Take a slow deep breath, and let go of any tension, as you feel yourself sinking into the surface you're resting on, becoming still more comfortable and relaxed. Take another slow, deep breath, and release your thoughts, letting them drift far away. And take another slow, deep breath, and know that in this moment, all is well.

Bring your awareness into your heart center, in the center of your chest, and notice a softness there. Imagine all the energy you've sent out into the world lately coming gently back to your heart, like the last pieces of a puzzle, making you feel more whole, and complete.

Follow your breathing, in, and out, as you relax and settle in still more. Breathing is your connection to life, and the natural world, and like all of nature, it has a rhythm. Take a few moments to do nothing more than simply follow the rhythm of your breath, and relax.

Imagine you've been invited for a summer vacation at a friend's country cottage, to look after things while they're away. You relish spending time alone in this quaint setting, where you can read, meditate, and just be for a while, on your own private retreat from the outside world.

And so you find yourself at the edge of the yard, stepping through the wooden gate, and making your way up the winding stone path toward the cottage.

There's a front porch with a comfy wooden rocking chair, and it's far too fine a day to spend inside, so you settle into the rocker, and take in the view. You have a front row seat for the colorful flower beds on either side of the stone path. And it feels wonderful to just sit here rocking, watching the flowers, the sky, and the trees in the distance; breathing in the softly scented air on this lovely summer day. Take a few moments to absorb this peaceful setting, enjoy the garden, and follow your breathing.

Soon you notice your friend's cat exploring the flower beds, stalking the tall plantings, and checking her favorite spots. With her paws wet from the damp ground, she crosses the stone path, then back again, leaving little footprints as she goes. Absorbed in the show you watch as her prints dampen the walkway, then dry, and disappear. Take some time to settle in further, enjoy this simple, hypnotic play, and follow your breath.

The cat finally decides she's had enough exploring for a while, and saunters up on the porch to visit. She rubs against your leg, and finding that satisfactory, jumps into your lap, where after a few pets from you she promptly falls asleep, purring all the while. Her contentment seems to carry you still deeper within, as you focus of the gentle rhythm of your own breath. Continue to let your breathing carry you inward, as you consider this question:

"What does life want me to know?"

Sit with this question for some time, without trying to analyze or think, and let any answers to come up from deep within. Take your time to simply let it be, as you ask, "What does life want me to know," and allow yourself to receive whatever might be helpful.

It will soon be time to bring this inner journey to a close. But first, take a moment to thank yourself for giving yourself this gift.

Bring your awareness gently back to your physical surroundings.

Take your time, and when you're ready, open your eyes, and feel awake, alert, and refreshed.

While it's still fresh in your mind, take time to write down anything you may have heard, felt, or learned in this exercise.

DEEP LISTENING 7: YOUR OWN QUESTION

INTRODUCTION

What question would you like to ask? This meditation is an opportunity to receive input from your own higher consciousness. Consider asking something about yourself, about your connection to life, or about your path in life. You can also use this as an opportunity to receive insight into the nature of life itself. Let your intuition guide you in choosing a question that will stimulate a rich response. You can also use this process to ask no question at all, and simply receive the peace and sense of connection that may be waiting for you within. Through deep listening, you may experience an answer to something beyond any question you might have imagined.

GUIDED MEDITATION

Make yourself comfortable, and close your eyes. Take a slow deep breath, and let go of any tension, as you feel yourself sinking into the surface you're resting on, becoming still more comfortable and relaxed. Take another slow, deep breath, and release your thoughts, letting them drift far away. And take another slow, deep breath, and know that in this moment, all is well.

Bring your awareness into your heart center, in the center of your chest, and notice a softness there. Imagine all the energy you've sent out into the world lately coming gently back to your heart, like the last pieces of a puzzle, making you feel more whole, and complete.

Follow your breathing, in, and out, as you relax and settle in still more. Breathing is your connection to life, and the natural world, and like all of nature, it has a rhythm. Take a few moments to do nothing more than simply follow the rhythm of your breath, and relax.

Imagine you're resting under a grand old maple tree, by a pond, on an autumn afternoon. The sky is deep blue with clouds of white and silver, and beyond the pond are rolling hills, trees in fall foliage, and perhaps a farmhouse in the distance. The surface of the pond reflects the sky and the leaves above you, yellow, orange and brown. And the water shifts between glassy stillness, and rippled patterns set in motion by the breeze, only to become still again.

It's quiet here, and as you settle in, you feel yourself becoming a part of this peaceful scene. Following your breath, it seams as if this whole setting were breathing softly with you. Take a few moments to enjoy the comfort of being here, as you gaze at the pond's changing reflection, and follow your breathing.

A soft wind rustles the leaves overhead, and one of them drifts down, coming to rest on the water. Perhaps you've become so still inside that this simple event seems quite rich. So you watch the leaf, floating on the water, now rippling, and now still. Take a little while to observe, as you follow your breathing, and go deeper.

The peace and quiet you feel carries you still deeper within, and the pond fades into the background. Now you're aware only of the gentle rhythm of your breath. Focus only on your breathing now, the in breath, the out breath, and the soft movement of your abdomen and chest. And allow yourself to become totally engrossed and fascinated by this simple experience. If thoughts occur, just let them go, and re-attune to your breathing. Enjoy this for some time now.

If there is a question that seems important for you to ask, listen deeply for an answer. There's no need to think or try to work on it. Simply let whatever comes, come. Or if you have no pressing question at this time, just continue to follow your breathing, enjoy the peace within, and be present with yourself.

It will soon be time to bring this inner journey to a close. But first, take a moment to thank yourself for giving yourself this gift.

Bring your awareness gently back to your physical surroundings.

Take your time, and when you're ready, open your eyes, and feel awake, alert, and refreshed.

While it's still fresh in your mind, take time to write down anything you may have heard, felt, or learned in this exercise.

PART SEVEN

HIGHER GUIDANCE
& HEALING

RECEIVING LOVE FROM ABOVE

Make yourself comfortable, and close your eyes.

Breathe deeply, and slowly.

Imagine that love is all around you. You may feel it as a delicate, pink energy, softly touching into you everywhere. It fills your body and your mind, warm and comforting.

Love is being brought to you by Spirit, and Spirit can include God, angels, spiritual masters, gurus, saints, loved ones, and your own higher self. Someone wonderful is watching over you right now, waiting for you to connect with them.

Think of a beautiful color, and imagine it flowing out from your heart, toward someone in Spirit, who is with you, right now. Just send them that color for a moment, to say hello.

And now notice the color they are sending back to you. Perhaps there are many colors.

Think of a positive word or phrase, and mentally send it to Spirit, to the one who is with you, now. And notice how it feels to send it to them.

Now notice the word or phrase they send back to you.

And think of a flower, something specific, and beautiful. There is no need to send it anywhere. That flower, the one that just came into your mind, was sent to you by Spirit. Just say thank you.

Now imagine that the one who is with you in Spirit now is standing behind you, with their warm hands on your shoulders, sending love into you. Just be still and receive.

And imagine another being in spirit has placed their warm hand on your heart, sending you love. Just be still and receive.

Loving beings in Spirit are with you, and you can connect with them at any time. Open your heart, open your mind, and use your imagination as a bridge between worlds, so you can meet.

Love is waiting for you to receive.

THE ARROW: CONNECTING TO HIGHER SUPPORT

INTRODUCTION

Imagine that somewhere above you, just outside your normal awareness, is a vast storehouse of higher wisdom and support, waiting just for you. This storehouse is constantly updating according to your needs, with all the latest information and most refined energies available. And contributing to this storehouse, and waiting to be of service, are higher beings with expertise in every conceivable area of your life, always available to help you in any way necessary.

For now, let's just call this vast resource, with all the beings there, "your higher support." There are many ways in which you can access your higher support, including meditation, writing, art, deep listening, and more. In this program, we'll use a technique called "The Arrow."

To begin, first consider something specific you'd like help with. It may be a problem you've been struggling with, or it might be something you're working on well, that you'd like to take to the next level. Take a moment to consider the one thing you'd most like to receive input on now. We'll come back to that during the following guided meditation.

GUIDED MEDITATION

Make yourself comfortable, and close your eyes. Take a slow deep breath, and let go of any tension, as you feel yourself sinking into the surface you're resting on, becoming still more comfortable and relaxed.

Take another slow, deep breath, and release your thoughts, letting them drift far away. And take another slow, deep breath, and know that in this moment, all is well.

Bring your awareness into your spiritual heart, in the center of your chest, and notice a softness there. Imagine that all of the energy you've sent out into the world lately is coming gently back home to your heart, helping you to feel more whole, and complete. Quietly receive this energy in your heart, and know there's nothing else you need to do right now. You can simply be here, relax, and receive.

As your energy continues to return to you, it's followed by a feeling of love, collecting within you, warm, and comforting. Allow yourself to soften and let go, and you can feel more of this love, as it gently gathers within your heart, easing everything, and helping you to know that all is well.

Bring your awareness more fully into your heart, as if you were standing there now, inside a cozy room. As your eyes adjust, you'll notice an opening in the floor of your heart, with a ladder leading down. Imagine you're climbing down that ladder within your heart, going deeper and deeper within. Down you go, past the place where words are important, and still further, into the deep, deep unknown. And when you can go no deeper into your heart, you find yourself stepping through a doorway, and into a beautiful mountain meadow.

The meadow is covered in green grass and wildflowers, and surrounded by tall evergreen trees. You can hear birds singing in the trees, and smell the scent of pine in the crisp mountain air. And the sky is the bluest blue you can possibly imagine.

Walk toward the center of the meadow, and there you'll find a beautifully made wooden bow, and one arrow. Pick up the bow, and notice the finely carved wood, inlaid with intricate patterns. Notice its sleek curves, and the taught bow string joining its two ends. The bow feels alive. It's perfectly weighted in your hand, and offers a fine feeling of quiet, dignified power.

As you pick up the arrow, you'll notice a colorful ribbon tied to the shaft, near the feathers at the back. Look more closely at the ribbon, and you'll find it has some words printed upon it—your own name, followed by a short sentence describing something you've decided to receive help with today. Although your situation may seem complicated in life, it all looks very clean and concise printed on this ribbon, and you marvel at how simple and direct it now appears. At this moment, the problem, the arrow, and the bow are all well within your grasp.

Place the arrow on a bow string, and point the arrow straight up into the sky, as if you were aiming for the farthest star in the universe. Pull back the bow as hard as you can, and hold it just for a moment, while you call upon your higher support, that vast resource of information, energy, and higher beings, all waiting to help you. Hold that arrow tight, as you simply ask for connection.

Now let the arrow fly, as it quickly carries your ribbon with it into the sky. Higher and higher it goes, until the arrow and your ribbon travel so high that you can barely see them. And then, they finally disappear.

A moment later, you hear a distant explosion. Your higher support has received your message, and is about to respond.

The sky bursts into a million colored light particles, like fine confetti, raining down. The particles keep coming and coming, forming patterns in the sky. Brilliant geometric shapes of light form symbols and images. And within this amazing array of shapes and colors, words begin to form above and all around you, along with whispered phrases.

Your higher support is speaking to you, sending messages that represent simple solutions, approaches, attitudes that will most help you take your next step. And at the same time, light begins flowing all around you, clearing, releasing, and transforming any negativity, blocks or illusions surrounding you, so that you can receive all of these messages, in just the way you need.

Take a few moments just to receive, and absorb whatever messages, information, and energies you many need right now.

Some of what you have received has gone into your unconscious mind, to be revealed gradually over the next 48 hours. Be sure to give yourself time to daydream, relax, and rest. No need to stress or strain, because everything will come to you in good time now.

It will soon be time to begin your return home, but first take a moment to thank your higher support for its input, and its connection with you.

And take a moment to thank yourself, for giving yourself this gift.

Gradually bring your awareness back to your physical surroundings. Take your time, and when you're ready, open your eyes, and feel awake, alert and refreshed.

Take a moment to write down anything you may have heard or learned during this experience, including any steps you need to take to put your learning into action.

THE HEALING LIGHT

Make yourself comfortable, and close your eyes. Take a slow deep breath, and let go of any tension in your body, as you settle into a more relaxed posture. Feel yourself dropping down from your mind into your body. Feel the weight of your body sinking into the surface you're resting on, as you become still more comfortable and relaxed.

Inwardly turn your attention up toward the heavens, and let your inner vision rise up higher, and higher, until you begin to notice a broad beam of pale golden light, reaching down toward you. And streaming down within that beam are delicate rays of all different colors, transmitting the most rarified and heavenly essences of love and healing.

As you continue to gaze upward, you recognize that this outpouring of heavenly light is being sent toward you by the angels, and realize that the beautiful energies they send are pristine, untouched by our world, and purer than the clearest water of the highest mountain spring. This light is their gift for you personally, containing a blessing of peace, love, and healing for your journey, here on Earth.

As this transmission reaches you, it forms itself into a perfect ball of healing light, collecting just a few inches away from the top of your head, golden white, with gem-like flecks of rose, emerald green, blue, purple and violet.

As the light continues to collect above you, you can feel your own body and energetic field relax, and prepare to receive it. All your cells are beginning to turn toward this light, as if each were a tiny satellite dish, turning to receive a new signal from above; and your energy field seems to expand, and open to attune to the message that's soon to be delivered.

Take another slow, deep breath, and invite the ball of light to come into your head. Imagine and feel it filling every part of your head and face, inside and out, bringing you a sense of peace and tranquility.

And take another deep breath, and breathe the ball of golden, multi-colored light down into your neck, and shoulders. Gently raise your shoulders for just a moment, and as you let them drop, let go of any tension there.

And breathe your ball of light down into your arms... elbows... wrists... and hands... until it flows out your fingertips. For just a moment, gently make a fist with both hands, and as you let them open again feel even more of the golden light flowing through your arms and out your fingertips.

Breathe the light into your chest and upper back... letting it fill your heart... lungs... and everywhere within and around your chest. Take a moment to experience the ball of light pulsing with your heartbeat, in the center of your chest.

Take another slow, deep breath and invite the golden, multicolored light into your abdomen and lower back... Give it time to find its way into all your internal organs, bringing balance and peace everywhere within. Imagine your organs all working together like a fine machine. The golden light has just given you a tune-up to make everything run smoother, and more freely.

And breath the ball of light into your hips and reproductive organs, as it balances and releases any tension within you. Imagine the light absorbing any sort of negativity or pressure, leaving you clear.

Invite the ball of light to travel through your upper legs... knees... calves... and feet. Lightly scrunch up your toes for a moment, and then let them relax, and the light flows freely throughout your legs and feet.

Now the golden white light, with its flecks of many different colors, is free to move all throughout your body, working its way everywhere within you. Connect within as deeply as you can, and ask your body, your mind, and your emotions to let go now of anything that doesn't serve your highest good. Take some time to be with the light in this way now, and imagine it going wherever it is most needed within you, doing it's healing work, and making everything just right.

Now imaging the light surrounds and fills your soul, and lifts you gently out of your body, to take you on a visit into the heavens.

Up you go, into the air, through the ceiling, and into the sky. And at the speed of light you're transported into a beautiful heavenly chamber, with transparent crystal walls, and a ceiling that's open to the infinite sky.

Here you're surrounded by a group of beings you may not recognize at first, but who nevertheless seem quite familiar, as if you had known and loved them for eons. They've gathered here to be with you now for one reason: To let you know, without the slightest room for doubt, that you are loved. As they look at you tenderly, you feel so well-understood by these old friends that your heart seems to open wider and wider. And as they reach forward and begin to pour love into you, first one by one, and then all together, you find you're able to let love in as you never have. Take some time to rest in this heavenly chamber, and receive this blessing.

It's almost time to bring this guided meditation to a close. So take a moment to thank yourself, for giving yourself this opportunity to relax, and heal from within.

Gradually bring your awareness back into your body, and your physical surroundings.

Take your time, and when you're ready, open your eyes, and feel awake, alert, and refreshed.

ABSENT HEALING: CALLING IN GRACE FOR SOMEONE IN NEED

INTRODUCTION

Here in Earth School, we operate under the principle of the "life plan." As souls, we come to earth to grow and learn, and as in most schools, we have a lesson plan all set up for us. Our life plan covers things like:

- Th e major lessons we need to learn.
- Our parents, family, and genetics.
- Experiences we're slated to have.
- Windows of opportunity for accelerated growth.
- Key people we'll be connected with.
- Struggles, challenges, and handicaps.
- Service we'll have the opportunity to perform
- Opportunities for successes, wins, and triumphs.

All of this is arranged for us to learn important lessons, build strength, balance karmic debt, build karmic equity, and experience fulfillment.

A related principle here is free will and accountability. Free will means we have some choice over the thoughts we think, the feelings we feel, and the actions we take. And accountability means we're responsible for the results of the choices we make.

Because we are accountable for our choices, angels can't just swoop down and go about fixing things for us. There's a kind of "no interference" clause in place that says if we get our struggle taken away, we'll miss our lesson, and that would defeat our whole purpose here. BUT, when we demonstrate a willingness to be open, to stretch, to listen, and to learn, sometimes help can be extended from above. And that's called "grace."

When we get sick, a whole variety of factors can be involved. It may be the result of conscious choices we made, it may have to do with our genetics, we may be slated to learn something of the human experience by way of the illness, we might be building strength through adversity, or we might be releasing accumulated negativity and stress through the body. Whatever the reason, our soul has something to learn from the experience, or growth to be gained. The question is, how much suffering is necessary for the growth to occur, and this is where grace can come in, if we're open to it.

Grace is the extension of God's love through creation. And by opening to grace, we may gain the growth and learning our soul needs, with less suffering. When we ask for grace, we put the whole situation—the illness, the suffering, the learning, and the outcome—into God's hands. Another way of saying this is we turn it over to our higher power, or we pray for the highest good of all concerned.

When it comes to grace, angels, saints, masters, and spiritual healers can play an important role, through the great love they transmit. When we're in the presence of love, and we open to it, it changes us. If we allow it to, pure love can help us let go of all sorts of negativity, and often it's the negativity that contributes to illness. And so depending upon the condition of the body, the negativity we hold, our lesson plan, and other factors, being in the presence of love can make a big difference in our recovery. And it always makes a big difference in our growth.

But what if you have a ton of love to convey to someone, but you're no where near them? Love is not limited by distance, and the level on which we give and receive pure love goes beyond the physical dimension. And that's why it's called "absent healing."

Use the following guided meditation to help connect with love at the deepest level within, call upon the support of all the positive beings you're connected to, and bring grace to the one you would most like to assist.

GUIDED MEDITATION

Make yourself comfortable, and close your eyes. Take a slow deep breath, and let go of any tension in your body, as you feel yourself sinking into the surface you're resting on, becoming still more comfortable and relaxed.

Imagine that waiting for you above, in another dimension, is a beautiful temple of light, and part of you is already there, waiting for the rest of you to arrive. Over the next few minutes you'll be bringing more and more of your awareness there, to call in grace for someone you know. In this meditation, we'll simply refer to that person as your friend.

Bring your awareness into your spiritual heart, in the center of your chest, and notice a softness there. Your heart is a great place to find peace, stillness, and connection to grace, within.

Imagine that all of the energy you've sent out into the world lately is coming gently back home to you, helping you to feel more whole, and complete. Quietly receive this energy in your heart, and know there's nothing else you need to do right now. You can simply be here, relax, and receive.

As your energy continues to return to you, it's followed by a feeling of love, collecting within you, warm, and comforting. Allow yourself to soften and let go, and you can feel more of this love, as it gently gathers within your heart, easing everything, and helping you to know that all is well.

Imagine you're hovering just outside your body, perhaps a foot or so above your head, and as you do, a column of light extends down from the heavens to surround and protect you. The light is a golden white color, a gift from above, and you can feel it reminding you of your own higher nature, your pure essence, and your connection to the divine.

As you continue to connect with this light, it becomes easy to lift higher, and soon you find yourself traveling within the light column, through the ceiling, above the roof, and into the sky. Going higher still, you reach the upper atmosphere, beyond the confines of Earth's gravitational pull, and into the upper heavens. Here, you experience a sense of expansion, a feeling of unlimited possibilities.

Soon you arrive at the temple of light, with its walls of majestic crystalline shapes, and it's ceiling open to the heavens still higher above.

Standing within this temple, you're joined by many beings of light; angels, masters, healers, and loved ones, all of whom have come to help channel God's grace, and bestow blessings upon your friend.

There is such a feeling of light-hearted love and warmth here among you, as if it were a quiet celebration. And there's a sense of great anticipation, and reverence in the air, because this meeting is an opportunity for a visit from the Creator.

Everyone forms a circle in the temple of light, and soon, in the center, your friend appears, perhaps as a physical presence, or quite possibly as a light form—a representation of their soul—because the healing they're about to receive will occur at the highest level of their being.

The work is about to begin. You and all of the light bearers silently bow your heads, and hold out your hands toward your friend. A powerful light pours forth from above, from the source of all creation, through all of you, and into your friend. The force of this energy moving through you is at first almost too powerful for you to bear, but you quickly adjust and find it easy to relax, open, receive, and transmit.

Take some time to continue to stay present with this energy, and allow it to pour through you, as you imagine your friend receiving it for their highest good.

While you and your friend are still open to this flow of divine love, take some time to speak directly to your friend now. Share with them your highest wishes, and let them know that your love is with them, whatever the outcome may be. Make sure to keep your expression neutral, with no emotional pressure or demand. Simply offer compassion, love, and positive wishes for their highest good.

Take this opportunity now for you to receive the blessings of everyone here. Stand in the center of the circle, and as the beings present bow their heads and hold out their hands toward you, that same powerful energy of love and grace is being poured into you. Take some time to simply open, receive, and allow it into every part of your being.

It will soon be time to bring this journey to a close. But first, take a moment to thank God, all of the light bearers, and your friend for this opportunity to be of service.

And thank yourself for giving yourself this gift.

Bring your awareness gently back to your physical surroundings.

Take your time, and when you're ready, open your eyes, and feel awake, alert, and refreshed.

CLEARING YOUR ENERGY

INTRODUCTION

If you're reading this script about clearing your energy, perhaps you or someone you know has been dealing with some uncomfortable feelings, have felt plagued by thought processes that you can't seem to let go of, or feel as though other people's negativity seems to get stuck to you, making you feel "yucky." Clearing your own energy can wipe away the yucky stuff, give you a fresh outlook, and allow you to be yourself again. Learning how to clear yourself takes some patience and practice, but it's a valuable skill, and once you have it you'll want to use it often.

GUIDED MEDITATION

Make yourself comfortable, and close your eyes. Take a slow deep breath, and let go of any tension, as you feel yourself sinking into the surface you're resting on, becoming still more comfortable and relaxed. Take another slow, deep breath, and release your thoughts, letting them drift far away. And take another slow, deep breath, and know that in this moment, all is well.

Imagine that all the energy you've sent out into the world over the last few days is coming gently back to you, like the last parts of a puzzle coming into place. And as your energy returns, you begin to feel more whole, more like yourself.

Imagine a column of golden, white light is streaming down from the highest heavens, surrounding, filling and protecting you, and going deep down into the earth, all the way to earth's core. This light is here to facilitate your clearing at the deepest level, and will allow anything you might release to be transmuted into love. Feel and visualize this light as it penetrates every part of you body, mind, and spirit. And call upon any spiritual figures or allies you feel connected to, to help support your inner work now.

Bring your focus into your spiritual heart, in the center of your chest. Your heart is a place to connect deeply within, find peace, and receive guidance from above, and it's the ideal place for you to be now, for clearing.

Become aware of your inner climate, and any feelings you may be experiencing. Notice whether you might feel sad, angry, worried, anxious, guilty, or upset in any other way.

Consider whether there is anyone you might have conflict with or concern about.

And consider whether there is any particular situation that's been bothering you, past or present.

Now refocus in your heart, and simply be present with whatever feelings you've discovered. Those are the feelings that are coming up to clear.

Begin to breathe deeply, and slowly. Take very full, deep breaths, as you breathe in through your nose, and out through your mouth. Place one hand on your belly, and notice whether your belly moves in and out with your breath. As you breathe in, let your belly expand, pushing out your hand, and as you breathe out, let your belly relax.

As you continue to breathe in this deep, even rhythm, stay present with the feelings you need to clear, and stay in your heart. Don't try to analyze, justify, argue with, or control the feelings. Simply observe them, stay in your heart, and breathe. Take some time to practice this.

Remember that the feelings you're experiencing are just stuff within you coming up to clear. It's not you, nor does it define you. It's only some baggage you've accumulated by being human, as we all do. Breathe, don't try to think about or control it, and remain neutral toward it. By not adding judgment to it or making it part of yourself, it has nothing to cling to, and your system can allow it to release, as it's doing right now. The key is neutrality. Even though it's a feeling within you, you can still stay neutral toward it, observe it, breathe and let it naturally dissipate, as you're doing. Take some more time to practice this now.

Refocus in your heart center, and become aware again of the column of light surrounding and filling you, and of any spiritual allies or figures you've invited to be with you. Consider one thing in your life that you feel grateful for, and focus on that for a few moments.

Now take some time to continue to focus in your heart, and simply receive love coming into you from the inside, the outside. Quietly receive, breathe, let go, and receive more.

Check your inner climate again, and notice whether what you were clearing before is still there, or if it has diminished, or gone away.

During the day, when you notice something coming up within you to clear, simply be present with it, breathe, stay neutral, and allow it to pass through.

Take as long as you wish to continue your meditation, and then bring your awareness gently back to your physical surroundings.

When you're ready, open your eyes, and feel awake, alert, and refreshed.

RIVER OF LIGHT

Make yourself comfortable, and close your eyes. Take a slow deep breath, and let go of any tension, as you feel yourself sinking into the surface you're resting on, becoming still more comfortable and relaxed. Take another slow, deep breath, and release your thoughts, letting them drift far away. And take another slow, deep breath, and know that in this moment, all is well.

Bring your awareness into your heart center, the energy center, in the middle of your chest, and notice a softness there. Imagine all of the energy you've sent out into the world lately coming gently back home to your heart, helping you to feel more whole, and more complete. Quietly receive this energy, and know that for now, it's OK to simply be here, relax, and receive.

Imagine a column of light, descending from the highest heavens, through the sky, through your ceiling, and into your room. This light contains a multitude of beautifully colored healing energies, angelic blessings, and whispered messages of love from above, all for you, in a never ending stream.

Just as this column of light touches your floor, it transforms into a river, flowing in front of you, a combination of living water and sacred light. All the healing energies, angelic blessings, and whispered messages of love are now streaming before you in a continuous offering, waiting for you to receive.

And so you remove your shoes, and place your feet in this river of light. Breathe deeply, and feel its blessings flowing up into your ankles...

legs… hips… torso… arms… shoulders and head… until your whole body is filled and overflowing with love. Continue to take full, deep breaths, and allow all the concerns of daily life to release, as you receive this gift.

Now you find yourself holding a baby in your arms—you, as a newborn. So much has happened in your life and a lot of it hasn't been easy. But today you can let go of the past, bless yourself, and return to that tender state of innocence, keeping all the wisdom you've gained along the way.

Open your heart as wide as you can, as you tenderly place yourself as that newborn into the river of light, just long enough to receive whatever you need. Healing can happen in an instant.

And now once again hold your newborn self to your chest, cradled in your arms, giving and receiving in a full circle of love. Take a few moments to experience this.

As you continue, the love you pour into yourself as a newborn begins to expand it, until it's so large that it surrounds and embraces you. Your newborn self has become your own soul, with all the higher wisdom, light, and energy you truly are. Feel the light and love of your soul pouring into you now, as you open, allow, and receive.

Now you and your soul begin to expand further, becoming larger, and larger, until you completely merge with the whole of creation. Feel yourself dissolve into pure love, held in the arms of the Creator.

Slowly begin to return to the river of light, flowing before you. Imagine it continuing to flow through your life over the next day, the next week, month, and year. Envision yourself touching into it through times of peace, and times of challenge, drawing support and encouragement, and being filled with its blessing, whenever you need it.

If there is anyone else whom you would like to share this with, imagine them now standing in the river of light, receiving whatever they may need, for their highest good.

It's almost time to bring this inner journey to a close. But first, take a moment to thank yourself for giving yourself this gift.

Bring your awareness gently back to your physical surroundings.

Take your time, and when you're ready, open your eyes, and feel awake, alert, and refreshed.

SOUL OVERVIEW ONE: A HIGHER PERSPECTIVE

Make yourself comfortable, and close your eyes. Take a slow deep breath, and let go of any tension, as you feel yourself sinking into the surface you're resting on, becoming still more comfortable and relaxed. Take another slow, deep breath, and release your thoughts, letting them drift far away. And take another slow, deep breath, and know that in this moment, all is well.

Bring your awareness into your spiritual heart, in the center of your chest, and notice a softness there. Imagine that all of the energy you've sent out into the world lately is coming gently back home to your heart, helping you to feel more whole, and complete. Quietly receive this energy in your heart, and know there's nothing else you need to do right now. You can simply be here, relax, and receive.

As your energy continues to return to you, it's followed by a feeling of love, collecting within you, warm, and comforting. Allow yourself to soften and let go, and you can feel more of this love, as it gently gathers within your heart, easing everything, and helping you to know that all is well.

Bring yourself more fully into your heart, as if you were standing there now, inside a cozy room. As your eyes adjust to this space, you'll notice there's an opening in the ceiling, with a ladder, leading up. Imagine you're climbing up that ladder, going higher and higher into your awareness.

Up you go, past the place where words are important, and still further, even beyond where emotions would distract you.

And when you can go no higher, you find yourself stepping through a door, outside of your body and into a state of pure consciousness, hovering like a cloud. You're in an expanded state of being—your own soul essence, pure and very present, in non-physical form.

Take a few moments to simply enjoy this sensation of being your essential self, with no distractions or attachments, floating free.

Soon you begin to feel the presence of others there with you, who feel very familiar. This is your soul group; your true family; the ones you're most deeply connected to. You may not always get to be with them on earth, but here in spirit you can join with them once again, feel unified and whole, and receive their unconditional love. Take some time to bathe in the love and support that they offer you now, and let it bring you deep peace.

Imagine that as a soul in this expanded, free state of being, you are between lifetimes on Earth, just prior to your current incarnation. You've been in human form many times, and you've learned much about life. But you still have more to do. Perhaps you feel a longing to experience more, to know more, and a yearning to expand and fulfill yourself more deeply. Something tells you it will soon be time to be in an Earth body again, to continue your journey.

And so you begin to feel a familiar pull toward the Earth. At first it's very faint, like a distant memory on the edge of your awareness. Then it begins to grow stronger, and you recall what it's like to have physical senses. You start to remember taste, then smell, touch, hearing, and sight.

Now as you draw closer, you begin to tune in to your mother. Drawing closer still, you perceive the outline of your life plan, taking shape like a holographic blueprint. Now you notice some of the particular life skills, gifts, talents and abilities you will have available, should you choose to engage with them. And you get a glimpse of some of the key relation-ships that will shape your journey ahead.

The closer you come to this new life, the stronger the attraction, because your soul knows how much you have to gain. And even though you can tell there will be some struggle, you have little hesitation, because of the great opportunities ahead.

Take a few moments to experience that unique state of being just before you come into your current lifetime, while you still have the overview of your life plan. Imagine you're looking ahead at your life, and being briefed by a team of loving guides and angels about what you're about to experience. Take some time to listen, receive messages, and let them help light the way ahead.

Soon you find yourself in a new infant body, held by your mother, perhaps surrounded by some of your new family. You've willingly left behind much of the awareness you had in the soul realm, in order to enter life here with your memory a clean slate.

But as you reenter your life, bring gratitude and appreciation for creation. This is the life that's been set up perfectly for you—for the most real part of you—to gain all the learning, growth, and evolution you possibly can. And even when it doesn't seem like it, even when it's uncomfortable or painful, remember that everything here has been orchestrated specifically for you. Life is precious to you, and you are precious to life.

Consider the one thing that you would like to bring forward into your present day life, from this experience. It might be an awareness of the overview of your life plan, or the appreciation of the opportunities you've been given. Perhaps it's the unconditional love of your soul group, or the sense of innocence or vulnerability you had as an infant, as yet unprogrammed. Take some time to be in touch with that feeling or awareness, and allow it to update and inform your present day consciousness.

As you come forward in time to the present day, you know that eventually you'll be back in soul consciousness again, and out of the form of creation known as Earth. So, while you're here, appreciate all you can, let go of judgment, and know that life's plan for you is far greater than you could ever imagine. Life isn't a party, but neither is it a nightmare.

It's a miraculous series of moments designed and orchestrated for you and your own highest good.

It's almost time to bring this inner journey to a close. But first, take a moment to thank yourself for giving yourself this gift.

Allow all the benefits of this experience to stay with you, as you gently bring your awareness gently back to your physical surroundings.

Take your time, and when you're ready, open your eyes, and feel awake, alert, and refreshed.

SOUL OVERVIEW TWO: SOUL AWARENESS

Make yourself comfortable, and close your eyes. Take a slow deep breath, and let go of any tension, as you feel yourself sinking into the surface you're resting on, becoming still more comfortable and relaxed. Take another slow, deep breath, and release your thoughts, letting them drift far away. And take another slow, deep breath, and know that in this moment, all is well.

Bring your awareness into your spiritual heart, in the center of your chest, and notice a softness there. Imagine that all of the energy you've sent out into the world lately is coming gently back home to your heart, helping you to feel more whole, and complete. Quietly receive this energy in your heart, and know there's nothing else you need to do right now. You can simply be here, relax, and receive.

As your energy continues to return to you, it's followed by a feeling of love, collecting within you, warm, and comforting. Allow yourself to soften and let go, and you can feel more of this love, as it gently gathers within your heart, easing everything, and helping you to know that all is well.

Bring yourself more fully into your heart, as if you were standing there now, inside a cozy room. As your eyes adjust to this space, you'll notice there's an opening in the ceiling, with a ladder, leading up. Imagine you're climbing up that ladder, going higher and higher into your awareness. Up you go, past the place where words are important, and still further, even beyond where emotions would distract you. And when you can go no higher, you find yourself stepping through a door, outside of your body and into a state of pure consciousness, hovering like a cloud. You're in an expanded state of being: Your own soul essence, pure and very present, in a non-physical form.

Take a few moments to simply enjoy this sensation of being your essential self, with no distractions or attachments, floating free.

Consider one of the challenges you currently face in life. From your limited perspective back on Earth, you may feel stuck, at a dead end, or unable to surmount certain obstacles that face you. But take a look at yourself from this higher perspective, this view of your soul's journey through life.

Visualize yourself from high above, as if you were on a road or pathway, representing your life. Your pathway stretches far into the past, and far into the future, and it intersects with many other paths, where others travel.

From above, you can see that there have been many obstacles already, from the moment you were born, up until the present day. And that there are still more challenges up ahead.

But you've faced and dealt with challenges time and time again, and kept going, and you will continue to do so. You have not done anything wrong to create these obstacles, nor made the wrong choices. They come and go as a natural part of life, here in creation, to help your soul grow and evolve during its journey. There is no success or failure, only experience. You're simply a soul in human form, learning, growing, and moving forward along your path on Earth.

And so, from your higher perspective, from your soul's point of view, take some time to send your Earth-self love, encouragement, and understanding. Offer yourself compassion for your struggle, and remove any doubt, self-judgment, or feelings of shame or remorse. Tell yourself that you're simply a soul in human form, doing your best. Take some time to do this now.

Take another look at your current situation on Earth, from your higher soul perspective. What wisdom or words of advice might you have to convey to yourself, to help you move forward more easily along your path? Take a moment for this now.

Begin to come gently back into your body, and your current physical surroundings. But before return to your normal consciousness, do one more thing. Invite your soul, with all its wisdom, love, and its natural connection to higher guidance, to come more fully into your body, and your life. Imagine this presence, your essential, true self, embracing you now, filling you with love. Take a moment for this now.

Envision your soul permeating your entire being, and manifesting more fully in your life on an ongoing basis, in the days ahead.

Notice how you might think, speak and behave differently as this occurs.

Notice how you might relate differently to your environment, to other people, and in your occupation. Let this experience take shape in your imagination now, as you invite your soul to come more fully into your life, on an ongoing basis.

It's almost time to bring this inner journey to a close. But first, take a moment to thank yourself for giving yourself this gift.

Allow all the benefits of this experience to stay with you, as you gently bring your awareness gently back to your physical surroundings.

Take your time, and when you're ready, open your eyes, and feel awake, alert, and refreshed.

THE HEALING WATERFALL

III

Make yourself comfortable, and close your eyes. Take a slow deep breath, and let go of any tension, as you feel yourself sinking into the surface you're resting on, becoming still more comfortable and relaxed. Take another slow, deep breath, and release your thoughts, letting them drift far away. And take another slow, deep breath, and know that in this moment, all is well.

Imagine you're a tiny version of yourself, clinging to a rope in the middle of your head, holding on tight, as the rope slowly lowers. Down you go, past your nose, your mouth, down your neck, and into your chest until you come gently into your heart.

Your feet touch down, the rope disappears, and you find you're in the middle of an enchanted forest, with tall trees, moss covered rocks, and a winding brook, leading to a tall waterfall, farther upstream. Birds are commuting in the tree tops; robins and jays, and some you've never seen before, and here and there red ground squirrels and tawny colored rabbits are busy going about their day. It's morning here, and everything is bursting with life, rich and resplendent.

A soft breeze brushes your face, and you feel a subtle shift in the energy. And as you turn to look at the waterfall, you see that way up at the top is a huge angel, pouring light into the falling water. The light and water mix, so that by the time they cascade into the pool below, they've transformed into something between water and light, a golden-white healing combination.

That pool looks so inviting, but there's no hurry. You have all the time in the world. And so you walk peacefully along the brook, smelling the delicious forest air, taking in the sounds, and exploring a little.

Looking around at the trees, you see that they're ancient; so tall they almost seem to fade into the sky above, even as they cast a dappled shade across the forest floor. The path beneath your feet is covered with leaves of green, yellow, brown and red, and bright blue and white wildflowers poke their way here and there through the rich, forest soil.

The silvery brook offers rippling reflections of the blue sky above. And through the surface you can see stones of copper, gold, and grey, layered on the stream bed below. Little fish are darting about in the current in search of their breakfast.

As you come closer to the pool beneath the waterfall, you notice a fawn, who looks up at you for a moment, and then goes back to her drink. And there on the other side is a magnificent blue heron, stalking the shallow edge. This must be a sacred place, for the wildlife isn't bothered by your presence in the least.

A fallen log nearby makes a perfect spot to sit, as you quietly remove your shoes and clothing, preparing for your immersion in the inviting pool. And as you dip your toe in the water, you find it's the perfect temperature, and the bottom is smooth and even, making it easy to wade in. And so you step slowly forward, immersing your feet, ankles, calves, and knees in this healing pool of water and light.

Soon you're up to your waist, letting your hands sweep softly back and forth in the water, so relaxing and soft. The pool is deep enough that you can easily dip fully below its surface, and the current here is slow and languid, making it the ideal place to relax and let go.

Looking up at the waterfall, you see the angel once again, still pouring light into the water. It seems as if she's been there forever, and your breath catches for a moment as she meets your gaze, and makes contact with you directly. She sees you, knows you've come to receive her gift, and welcomes you to her world.

If you like, float on your back, and feel your whole body embraced by the light-filled water, as it seems to cradle and invite you to feel totally relaxed and free.

Soon you can hear the angel begin to sing to the waterfall, to the forest, the earth, the sky, and to you. She opens her heart wide, pouring out love that seems to come from the very source of all creation, her blessing resonating everywhere within you, bringing harmony to every cell in your body. Take some time to open, listen, and receive.

Before long you notice that her song has called forth four more angelic beings, now at your head, feet, and on either side of you, as you continue to float in this healing pool. They're helping channel positive, loving energy into your body, mind, and emotions, bringing you into greater and greater harmony with love.

Everything seems to be vibrating in harmony now; the earth, sky, water, and you, until all is one. Take some time to simply be at peace now, let go of anything you no longer need, and receive more of this healing energy of love.

The four angels are standing back, signaling that their work is done for now. So take a moment to listen and receive any further message that may be here for you at this time.

The heron that's been so quietly standing by the pool takes off in flight. The fawn has also gone away, and it feels like it's time for you to leave as well, for now. Take a moment to thank the waterfall angel for her gifts. And thank yourself for taking the time to be here now.

Gradually bring your awareness gently back to your physical surroundings.

Take your time, and when you're ready, open your eyes, and feel awake, alert, and refreshed.

PART EIGHT

CONNECTING WITH SPIRITUAL FIGURES

MEET YOUR GUARDIAN ANGEL

Make yourself comfortable, and close your eyes. Take a slow deep breath, and let go of any tension, as you feel yourself sinking into the surface you're resting on, becoming still more comfortable and relaxed. Take another slow, deep breath, and release your thoughts, letting them drift far away. And take another slow, deep breath, and know that in this moment, all is well.

Consider a time when you first met someone important to you, and the circumstances around that meeting. Imagine a kind and loving presence there with you, standing by, making sure this meeting took place. Your guardian angel was there, pulling strings, making arrangements, and orchestrating all the events necessary to bring you together with that person. Notice the feeling of Divine intervention, the blessing surrounding that meeting, from on high.

Consider a time when you made a decision that had a positive impact on your life, and remember the feeling of knowing you needed to do this. Imagine your guardian angel there with you, brightening your awareness, helping you focus on what mattered most, insuring you made the best decision possible. Your angel could see far down the road, and knew what you needed. And he or she was right there with you, making sure you were headed in the right direction.

Consider one time in your life when circumstances led you to something special you wanted, or needed, perhaps without even knowing you needed it beforehand. See your guardian angel there, coordinating the events, standing by, making sure that things fell your way, so that you would receive exactly what you needed, just when you needed it.

And consider a time when you were concerned and uncertain about something, perhaps about yourself or someone near to you, and prayed for help. Envision your guardian angel at your side, hearing your prayers, and taking them directly to God on your behalf. Whatever the outcome of that situation, know that your angel was there for you, helping to insure that God's will was delivered.

Your guardian angel has been right there with you, from the moment you were born, has stayed by your side, and will continue to assist you throughout your life. He or she is a faithful servant, born of God's love, and devoted entirely to helping you, for your highest good.

And your guardian angel is with you right now, right in front of you. Your angel knows you seek a deeper connection with them, and is projecting their image, and their presence, into your higher mind, so that you might know them more closely.

Without stress or strain, simply relax into your heart, and allow your imagination to be set free. Let whatever images seem come before you appear in your mind's eye, without trying to modify or edit what you see. Ask your angel to show you their face, and just breathe, relax, and envision.

Whatever does or doesn't come up in your mind's eye is just fine. Simply open, and allow yourself to freely see. Let whatever comes into your mind be real for you, and allow it to fill in and become richer. Even if you seem to see nothing at all, continue to hold your focus and be open. This is a practice of receiving from the Divine. There is no way to fail, because all you need do is be open, and patiently wait. Do this for a few moments now.

Continue to hold your focus as you bow your head slightly forward as you take a moment to give thanks to God for your guardian angel. Hold our your hands before you, and feel your angel touching you, sending you a gentle wave of loving energy. Take some time to open, breathe, and receive.

If there is anywhere within your body that hurts or needs healing, ask your guardian angel to send God's love and healing energy there now.

Your guardian angel is networked with all the angels, saints, masters, and others throughout heaven. Ask your guardian angel to bring another being into your presence now, to connect with you in love. This may be someone you know or wish to know better, or someone new to assist you through the next stage of your journey. You may ask for someone specific, or allow your guardian angel to bring you whomever would be best for you right now. Take some time to breathe, open your awareness, and receive your visitor, now.

Now ask your guardian angel to take a message of love or healing from you, to someone you know. Tell your angel what you'd like to convey, and give them a moment to deliver that message from your heart, to the heart of your friend or loved one, now.

Ask your guardian angel if they have carried any message for you in return.

Ask your guardian angel to bring a blessing of love and healing from on high, directly into your room now. See and feel your room filling with heavenly light, a beautiful scent, and a wonderful feeling of love and peace. Take a moment to allow this experience to expand, as you simply receive love from above.

You've asked your guardian angel to assist you in many ways today, and in doing so you've grown closer to them in spirit. Take a moment to open your heart as wide as you can, and be in a state of loving gratitude with your guardian angel now. Feel God's love pouring from their heart into yours, and receive.

Cast your mind forward in time, as you envision your guardian angel standing by you, protecting you, and serving you with God's love, day after day, and night after night, for the rest of your life. Imagine yourself opening more and more to your angel's presence. Ask that you might be helped to notice all the miracles, large and small, being delivered to you, in perfect timing.

It will soon be time to bring this inner journey to a close. But first, take a moment to envision your angel before you, one more time, and see, feel, hear, or simply know of their presence there with you.

Thank your guardian angel for their blessing, and give them yours.

Bring your awareness gently back to your physical surroundings.

Take your time, and when you're ready, open your eyes, and feel awake, alert, and refreshed.

VISITING PADRE PIO

INTRODUCTION

Padre Pio was a great spiritual master, priest, and monk known for countless miracles. Though he passed on in 1968, his spirit continues to touch all who reach out to him. He offers us wisdom, solace, blessings, and boundless love from above.

Though he became famous for bearing the stigmata, he was best appreciated for the love emanating from his presence, and for the miracles stemming from his touch, or from simply asking for his help in prayer.

Padre Pio lived most of his life in a small Italian village as a simple priest in the Capuchin order, an offshoot of the Franciscans. As word of his spiritual gifts spread, thousands came to receive his blessing from around the world, and letters poured in asking for his intervention. He was canonized in 2002 by Pope John Paul II. His most famous words are "Pray, hope, and don't worry."

Use this guided meditation to make a deep and lasting spiritual connection with this great teacher and lover of God and humanity.

GUIDED MEDITATION

Make yourself comfortable, and close your eyes. Take a slow deep breath, and let go of any tension, as you feel yourself sinking into the surface you're resting on, becoming still more comfortable and relaxed. Take another slow, deep breath, and release your thoughts, letting them drift far away. And take another slow, deep breath, and know that in this moment, all is well.

Bring your awareness into your spiritual heart, in the center of your chest, and notice a softness there, a feeling of peace. Take a moment to enjoy this feeling, as you quietly focus in your heart, and follow your breath, in, and out.

Bring yourself more fully into your heart, as if you were standing there now, inside a cozy room. Soon, you'll notice a doorway, and as you walk through it, you'll find yourself transported to a lovely garden, on the grounds of an ancient monastery.

The garden is a rustic one, with flower beds, shrubs, and olive and fig trees, all lovingly cared for. The plants and trees seem to glow with a heavenly light, their colors soft, and radiant. The bird songs here are sweet, and musical. And the air is filled with a delicate scent of roses, lilacs, and other flowers, all fresh from a recent rain shower.

There's a pretty stone path, edged with tiny flowers and moss, winding its way through the garden. As you make your way along the path, you come to a wooden bench, worn and inviting, the perfect spot to relax, and take in your surroundings. Have a seat, and enjoy.

Through the years, many have visited this garden, and rested on this very bench, to contemplate nature, meditate, and pray. And as you sit, you begin to feel the spiritual energy and love so present here today. Take a moment to enjoy this feeling, and your kinship with all those who have come before you, on this spiritual path.

Soon you hear quiet footsteps coming toward you. And as the sound draws nearer, you also hear the soft click of rosary beads. Before you know it, Padre Pio has come, and has taken the seated beside you, in his brown monk's habit, eyes closed, deep in prayer.

To join him within, you go deeper into your own meditation, focusing on God's love, now so present within you. You and Padre Pio become wrapped in a profound, sacred silence. Take a moment to enjoy the sweetness of God's love, together with Padre Pio.

Padre Pio turns to face you now. His eyes are an endless well of compassion and understanding, and it feels as if you could fall completely into his gaze. He sees into the very depths of your soul, and knows your struggle, and your shortcomings. Yet he looks at you with only love, as the beloved child of God you truly are.

If you would like, Padre Pio will lift whatever may be weighing on you inside, and clear any suffering you're ready to release. Take a moment to look into his eyes, and allow his gaze to purify your soul, and let all else fall away. Open, receive God's love, and be restored.

Do you have a question for Padre Pio, about your life, or your spiritual path? Ask now, listen, and inwardly receive his answer.

Project your mind forward in time to a challenge or situation you may be facing, and imagine Padre Pio praying by your side. Envision Padre Pio leading you through that situation now, with grace and ease. He encourages you to accept whatever may come, act in the most positive way possible, and turn your focus upward to God.

Padre Pio's presence brightens the air, and creates an opening between heaven and earth for miracles to occur. And he helps you recognize the miracles already present, all around you. Take some time to envision your situation unfolding, in the most positive way possible, with Padre Pio by your side.

Padre Pio commands the mightiest of angels, and can perform miracles in God's name. Only God knows our spiritual needs, but Padre Pio's blessing can accelerate our growth and healing, for our highest good. Ask for Padre Pio's blessing now, as he offers his gift, with a touch, a look, or a sacred gesture. Open your heart, and receive Padre Pio's blessing.

It will soon be time to bring this inner journey to a close. But first, take a moment to thank Padre Pio for his presence, and his blessing.

And take a moment to thank yourself for giving yourself this gift.

Gradually bring your awareness back to your physical surroundings.

Take your time, and when you're ready, open your eyes, and feel awake, alert, and refreshed.

VISITING MOTHER MARY

Make yourself comfortable, and close your eyes. Take a slow deep breath, and let go of any tension in your body, as you settle into a more relaxed posture. Feel yourself dropping down from your mind into your body. Feel the weight of your body sinking into the surface you're resting on, as you become still more comfortable and relaxed.

You will soon be receiving a visit within, and so, much as you might prepare your home to welcome a special guest, let's take a few moments to clear your mind, and open your heart, as you prepare to welcome Mother Mary.

Imagine a soft shower of silver light is being sent down toward you from heaven. See and feel the light, sparkling raindrops falling all around and through you, clearing your energy, lifting your spirit, and leaving everything sweet and fresh, as it would be after a light summer rain.

Now imagine a warm current of love is softly pulsing in the center of your chest, in your spiritual heart. As this love continues to pulse, your heart becomes warmer, and softer, and begins to open like a flower in the sunshine. And as your heart opens, everything seems to fade away but love, and love begins to fill your whole being with this warm, soft feeling.

Imagine your love begins to overflow, and spread out from you in every direction. And as your love continues to expand, it meets another outpouring of love that's coming down from heaven. And where your love, and this heavenly love meet, rose petals begin to appear, delicate and pink, manifesting in the air, and drifting softly down around you.

The petals are a gift from Mary, letting you know that she is coming. Down they float, settling all around you, and bringing the sweetest scent, the most wonderful feeling, and a blessing of peace from Mother Mary. Take a few moments to receive this blessing, as it continues to help you open and expand your heart.

As the blessing unfolds, Mary herself comes closer, and closer, so that you can begin to feel her enfolding you with her love.

And now, soft as a whisper, she is with you, seated before you, and surrounded by heavenly light. Mary asks nothing, and offers everything, with her kind attention focused entirely upon you. She sees you, knows your struggle, and knows your heart. And she loves you completely, for the precious child of God that you are. Sit with her here for a few moments, and simply enjoy her company, and her love.

Remember how you were as a little child, so innocent, and open to everything. Perhaps when you were little, things were difficult, and you sometimes felt afraid, or frustrated, unable to manage the world around you. Allow Mother Mary to hold you now, as if you were that precious, innocent child, and receive her love and comfort.

What would you most like to ask Mother Mary? Let the questions come up from your heart, and listen within as she softly responds. Take some time and allow this conversation to unfold naturally. Ask, be still, listen, and know.

Mother Mary would like to show you something about God's love, and extends her hands, asking if you would take them in yours. As soon as you feel her touch you begin to travel inwardly with her, toward the heart of God, going deeper, and deeper, and still deeper still, as the energy of love becomes stronger and stronger. And when it seems that you couldn't possibly go any deeper within, you find yourself fully embraced in Mother Mary's arms, while she is fully embraced by God. It's as if she were receiving Gods love in all its power, softening it in her own heart, and pouring it tenderly into you. Allow Mary to continue to hold you in this way for a while, as you simply receive.

Stay with Mother Mary a little longer, and allow the meaning of the following simple prayer, to reveal itself.

Oh, Divine Mother,
Bless my heart
Embrace my soul
And with your tender love and mercy
Dissolve my fear to help me better know God's love.
Show me where I can extend kindness to others.
Mother Mary, who shall I pray for today?

It will soon be time to bring this journey to a close, so take a few moments to thank Mother Mary for her love, and if you wish, ask her to remain with you in your heart over the coming days.

Take your time, and when you're ready, bring your awareness gently back to your physical surroundings.

Bring with you all you have learned, and when you're ready, open your eyes, and feel awake, alert, and refreshed.

VISITING SAINT FRANCIS

Make yourself comfortable, and close your eyes. Take a slow deep breath, and let go of any tension in your body, as you settle into a more relaxed posture. Feel yourself dropping down from your mind into your body. Feel the weight of your body sinking into the surface you're resting on, as you become still more comfortable and relaxed.

Imagine you're walking in a beautiful mountain meadow, along a path by a quiet stream. It's a late summer morning, and the air is soft and warm. You can smell wildflowers blooming, and the plants along the water's edge, and as you walk along you can feel the soft ground beneath your footsteps.

Birds are singing to each other in the nearby trees, and you hear the sound of water running over the smooth, copper colored rocks on the streambed. A feeling of peace seems to encompass everything here, and you feel it begin to it settle over you as well. Breathe this peaceful feeling in, deeply and slowly now, and let it find its way everywhere within you.

As you continue to walk along this path, you sense the warm, familiar presence of an old friend, someone kind and gentle, and you have the unmistakable feeling he's come especially to see you. As he draws nearer, you feel your spirit lighten, and your heart open. And now, as if it were the most natural thing in the world, you feel Francis's hand resting gently on your shoulder, as you walk together along the path.

Francis has the touch of an older, wiser, and most compassionate brother. Of someone who's experienced tremendous joy, profound sadness, and most of all, a deep and constant bond of love with God the Creator.

And by his hand upon your shoulder you know that he's here to share that bond of love with you.

Turn and face Francis, and allow his presence to fill you. As more song birds come to visit, one by one, in the grass and trees nearby, you can feel Francis' love, and the grace surrounding him, growing stronger, expanding, and touching your heart.

Something within you stirs awake, and you know that this visit, this experience, is a doorway through which Francis' love, and God's grace, are coming into your life, to grow and blossom, like flowers in the meadow. Take some time to feel Francis' love for you now, and allow the grace that surrounds him to also surround and fill you.

Walking further along the path with Francis, you now begin to notice things differently. Everything in the meadow seems to have become enchanted with love and beauty. Colors have taken on a soft luster. The river seems to be alive and shining with light. The bird songs have grown sweeter and more innocent, and a light breeze has set the grasses and flowers swaying in unison, as if they were all listening to a song.

Francis guides you over to the stream, and the two of you sit side by side, your bare feet resting in the cool water. As you sit, look around and notice God's incredible handiwork. At your feet a few fish dart here and there in the gentle current. A butterfly visits a flower on the bank. A rabbit hops by on the opposite side of the stream, and takes a moment to sniff the air. Everywhere before you is the beauty of Creation, the world in which you are so intimately connected. This is God's world, and you are God's most precious creation. And in this moment, you know what Francis knows, that God's love lives within you always, now and forever.

The stream has become a luminous current of heavenly light, and it flows around your feet, lifting your spirit, clearing your mind, and healing your body. Ask now in deepest prayer that you be helped to release anything that stands between you and your greater awakening, and open to the fullness of God's grace.

In answer to your prayer, waves of love flow from the Creator toward you and Francis, bringing blessings beyond measure. Take some time to breathe deeply, and receive.

As you continue to sit together, Saint Francis asks you to pray with him. Together, you say the following prayer, and you allow its meaning to go deep within you.

Lord, make me an instrument of your peace.
Where there is hatred, let me sow love.
Where there is injury, pardon.
Where there is doubt, faith.
Where there is despair, hope.
Where there is darkness, light.
And where there is sadness, joy.
Oh, Divine Master
Grant that I may not so much seek to be consoled, as to console;
To be understood, as to understand To be loved, as to love.
For it is in giving that I receive In pardoning that I am pardoned.
And it is in dying that I am born to eternal life.

If there is anything that has been troubling you, take a few moments to share it with Saint Francis now. With his kind, wise eyes full of compassion, he sees you, understands all you've gone through, and knows who you truly are, beyond all the trappings of your worldly existence. Allow him to comfort you in whatever way he feels is best, as you receive his blessing, through his words, his touch, or his gaze.

It will soon be time to bring this journey to a close, so take a few moments to thank Francis for his love, and if you wish, ask him to remain with you in your heart over the coming days.

Take your time, and when you're ready, bring your awareness gently back to your physical surroundings.

Bring with you all you have learned, and when you're ready, open your eyes, and feel awake, alert, and refreshed.

VISITING ARCHANGEL MICHAEL

Make yourself comfortable, and close your eyes. Take a slow deep breath, and let go of any tension in your body, as you settle into a more relaxed posture.

Feel yourself dropping down from your mind into your body. Feel the your body sinking into the surface you're resting on, as you become still more comfortable and relaxed.

Continue to breathe deeply and slowly, and enjoy the feeling of becoming lighter, and lighter. Imagine you're suspended in the air, and surrounded by clouds so thick it's impossible to see where you are. It feels good to be floating like this, and you don't really mind not knowing what's around you. In fact, it's nice for a change not to know, and to just let everything go, as you simply breathe in, and out.

As the clouds around you begin to dissipate, you find you're in the center of a huge, white room that's floating in the air, with its ceiling open to the sky. And coming down from the heavens, right into this room, is a beam of golden light, enveloping and embracing you. Slowly breathe this light in and out, as you become accustomed to it, and allow your focus to shift up along its beam, into the heavens.

As you look up, you see that within the beam of light is a staircase. And this is staircase is a symbolic welcome, an invitation to you, from Archangel Michael. And although the stairs are steep, you feel light as a feather, and know it's perfectly safe to climb.

As you step on the first step, you hear Michael call your name and say, "I am here to help you use love, to overcome every obstacle." Take a deep breath, and breathe in love.

As you climb higher, the golden light from above becomes a little brighter, and you hear Michael say, "I am here to help you surrender your anger and frustration." Take a deep breath, and let it go.

As you climb higher, and step upon the third step, the golden light begins to shift to white, and you hear Michael say, "I am here to help you use love to answer your heartfelt prayers." Take a deep breath, and breathe in love.

And as you climb higher, and step upon the fourth step, the golden light becomes pure white, and you hear Michael say, "I am here to help you surrender your pain and sadness." Take a deep breath, and let it go.

As you climb higher, and step upon the fifth step, the light from above begins to expand, and intensify, and you hear Michael say, "I am here to help you use love to break through your resistance." Take a deep breath, and breathe in love.

And as you climb higher, and step upon the sixth step, the light from above becomes brighter, and more powerful still, and you hear Michael say, "I am here to help you surrender your doubt and fear." Take a deep breath, and let it go.

As you climb higher, and step upon the top step, the light from above becomes all encompassing, and glows with every color of the rainbow. And you hear Michael say, "I am here to support you with love, in every way possible, whenever your motivation is pure." Take a deep breath, and breathe in love.

Your next step places you into the midst of Michael's heavenly realm, where love pours forth from the Creator in its purest form, and color and sound is everywhere, rich and resplendent. Michael stands before you, tall and majestic, with his gleaming sword of truth and discernment at his side, ready to be of service to you.

Michael looks directly into your eyes, and says:

"Every difficult situation you face is an opportunity to transform darkness into light. Meet me on the inner battlefield of life, and I will bring my angels and my sword to help you conquer fear, doubt, and every kind of illusion."

Michael approaches, and extends his hands, focusing his love upon you. Rays of every color pour forth from his hands, and powerfully flow into your head, your heart, and everywhere within you. Experience yourself becoming filled with these rays of light, driving out darkness, and charging you with God's love, until you become totally radiant. Take some time to experience this, as love and light pour into you, purifying your mind, and strengthening your heart.

From this vantage point, within Archangel Michael's heavenly realm, and steeped in the love and light that he brings, consider a situation in your life that you find challenging, and take a new look. See yourself being the kind of person you would most like to be, acting for the greatest good, and handling the situation with natural grace and ease. Take some time, and allow the scene to unfold in a new way—the most positive way possible. Allow Michael to help shape your vision.

Now consider something in your life that you know doesn't currently serve your highest good. This could be a behavioral pattern, an attitude, or an association with something negative. Whatever it might be, imagine it's represented by a dark cloud several feet away, that contains everything you'd like to be free of. Get a good look at that cloud, and imagine it's connected to you by a dark cord that extends from your solar plexus, just below your chest.

Ask Archangel Michael to intervene on your behalf, to help you let go of this darkness. With one swift movement, Michael brings down his gleaming sword, cuts the cord cleanly, and that dark cloud and cord completely dissolve, into heavenly light.

Michaels says,

"It is my honor to assist you in your process of becoming free. And it is your responsibility to remain free, by being vigilant. Always remember to make the choices that help you focus upon love, and let go of everything else."

Ask Michael to reveal anything specific about you and your life that you need to know in order to follow his advice, including whatever you've not yet had the courage to hear or see. Listen, look, and know his answer.

Take a moment to allow the meaning of the following prayer to go deep within you:

Dear Archangel Michael,
Through the grace of God
Please help me to embrace every challenge as an opportunity
To look deep within my heart for truth
To let go of fear
To expand in love
To engage fully in life
And to learn to trust in God's plan.

It will soon be time to bring this journey to a close. So take a moment to thank Michael the Archangel for his love, and to thank yourself for giving yourself the opportunity to be open to receive it.

Bring your awareness gently back to your physical surroundings.

Take your time, and when you're ready, open your eyes, and feel awake, alert, and refreshed.

VISITING ARCHANGEL GABRIEL

Make yourself comfortable, and close your eyes. Take a slow deep breath, and let go of any tension, as you feel yourself sinking into the surface you're resting on, becoming still more comfortable and relaxed. Take another slow, deep breath, and release your thoughts, letting them drift far away. And take another slow, deep breath, and know that in this moment, all is well.

Bring your awareness into your spiritual heart, in the center of your chest, and notice a softness there, a feeling of peace. Take a moment to enjoy this feeling, as you quietly focus in your heart, and follow your breath, in, and out.

Imagine that you are where you most often do your creative work, or if you don't currently have such a place, imagine somewhere you would like to work. This could be an office, studio, workshop, gymnasium, outdoor setting, or anywhere that you feel comfortable. Bring yourself into that setting as fully as you can, and notice any other people, equipment, instruments, or materials, that might be part of your creative process. Take a moment to see, feel, and hear what it's like to be there.

Now imagine this setting is filling with light. Colors are intensifying, sounds are becoming richer, and there's a rarified, uplifting feeling in the air, something like the way it feels just after a spring rain.

Gabriel the Archangel is sending her love into your space, and into you, in preparation for her visit. All your senses are becoming heightened, so that you can attune to her spirit, and to the light and love she brings. Take a moment to begin to tune into her energy, and her love.

Now hundreds of small angels appear in the air around you, who have come to announce her presence, filling the air with color and sound.

She's coming closer now, huge, and magnificent, her capacity beyond measure.

And yet she brings her presence down to a form in human scale, to make it easier for you to relate to, to share her blessing with you, and offer her love. She loves all humans, and is especially glad to help you in your creative endeavors, to bring more beauty and love to Earth.

Archangel Gabriel stands and faces you now, in all her magnificence, and allows you to take in her. Take a moment to experience the presence of Gabriel now.

Archangel Gabriel now speaks to you, saying, "I am here to send God's light, beauty, and inspiration through you, to Earth. All of your study, practice, and preparation to become a vessel for God's love are so supported and appreciated. Indeed, your path of creativity is overseen by myself and all the angels. You've been led from above through every twist and turn. God's love and influence is woven all around and through you."

If there is anything you believe stands in the way of your creative expression, inwardly offer it to Archangel Gabriel now, and ask that she help clear it away.

In response to your prayer, she speaks again, saying, "Your perceived limitations and limiting beliefs are of little consequence. There are countless ways around and through your imaginary obstacles. Your reasons why it can't happen mean nothing unless you believe in them. Move forward, find a way, and I will support you."

Allow any negative thoughts, feelings, or limitations to be swept away in her loving grace. Take some time to receive her blessing now, helping you to break free, release the past, and be restored.

Archangel Gabriel stands behind you now, sending her love through you, inspiring your mind, opening your heart, triggering your imagination. Take some time to receive her blessing, as you experience yourself expanding, beyond normal, into true greatness. Take some time to experience this now.

Imagine you are going about your creative work, in the coming days and weeks, and envision Gabriel and her countless angels surrounding you, inspiring you, and filling your heart and mind with love. Take a moment to watch, listen and feel as your abilities expand, and your work becomes more effortless and inspired.

Notice how much satisfaction and fulfillment you gain by allowing this flow of love to influence all that you do. And notice the elation you feel from the energy of the angels as it moves through you.

Watch as Gabriel oversees the influence of other angels, masters, and teachers who channel their gifts through you and your work. Feel, hear and see them working through you.

Imagine your work being shared with others, and notice how they're uplifted and transformed. They may not be aware of Gabriel's influence, but it flows all around and through the experience, from her, through you and your work, and to all who receive it.

Remember that your creative expression is not only your own, but much more. It's a gift from above that you've helped bring into form, through cooperation with the Creator.

It will soon be time to bring this inner journey to a close. But first, take a moment to thank Archangel Gabriel for her blessings. And thank yourself, for giving yourself this gift.

Gently bring your awareness back to your physical surroundings. Take your time, and when you're ready, open your eyes, and feel awake, alert, and refreshed.

WALKING WITH JESUS BY THE SEA: LOVE

Make yourself comfortable, and close your eyes. Take a slow deep breath, and let go of any tension, as you feel yourself sinking into the surface you're resting on, becoming still more comfortable and relaxed. Take another slow, deep breath, and release your thoughts, letting them drift far away. And take another slow, deep breath, and know that in this moment, all is well.

Bring your awareness into your heart center, in the middle of your chest, and notice a softness there. Imagine all of the energy you've sent out into the world lately coming gently back home to your heart, helping you to feel more whole, and more complete. Quietly receive this energy, and know that all is well, and you can simply be here, relax, and receive.

Bring yourself more fully into your heart, as if you were standing there now, inside a cozy room. Soon, you'll notice a doorway, and as you walk through it, you find yourself on a secluded beach, walking barefoot on the sand, close to where the surf thins out onto the shore, and then recedes again. Perhaps you'd enjoy letting the water softly lap up to your ankles, or prefer to make your way just out of its reach.

It's a beautiful, warm day, with just the right amount of cloud cover. As you walk along, you can feel the packed sand beneath your feet, as you sink in a little with each step. A light breeze brings a touch of ocean mist to your face, and you can smell the clean scent of the sea. The rhythmic sounds of the waves and the sea birds soothe and comfort you, and all the sights, sounds, and feelings here convey a deep sense of peace, and harmony with nature.

Before long, you notice the sound of the ocean has become softer, the feeling of the air around you lighter, as if nature were making a place for something special to occur. And within, you also begin to feel lighter, clearer, and more open, as if you were making room inside yourself for something important to shift. And in this moment, the conditions are perfect for a spiritual intervention.

Soon you feel the presence of the Christ, and notice Jesus walking along the shore beside you, as if he'd been there all along. His company feels perfectly natural, familiar, and warm. And from the moment he joins you, you feel that love is everywhere, coming from him, from the sea, the sky, the sand, and especially from your own heart. Love is present, and very apparent, as if it were being amplified within you so there can be no mistaking it.

Take a few moments to experience this, and to simply be with Jesus, as you walk along together, where the sea meets the sand.

Face Jesus now, and ask, from the depth of your being, for his guidance and support. In answer, Jesus leads you through the salt water to a quiet pool, and helps you to float on your back before him. The ocean seems to cradle you in God's love, as Jesus supports you with his left hand, and places his right hand on your heart. Receive the love that pours into you through his hand, and allow it to go anywhere and everywhere within you, opening, clearing, and helping you release. Allow anything within you that might be in the way of God's love to break loose and dissolve. Take time to receive, let go, and receive more.

Jesus leads you back along the shore to a quiet cove where the two of you can comfortably sit and rest. Here, he instructs you to close your eyes, and bring your focus into your spiritual heart, in the very center of your chest. Take some time now to practice being still, focus within, and quietly feel God's love in your heart, as you simply relax and receive.

Consider the people you feel closest to, focus on them one by one, and feel love flowing from your heart to each of them. Take some time to do this now.

Consider one person you know not so well, whom you might enjoy knowing better. Focus inwardly on that person now, and feel your love flowing freely from your heart to them.

Consider someone whom you do not like very much, who perhaps threatens you in some way. Ask Jesus to help you let go of any negativity you may hold toward that person, as you focus inwardly on them now, and feel your love flowing freely from your heart to them.

And consider the person you most dislike. Ask Jesus to help you let go of any negativity you may hold toward that person, as you focus inwardly on them now, and feel your love flowing freely from your heart to them.

It's almost time to bring this inner journey to a close. But first, take some time to listen and look within your heart for any messages or images Jesus may have for you now.

Take a moment to thank Jesus for his love and support.

And thank yourself, for giving yourself this gift.

Gradually bring your awareness back into your body, and your physical surroundings.

Take your time, and when you're ready, open your eyes, and feel awake, alert, and refreshed.

WALKING WITH JESUS BY THE SEA: HUMILITY

Make yourself comfortable, and close your eyes. Take a slow deep breath, and let go of any tension in your body, as you settle into a more relaxed posture. Feel yourself dropping down from your mind into your body. Feel the weight of your body sinking into the surface you're resting on, as you become still more comfortable and relaxed.

Imagine you're walking barefoot along a secluded beach, close to where the surf thins out onto the shore, and then recedes again. Perhaps you'd enjoy letting the water softly lap up to your ankles, or would prefer to make your way just out of its reach. It's a beautiful, warm day, with just the right amount of cloud cover. As you walk along, you can feel the packed sand beneath your feet, as you sink in a little with each step.

A light breeze brings a touch of ocean mist to your face, and you can smell the clean scent of the sea. The rhythmic sounds of the waves and the sea birds soothe and comfort you, and all the sights, sounds, and feelings here convey a deep sense of peace, and harmony with nature.

Before long, you notice the sound of the ocean has become softer, the feeling of the air around you lighter. And within, you also begin to feel lighter, clearer, and more open. And soon you feel the presence of the Christ, and notice Jesus walking along the shore beside you, as if he'd been there all along. His company feels perfectly natural, familiar, and warm. And from the moment he joins you, you feel that love is every-where, coming from him, from the sea, the sky, the sand, and especially from your own heart. Love is present, and very apparent, as if it were

being amplified within you so there can be no mistaking it.

Take a few moments to experience this, and to simply be with Jesus, as you walk along together, where the sea meets the sand.

Jesus leads you back along the shore to a quiet cove where the two of you can comfortably sit and rest. Consider one situation in your life today, where despite your best efforts, things do not go the way you believe they should. Take a moment to get a good look at that situation, and be especially aware of the way you feel about it.

Now consider one situation in the world that you believe is tragic and unfair, over which you believe you have little or no influence. Take a moment to get a good look at that situation, and become keenly aware of how you feel about it.

Now Jesus leads you toward a small cave nearby, and you enter together. At first it's very dark, but as you move forward you find a faint light is drawing you deeper into the cave. Finally, you come to an opening, where Jesus holds you securely, as you look out. There before you is the universe in a night sky, filled with more stars than you've ever seen. The scene is breathtaking, and overwhelming in its vastness. Without Jesus saying anything, you know he is showing you the creation before you to illustrate the magnitude of what God can do. Take a moment to let this experience into your heart, and absorb it as fully as possible.

Quietly Jesus now leads you back to the cove where you were seated before, and he kneels down, pointing to something in the sand, for you to pick up and examine. It's a seashell, and embedded in it is the fossil imprint of a tiny fish that swam in the sea millions of years ago. Jesus looks at you. God made this also, and the ocean, and the land, and the sky, and all the millions of creatures that swim, walk, and fly. And God made Jesus. And God made you.

Life is unfolding within you, and around you, according to God's plan. You are being extended an invitation now to release the need to know God's plan, in order to come gracefully into humble appreciation of a world of miracles.

Look once more at the current situation in your life you first examined earlier in the meditation, and see it, in all its apparent imperfection, surrounded by the light of God. Remember the way you felt about that situation before, and consider how you can adjust your attitude to best support yourself and any others involved. Jesus places his hand upon your heart to help you come into the harmony of humility, as you take some time to make a shift. Take several slow, deep breaths, release that situation from your own ego, and turn it over to God, where it belongs.

And now once again consider the situation in the world you earlier looked at, that you consider unfair. Go deep into your heart, and ask God to help you let go of any judgment, about the world, life, God, or Creation. Open your heart, and send love, without any condition on how it is to be used, to that situation. As you do this, Jesus places his hand again upon your heart. Feel a shift within you, as any bitterness you may have held is dissolved and released. Release that situation from your ego, and turn it over to God, where it belongs. Take some time to let this unfold.

Jesus turns and you stand facing each other, as he blesses you with his deepest love and compassion. Take some time to experience the love that radiates from Jesus' heart toward your own. Open your own heart and expand it as wide as you can. Receive all the love your heart can receive.

It's almost time to bring this inner journey to a close. So gather together anything you have learned, that you'd like to bring with you.

Take a moment to thank Jesus for his love and support.

And thank yourself, for giving yourself this gift.

Gradually bring your awareness back into your body, and your physical surroundings. Take your time, and when you're ready, open your eyes, and feel awake, alert, and refreshed.

WALKING WITH JESUS BY THE SEA: FORGIVENESS

INTRODUCTION

Forgiveness is normally thought of as being focused outwardly toward others:

I forgive you for the hurt you caused,
I forgive your debt,
I forgive you for backing into my car,
I forgive you for forgetting my birthday...

and so on.

But to completely forgive another person is an inside job, and more difficult than just the outer expression: "Not only will I erase your debt, I'll release my anger and resentment toward you, and let love, or at least neutrality, take its place. And, I won't revisit it in the future and bring it up again." Sometimes that can be a tall order.

Taken a step further, and harder still, is self forgiveness: Forgiving ourselves for the mistakes we've made, the hurt we've caused, and things we're ashamed of.

True forgiveness is challenging because it requires stepping out of our ego, where we tend to feel comfortable, safe, and in control, and entering into that dicey territory where it feels as if anything can happen.

And this is where we most often get stuck. We can't forgive and hold a grudge at the same time, and letting go is not easy. But worth doing. Because when we step out of our ego we step into a state of grace, where we can experience miracles and know love. And by letting go we have the opportunity to receive.

The posture of holding hands up to the heavens to receive love from God is exactly the same as the universal posture for surrender:

I surrender to a higher power, and I'm open to receive.

I forgive, and I'm open to life.

I forgive myself, and I free up my energy to make a new start and see what's possible, and discover what God can do.

Forgiveness is an inside job, it can feel a risky, and it opens up a world of possibility. Use the following guided meditation as a starting point and catalyst.

MEDITATION

Make yourself comfortable, and close your eyes. Take a slow deep breath, and let go of any tension in your body, as you settle into a more relaxed posture. Feel yourself dropping down from your mind into your body. Feel the weight of your body sinking into the surface you're resting on, as you become still more comfortable and relaxed.

Imagine you're walking barefoot along a secluded beach, close to where the surf thins out onto the shore, and then recedes again. Perhaps you'd enjoy letting the water softly lap up to your ankles, or would prefer to make your way just out of its reach. It's a beautiful, warm day, with just the right amount of cloud cover. As you walk along, you can feel the packed sand beneath your feet, as you sink in a little with each step.

A light breeze brings a touch of ocean mist to your face, and you can smell the clean scent of the sea. The rhythmic sounds of the waves and the sea birds soothe and comfort you, and all the sights, sounds, and feelings here convey a deep sense of peace, and harmony with nature.

Before long, you notice the sound of the ocean has become softer, the feeling of the air around you lighter. And within, you also begin to feel lighter, clearer, and more open. And soon you feel the presence of the Christ, and notice Jesus walking along the shore beside you, as if he'd been there all along. His company feels perfectly natural, familiar, and warm. And from the moment he joins you, you feel that love is everywhere, coming from him, from the sea, the sky, the sand, and especially from your own heart. Love is present, and very apparent, as if it were being amplified within you so there can be no mistaking it.

Take a few moments to experience this, and to simply be with Jesus, as you walk along together, where the sea meets the sand.

Jesus leads you back along the shore to a quiet cove where the two of you can comfortably sit and rest. As you sit with Jesus, bring your focus into your spiritual heart, in the very center of your chest. Take some time now to practice being still, focus within, and quietly feel God's love in your heart, as you simply relax and receive.

Consider someone toward whom you currently hold a grudge, because you feel they treated you unkindly, or unfairly. Imagine that the three of you—you, Jesus, and that person—are now standing together by the sea, listening to the waves, feeling the breeze, and appreciating the beauty of creation, each in your own way.

Jesus looks at that person, and sees them for who they are: a soul here on Earth with their own challenges, struggles, and hardships to overcome. And Jesus, knowing the depths of that person's soul, as well as all the mistakes he or she has made, has nothing but love and respect for them and their journey here. Jesus looks at them with love, and looks at you with love, as if to extend you an invitation. He's inviting you to give up your grudge, here and now, and join him in love.

Jesus places his hand on your back, as if to send healing energy into your heart, as you turn to face this person. Take a deep breath. Feel your heart, and receive God's love, as you look into their eyes, and see, not the person who did you harm, but one of God's children, just trying to find their way. Let whatever hard feelings you've been holding onto dissolve, and melt into the love that's present with you now. Take some time to breathe deeply now, and let it be.

Now it's just you and Jesus, standing together again by the shore. Consider the one thing most hold against yourself. This may be something that happened recently, or a long time ago, that you've always felt bad about, and have never truly forgiven yourself for.

Jesus looks into your eyes, and places his hand on your heart. The love pouring from him is so powerful now that it seems to block out everything else. Experience Gods love moving within you now, touching everywhere inside. We've all done things we regret, and no matter what we've done, God forgives us immediately. To live in guilt or self reproach is to deny God's love.

So know this now: You are a good, good person, worthy to receive love without exception. Whatever you may have done, forgive yourself, and let it go. Take a deep breath, and let it dissolve, and melt into the love that's present. Take some time to breathe deeply, and let it be.

The evening is approaching, and the sun has dropped close to the horizon, casting a warm, golden hue across the ocean, its gentle waves lapping the sand. Would you like to swim with Jesus, in the sea of total love and mercy, forgiveness and joy? Now would be a good time. Jesus takes your hand, as you both wade in to the warm water together, until you can float and drift. Enjoy some time here now, with nothing to do but relax and enjoy being in love, with the master by your side. All is well.

It's almost time to bring this inner journey to a close. But first, take some time to listen and look within your heart for any messages or images Jesus may have for you now.

Gradually bring your awareness back into your body, and your physical surroundings.

Take your time, and when you're ready, open your eyes, and feel awake, alert, and refreshed.

WALKING WITH JESUS BY THE SEA: FAITH

Make yourself comfortable, and close your eyes. Take a slow deep breath, and let go of any tension in your body, as you settle into a more relaxed posture. Feel yourself dropping down from your mind into your body. Feel the weight of your body sinking into the surface you're resting on, as you become still more comfortable and relaxed.

Imagine you're walking barefoot along a secluded beach, close to where the surf thins out onto the sand, and then recedes again. Perhaps you'd enjoy letting the water softly lap up to your ankles, or would prefer to make your way just out of its reach. It's a beautiful, warm day, with just the right amount of cloud cover. As you walk along, you can feel the packed sand beneath your feet, as you sink in a little with each step.

A light breeze brings a touch of ocean mist to your face, and you can smell the clean scent of the sea. The rhythmic sounds of the waves and the sea birds soothe and comfort you, and all the sights, sounds, and feelings here convey a deep sense of peace, and harmony with nature.

Before long, you notice the sound of the ocean has become softer, the feeling of the air around you lighter. And within, you also begin to feel lighter, clearer, and more open. And soon you feel the presence of the Christ, and notice Jesus walking along the shore beside you, as if he'd been there all along. His company feels perfectly natural, familiar, and warm. And from the moment he joins you, you feel that love is everywhere, coming from him, from the sea, the sky, the sand, and especially from your own heart. Love is present, and very apparent, as if it were

being amplified within you so there can be no mistaking it.

Take a few moments to experience this, and to simply be with Jesus, as you walk along together, where the sea meets the sand.

Jesus leads you back along the shore to a quiet cove where the two of you can comfortably sit and rest. As you sit with Jesus, bring your focus into your spiritual heart, in the very center of your chest. Take some time now to practice being still, focus within, and quietly feel God's love in your heart, as you simply relax and receive.

Consider something in your life that you worry about, something you believe needs to be different than it is, but that you seem to be at a loss to change. Feel the heaviness of that problem, and how it weighs upon you, almost like a lead jacket over your back and shoulders. Perhaps the reason it feels so heavy is it's a burden you are not meant to carry. You've chosen to feel personally responsible for something you can't control or change, something that should be left up to God, that you've taken as your own. This is an opportunity to give it back.

As you sit with Jesus, cup your hands together, and imagine placing that situation, and all the fear, worry, and concern you've accumulated about it into your hands. Get a good solid feeling of all that negativity accumulating now, and notice how heavy your hands become, as you allow it to all pour into them from your back and shoulders.

Jesus stand before you now, the light at his back, and embodiment and representative of your God, and holds out his hands to receive your burden of worry. Turn it all over to him now, and let go. Feel flooded with light and love from your heavenly Father, as his love rushes in to replace all that you release.

Faith is knowing that God's way is best for us, though it often goes beyond our understanding. Once you have done what you can to resolve a situation, and made good use of the resources available, you can rest assured God wants it that way. Make a commitment now to spend no more of your energy on worry, and turn over your wellbeing and the wellbeing of others to God.

Face Jesus now, and ask, from the depth of your being, for his guidance and support. In answer, Jesus leads you through the salt water to a quiet pool, and helps you to float on your back before him. The ocean seems to cradle you in God's love, as Jesus supports you with his left hand, and places his right hand on your heart. Receive the love that pours into you through his hand, and allow it to go anywhere and everywhere within you, opening, clearing, and helping you release. Allow anything within you that might be in the way of God's love to break loose and dissolve. Take time to receive, let go, and receive more.

Once again, take some time to simply be with Jesus, as you walk along together, where the sea meets the sand. Pelicans fly by and dive into the water, catching fish, a symbol that our needs are provided for, and life is sustained, as God's gift to us. As you walk together, look and listen within your heart for any message Jesus may have for you.

It's almost time to bring this inner journey to a close. But first, take a moment to thank Jesus for his love and support.

And thank yourself, for giving yourself this gift.

Gradually bring your awareness back into your body, and your physical surroundings.

Take your time, and when you're ready, open your eyes, and feel awake, alert, and refreshed.

WALKING WITH JESUS BY THE SEA: DEVOTION

Make yourself comfortable, and close your eyes. Take a slow deep breath, and let go of any tension in your body, as you settle into a more relaxed posture. Feel yourself dropping down from your mind into your body. Feel the weight of your body sinking into the surface you're resting on, as you become still more comfortable and relaxed.

Imagine you're walking barefoot along a secluded beach, close to where the surf thins out onto the shore, and then recedes again. Perhaps you'd enjoy letting the water softly lap up to your ankles, or would prefer to make your way just out of its reach. It's a beautiful, warm day, with just the right amount of cloud cover. As you walk along, you can feel the packed sand beneath your feet, as you sink in a little with each step.

A light breeze brings a touch of ocean mist to your face, and you can smell the clean scent of the sea. The rhythmic sounds of the waves and the sea birds soothe and comfort you, and all the sights, sounds, and feelings here convey a deep sense of peace, and harmony with nature.

Before long, you notice the sound of the ocean has become softer, the feeling of the air around you lighter. And within, you also begin to feel lighter, clearer, and more open. And soon you feel the presence of the Christ, and notice Jesus walking along the shore beside you, as if he'd been there all along. His company feels perfectly natural, familiar, and warm. And from the moment he joins you, you feel that love is everywhere, coming from him, from the sea, the sky, the sand, and especially from your own heart. Love is present, and very apparent, as if it were

being amplified within you so there can be no mistaking it.

Take a few moments to experience this, and to simply be with Jesus, as you walk along together, where the sea meets the sand.

As you continue to walk with Jesus on the shore, you feel as though a question is beginning to come up inside you, one that's long been waiting to be addressed, about your life, and your spiritual connection. And before you can ask, Jesus turns to you and begins to answer, saying

"If you call me to help you, I will point to the Father of Creation, and his love. God brings every challenge to help you build strength, grow in faith, and discover his love within you.

"All that happens here is of God, so do not reject life, or God, or other people for making you uncomfortable, or you will only compound your suffering.

"If you want to grow quickly, accept, let go and forgive without hesitation. Be the love you seek. Then you will know me in your heart."

As evening approaches, the sun sits lower in the sky, approaching the horizon. Jesus stops walking now, and you turn to face him, with his back to the sea and the sun, and rays of sunlight all around him.

Jesus continues...

"I am here to support you with love. To provide a template, and a pathway, to show you the way home to God. The way is through love. Love. The same love that brought you into form is here to feed and nourish your soul. Receive God's love and let all else go."

You can now experience his radiance, as if light and love were pouring out from the Creator through Jesus, directly from his heart into yours. Take time to receive his blessing, and allow his light and love to fill you.

Consider the thing in your life you are most uncomfortable with, or most afraid of. Turn it over to God. Breathe, let go of your fear of discomfort, and go deeper into your heart.

Feel your heart-space open and expand, until it encompasses your entire chest, shoulders, and upper back. Let your heart fill with God's love. Jesus stands with you, reflecting love back to you, showing you what is possible, who you can be. God's love wants to express in and through you, without fanfare, simply and easily, in this moment. Receive it, experience it, be it now. Your heart was designed to do this, to be fulfilled in this way. Allow it to unfold.

As you continue to walk along the shore with Jesus, you see dolphins swim by, representing absolute joy at being here in creation. Take a few moments to appreciate life, and to simply be with Jesus, as you walk along together, where the sea meets the sand.

It's almost time to bring this inner journey to a close. But first, take some time to listen and look within your heart for any messages or images Jesus may have for you now.

Gradually bring your awareness back into your body, and your physical surroundings.

Take your time, and when you're ready, open your eyes, and feel awake, alert, and refreshed.

WALKING WITH JESUS BY THE SEA: COMPASSION

INTRODUCTION

Compassion is the ability to recognize suffering in another, and the willingness to take action to relieve it. It's the desire to relieve another's suffering as if it were one's own.

Being compassionate doesn't necessarily mean dedicating one's life to serving others, feeding the homeless, or joining the Peace Corps. It means being sensitive to the needs of those in our lives, listening to the calling of our heart and higher guidance, and being open to what is asked of us. It doesn't requires a lot of thought and interpretation to know what to do. It flows naturally as we open to life.

To lack compassion is to close the valves to our spiritual heart, so that love can not pour out. And if God's love can't pour out, it can't pour in, and we loose.

Compassion is a form of love in motion.

MEDITATION

Make yourself comfortable, and close your eyes. Take a slow deep breath, and let go of any tension in your body, as you settle into a more relaxed posture. Feel yourself dropping down from your mind into your body. Feel the weight of your body sinking into the surface you're resting on, as you become still more comfortable and relaxed.

Imagine you're walking barefoot along a secluded beach, close to where the surf thins out onto the shore, and then recedes again. Perhaps you'd enjoy letting the water softly lap up to your ankles, or would prefer to make your way just out of its reach. It's a beautiful, warm day, with just the right amount of cloud cover. As you walk along, you can feel the packed sand beneath your feet, as you sink in a little with each step.

A light breeze brings a touch of ocean mist to your face, and you can smell the clean scent of the sea. The rhythmic sounds of the waves and the sea birds soothe and comfort you, and all the sights, sounds, and feelings here convey a deep sense of peace, and harmony with nature.

Before long, you notice the sound of the ocean has become softer, the feeling of the air around you lighter. And within, you also begin to feel lighter, clearer, and more open. And soon you feel the presence of the Christ, and notice Jesus walking along the shore beside you, as if he'd been there all along. His company feels perfectly natural, familiar, and warm. And from the moment he joins you, you feel that love is everywhere, coming from him, from the sea, the sky, the sand, and especially from your own heart. Love is present, and very apparent, as if it were being amplified within you so there can be no mistaking it.

Take a few moments to experience this, and to simply be with Jesus, as you walk along together, where the sea meets the sand.

The sun is beginning to set, and Jesus leads you back along the shore to a quiet cove, where a small driftwood fire is burning softly within a circle of rocks on the sand. Here the two of you can comfortably sit, enjoy the flames, and contemplate life.

When you were born, you were completely helpless, and lived entirely by your parents care and compassion for you. Although there were probably times when taking care of you was more work than they would have liked, their support continued, and their love allowed you to grow until you could make your own way. Perhaps you've been a parent yourself, or have experienced taking care of others, without payment or reward. It's natural for us to see a need, and act to fill it, and when we do, God's love can pour through us into another.

But it also happens that we sometimes don't see the need around us, or hold ourselves back from giving, because we feel tired, weak, or needy ourselves, or when we're in judgment of others.

Who in your life have you overlooked or closed your heart to, who could use a kind word, a touch, or some simple act of support and kindness? Imagine that person standing before you now, ready to receive your compassionate support. And imagine Jesus standing behind you, his hand on your back, sending God's love into your heart. Take some time to experience your heart opening, receiving God's love, and pouring out love and compassion toward this person, now.

Perhaps there are others to whom you'd like to offer your compassion. Imagine them standing before you now, open to receive. As Jesus stands behind you, sending love into your heart, continue to open, receive God's love, and pour love and compassion toward them.

For those whom you've just touched, consider whether there may be steps for you to take, to reach out to them in the near future, whether that might mean a visit, a call, or some other compassionate gesture. What would be right for you to do?

Jesus now turns to face you. Compassion can also be directed toward oneself. What is there within you that you've given yourself a hard time about, where compassion is needed instead? Open your heart, let go of anything you've held against yourself, and receive Gods love from Jesus. Allow love to flood your heart, and make its way all through you, softening, dissolving, and clearing any hurt within.

As this process continues, you might begin make out a group of angels now surrounding you and Jesus. They're naturally attracted to love, and they've come to witness your opening heart, and your healing, and amplify all the love that's here for you now. Take a little longer to let it in, and let it be.

It's almost time to bring this inner journey to a close. But first, take some time to listen and look within your heart for any messages or images Jesus may have for you now.

Gradually bring your awareness back into your body, and your physical surroundings.

Take your time, and when you're ready, open your eyes, and feel awake, alert, and refreshed.

WALKING WITH JESUS BY THE SEA: ACCEPTANCE

Make yourself comfortable, and close your eyes. Take a slow deep breath, and let go of any tension in your body, as you settle into a more relaxed posture. Feel yourself dropping down from your mind into your body. Feel the weight of your body sinking into the surface you're resting on, as you become still more comfortable and relaxed.

Imagine you're walking barefoot along a secluded beach, close to where the surf thins out onto the shore, and then recedes again. Perhaps you'd enjoy letting the water softly lap up to your ankles, or would prefer to make your way just out of its reach. It's a beautiful, warm day, with just the right amount of cloud cover. As you walk along, you can feel the packed sand beneath your feet, as you sink in a little with each step.

A light breeze brings a touch of ocean mist to your face, and you can smell the clean scent of the sea. The rhythmic sounds of the waves and the sea birds soothe and comfort you, and all the sights, sounds, and feelings here convey a deep sense of peace, and harmony with nature.

Before long, you notice the sound of the ocean has become softer, the feeling of the air around you lighter. And within, you also begin to feel lighter, clearer, and more open. And soon you feel the presence of the Christ, and notice Jesus walking along the shore beside you, as if he'd been there all along. His company feels perfectly natural, familiar, and warm. And from the moment he joins you, you feel that love is every-where, coming from him, from the sea, the sky, the sand, and especially from your own heart. Love is present, and very apparent, as if it were

being amplified within you so there can be no mistaking it.

Take a few moments to experience this, and to simply be with Jesus, as you walk along together, where the sea meets the sand.

Jesus leads you back along the shore to a quiet cove where the two of you can comfortably sit and rest. As you sit with Jesus, bring your focus into your spiritual heart, in the very center of your chest. Take some time now to practice being still, focus within, and quietly feel God's love in your heart, as you simply relax and receive.

There is a reason for everything in God's world, but from our limited perspective, we can't often understand why things appear as they do. It's easy to fall into the trap of looking out from our ego, thinking we know more than we do, and judging what we perceive. But judgment stops us from knowing what's real, closes us off from love, and keeps us stuck. Acceptance allows us to open up, embrace life, and become a vessel for God's love to unfold within and around us.

As you sit by the sea with Jesus, consider the situations in your own life you find hard to accept, and judge as wrong. As you think about each one, cup your hands, imagine you're spilling out all of your judgment into them, and then release your judgment into the surf, letting it wash it away in the sea. Take some time to allow every judgment you hold against yourself and your life to come up, pour out, and dissolve into the ocean of God's love.

Who are the people you hold judgment against; those you know personally, as well as those you've seen or heard about? Invite them all to come and form a circle around you now, as Jesus stands just behind you, supporting you with God's love. Look into the eyes of each person, one after another. There you will see other human beings, like you, each with their own struggles, challenges, and pain to endure. And like you, each is trying to live, grow, and find happiness.

Take time to focus upon each person, breathe deeply, and allow Jesus to pour God's love into you, as you feel yourself open, expand, and accept every one before you. Let go of your judgment, open your heart, and find peace.

Finally, Jesus turns to face you, and says,

"God is love. Look deep within your heart, beyond the illusion of life, and you will know love. Meet me there."

It's almost time to bring this inner journey to a close. But first, take some time to listen and look within your heart for any messages or images Jesus may have for you now.

Gradually bring your awareness back into your body, and your physical surroundings.

Take your time, and when you're ready, open your eyes, and feel awake, alert, and refreshed.

VISITING YOGANANDA

Make yourself comfortable, and close your eyes. Take a slow deep breath, and let go of any tension, as you feel yourself sinking into the surface you're resting on, becoming still more comfortable and relaxed. Take another slow, deep breath, and release your thoughts, letting them drift far away. And take another slow, deep breath, and know that in this moment, all is well.

Bring your awareness into your spiritual heart, in the center of your chest, and notice a softness there, a feeling of peace. Take a moment to enjoy this feeling, as you quietly focus in your heart, and follow your breath, in, and out.

Bring yourself more fully into your heart, as if you were standing there now, inside a cozy room. Soon, you'll notice a doorway, and as you walk through it, you'll find yourself transported to a footpath, where you're making your way around a beautiful lake, on a warm summer afternoon.

A group of lily pads cover the lake's surface nearby, and a pair of majestic swans lazily float around them, perhaps looking for their lunch.

The lake is surrounded by shade trees, some flowering in white or orange blossoms, and you can smell their delicate, intoxicating scent. The sky above is crystalline blue, decorated with puffy white clouds. And now and then a fish touches the glassy surface of the water, makes circles in the reflected sky, and then swims out of sight.

There is a profound sense of peace and tranquility here, and you're walking along quite slowly, taking in everything. And as you make your way around the lake, you soon find that all your cares have lifted, and your mind has become open, curious, and receptive.

Someone is walking toward you on the path. In his saffron colored robe, and his long, dark wavy hair, he stands out like a bright jewel in this setting. And as he approaches, you feel a wave of love sweep through you, as your heart begins to open.

Soon you're standing face to face with Yogananda, who greets you with a small bow and salutation. Yogananda's dark eyes draw you in, inviting you into an endless well of compassion. Take a moment to be with Yogananda now, look into his eyes, and receive his love.

As you continue to gaze into Yogananda's eyes, you soon find yourself transported to a mountain sanctuary, high in the Himalayas. Now you're seated in a circle next to Yogananda, along with a number of extraordinary individuals. These great yogis are a part of Yogananda's spiritual lineage. All are spiritual masters whose profound devotion and unceasing inner work has allowed them to transcend the limitations of time and space. These amazing beings operate in a state of interdimensional awareness, and things we would consider miracles are to them quite commonplace.

Everyone has come together for your benefit, to help you boost your spiritual progress, and make a positive shift. The group is just now in a very a deep meditation, one that will lead to a spiritual initiation for you. The vibrational energy here is so profound that you can actually begin to feel yourself begin to lift slightly off the ground, and your body begins to tingle with heightened sensitivity. Yogananda telepathically instructs you to focus on your third eye, simply follow your breath, relax, and receive. Take some time to do this, now.

All of the masters are in telepathic union with you now, and are infusing your being with loving vibrations, helping you to open and expand your awareness. Take a few more moments to open, receive, and enjoy their transmission.

Yogananda now transports you to the front door of your home, where you stand outside, looking out at your surroundings. He stands behind you. He's prompting you to view your world in a new way. He asks that you open your heart and mind to the perfection of God's Creation. See every atom vibrating with God's love, all unfolding in unified perfection. It's a way of truly seeing Creation without judgment. Take some time to imagine this, now.

If there is any part of your life that you would like higher perspective and input on, ask Yogananda to help you with it now. His help may come in the form of words, images, feelings, or simply an inner knowing. Listen, watch, and receive.

Take a moment to ask Yogananda to remain with you inwardly, to help you in the coming days and weeks, to deepen your meditation practice, and your awareness of God's presence in your life.

It will soon be time to bring this inner journey to a close. But first, take a moment to thank Yogananda for his love and support.

And thank yourself, for giving yourself this gift.

Let all the benefits of this experience stay with you, as you gradually bring your awareness back to your physical surroundings.

Take your time, and when you're ready, open your eyes, and feel awake, alert, and refreshed.

PART NINE

FOR KIDS & FAMILY

A GOOD DAY FOR A PONY

You're about to take a most enjoyable journey, within your own mind. So get comfortable, relax, and close your eyes. When you close your eyes, the inside of your eyelids become like a big movie screen, and your imagination becomes the movie projector. So settle in, and for a little while, listen and watch, as I lead you upon an inner adventure; a movie all about you.

Imagine you're at home one fine summer day, when you hear a knock at your front door, and maybe the doorbell too. "I wonder who that could be," you think to yourself. And as if to reply, you hear someone say, "Special Delivery for..." and they say your name.

Now, you know you're not supposed to open the door for anyone you don't know, but after all, this is a movie. So, just this time, you do! And there, tied to a post right by your door, is a fine looking pony, looking right at you.

Well, some ponies are black, and some are brown, some are tan, and some are white, and some are more than one color. What color is your pony? Does it have a long mane and tail?

Ponies enjoy a good rub, so go on up to your pony, and rub its neck and back, touching it firmly, but softly, and feel it's warm fur.

If you reach in your back pocket, and I bet you'll find a carrot. Ponies love carrots, so give it a snack, and your pony will love you too! Watch your fingers!

It's a little known fact that ponies can talk—if you know how to hear them. So, if you introduce yourself in a very friendly way, and ask your pony its name, it might just tell you. What does it say?

Ponies are good at eating carrots and talking, and especially good at taking children places, and this one loves to do just that. In fact, it looks right at you again, and says, "Hey! Are we going to stand here all day, or would you like to go somewhere?" To which you reply, "Absolutely!"

So you hop up on your pony, and as soon as you do, an idea pops into your mind about where you'd like to go. Maybe it's one of your favorite places, or someplace you've heard about but never been. Maybe it's the beach, or the park, or a store, or a friend's house. Or maybe you want your pony to surprise you. But whatever you decide, you're moving!

Off you go, and you can feel the gentle rocking of your pony's back as it clip clops, clip clops, walking along. It's a great way to enjoy the scenery, and you have plenty of time to look around. What do you see?

Would you like to have some friends along? If you would, pretty soon you'll find them riding with you, on ponies of their own. How many are there, one or two, or a whole bunch? Do you talk to each other? Do the ponies talk to each other?

How fast would you like to go? Your pony has 4 speeds: walk, trot, gallop, and "fly-pony-fly." You're walking now, so ask for a trot, and notice how much faster you go. Notice how the scenery changes, and how your pony feels under you.

Want to try a gallop? Ask your pony for a gallop, and you'll be moving twice as fast, so hang on! Notice the scenery going by now, and how your pony feels.

For the ultimate pony ride, ask your pony to "fly-pony-fly," and you'll really take off! Hold on, cause you'll be zooming. The scenery is a blur, and the ride becomes silky smooth.

Soon you arrive at your destination. Hop off your pony, and tie it up safe. Now you're free to spend some time doing whatever you wish. What's it like, being here? What do you see? Take as long as you like to be here, and enjoy. And whenever you want to go back home, just think of it, and there you'll be.

CIRCLE OF LIGHT

INTRODUCTION

Do this meditation with one or more children and family members.

MEDITATION

Make yourself comfortable, and close your eyes. Take a slow deep breath, and let go of any tension, as you feel yourself sinking into the surface you're resting on, becoming still more comfortable and relaxed. Take another slow, deep breath, and release your thoughts, letting them drift far away. And take another slow, deep breath, and know that in this moment, all is well.

Consider something you'd like help with. It could be a problem at home, at school, or at work. It could be something you're doing OK with, but you'd like to be doing even better. Or it might be something you want, and don't know how to get.

Now set that aside for a moment, and imagine a column of light is coming down from the highest heavens, through the sky, directly through the ceiling of your home, through your room and your family, and going deep into the earth. This light contains the most positive, loving energy in the universe, and it's here to help you, and make all things better, in every way.

Feel and see the light filling you, and everything around you. Just let it in, and it will help clear your mind, tune up your body, and bring you happiness and peace.

Imagine placing the problem or concern you thought of a moment ago directly in the middle of the room, in the column of light, here and now, with the light filling and surrounding it. Just picture you and whatever situation you're dealing with, becoming filled with it and surrounded by the light. Soon that situation becomes lighter, and lighter, until it's overflowing with light and love.

Now slowly begin to change the color of the light, beginning with red. Picture the most beautiful red color your can imagine, filling your house, your family, you, and any problems or situations you'd like help with. The red color brings you all the energy you need to work through any challenge. Take a deep breath, and let it in, and let all your problems go.

Now the light changes to orange, so allow the orange color to fill and surround you, and any challenges you face. The orange color is bringing you whatever help you need, for as long as you need it. Take a deep breath, and let it in, and let all your problems go.

Now the light column changes to a bright, golden yellow, and it surrounds and fills you, and everything and everyone around you. The yellow color brings happiness and joy to your day, and helps you know you can do whatever you need to do. Take a deep breath, breathe in the yellow color, and let all else go.

The light changes to a deep emerald green, and fills and surrounds you, your home, and everyone in your life. The green color fills you with love for yourself and for others, and helps you feel as if everyone is your friend, even if they don't know it yet. Take a deep breath, breathe in the green color, and let all else go.

Now the light changes to a beautiful blue. The blue color fills you, your home, your family, and your life. It brings clarity to your thinking, and peace to your mind. Everything is happening as it should, and all is well. Take a deep breath, breathe in the blue color, and let all else go.

The light column in your home now becomes a rich purple. Your life is part of a much bigger plan, and you are seen, known, and loved from above. All you need to do is be still and listen, and you can know whatever you need to know. Take a deep breath, breathe in the purple color, and let all else go.

Take a few moments now to just follow your breathing, and quietly listen and look inside for anything you need to know today. Don't force it. Just let whatever comes, come, even if for now it's just peace and quiet.

It will soon be time to bring this meditation to a close. Inwardly thank yourself and your family for taking the time for peace.

Gradually bring your attention back to your physical surroundings.

Take your time, and when you're ready, open your eyes, and feel awake, alert, and refreshed.

GUEST OF HONOR

INTRODUCTION

This is a short guided meditation for several or more family members to do together. Have the family member you'd like to honor today sit or lie down in the middle of the room, and have everyone else seated around them or nearby.

GUIDED MEDITATION

Everyone make yourself comfortable, and close your eyes. Take a slow deep breath, and let go of any tension, as you feel yourself sinking into the surface you're resting on, becoming still more comfortable and relaxcd. Take another slow, deep breath, and release your thoughts, letting them drift far away. And take another slow, deep breath, and know that in this moment, all is well.

Imagine a column of light is coming down from the highest heavens, through the sky, directly through the ceiling of your home, through your room and your family, and going deep into the earth. This light contains the most positive, loving energy in the universe, and it's here to help you, and make all things better, in every way.

As the light begins to touch you, your family, and your home, just let it in. Feel and see the light filling you, everyone, and everything around you. As you continue to receive the light, it clears your mind, tunes up your body, and brings you happiness and peace.

For the rest of this meditation, if you're the person in the center, all you need to do is rest, relax, and receive love and light. Just allow it in, let go of any tension or worry, and enjoy all the good feelings on their way to you now.

For everyone else in the circle, imagine that light is filling you from head to foot, and pouring out through your heart, and your hands. Place your hands face up in your lap, or hold them out in front of you, facing your guest of honor. Empty your mind, and simply allow light and love to flow out from your heart, and your hands toward them. As you breathe in, breath in light and love, and as you breathe out, breathe it toward your guest. Continue peacefully in this way for a while.

WORRY TAKES THE TRAIN

Settle in so you're nice and comfy, and close your eyes.

Imagine you're walking down a city street, late in the afternoon. And walking right next to you, holding your hand, is Worry; that scary, sad, uncomfortable feeling you have, when you're not sure how things will turn out. You know, worrying!

Worry is about four feet tall, and looks like a very sad and funny cartoon. Its face is frowning and crooked-looking. It wears a slouchy hat that's too big. It has dirty, and wrinkled clothes that don't fit properly. And the colors don't even match. Then you notice that it's pants are on backwards, and it's shoes are on the wrong feet!

Worry is trying to sing a sad little song, but it keeps forgetting the words, and can't sing in tune, so it sounds like a warped, scratched old record or CD that keeps losing it's place. And I hate to say this, but worry even smells bad. Poor, sad worry.

There you are, the two of you, walking down the street, hand in hand. Both of you are unhappy, and it feels like you've done this many times before. But on you go, with cars whizzing by, and other people passing on the sidewalk. Some of them are walking with their own Worries, and all of the worries look kind of the same, like you and your Worry: sad, dirty, twisted and uncomfortable, holding on tight to their people.

As you walk with Worry, you feel worse and worse. Suddenly you get an idea where to go and what to do. You hold onto Worry's hand tighter and start leading the way.

Pretty soon you come to a huge train station, and you and your Worry go through the big revolving doors into the gigantic lobby. There are signs pointing to places to go all over the world, and for a moment you're not sure which way you and your Worry are meant to go. There's a row of ticket counters on the side, so you walk up to one. There's a man behind a glass window, with a small circular hole so you can talk, and a place to slide in money.

"Where to?" says the man. And all of a sudden you hear yourself say, "Way Far Away. I'd like to buy one ticket to Way Far Away!"

"One way or round trip?" he asks. To which you reply in a strong voice, "One way. Definitely one way."

"That will be a dollar," the man says. And so you pay one dollar, and the man gives you a big, red ticket, and says, "Track 12."

So you and your Worry take the escalator down to the tracks, and walk quickly over to track 12. There's no train there, so the two of you sit down on a bench to wait.

Worry says, "Are we going on a vacation?"

And you say, "Not really."

And Worry says, "Are you going away?"

And you say, "No, not really."

And Worry says, "Am I going away?"

And you say, "Yes. Yes you are."

"And Worry says "Will I be gone long?"

And you reply, "Yes, Worry, you will be gone a very, very long time."

And Worry says, "I'm worried."

And you say, "I know but I'm not worried. I know you'll be okay."

Pretty soon, a train pulls into the station, on Track 12. And the sign on the front of the train, and the sign on the side of the train, both say "Way Far Away." The train looks very sleek, shiny, very powerful, and very fast. A conductor steps off the train and says "All aboard."

You and Worry walk up to the conductor, and you give him the big red ticket. And you say to Worry, "I don't need you anymore. I don't want you anymore. Goodbye!"

And before Worry can say anything back, you give Worry a little push, just enough to help Worry get on the train.

And you say once more, "Bye Worry, I don't need you any more. You'll be fine."

And the conductor says, "I'll take good care of your Worry." And then asks you: "Will YOU be okay without Worry?"

And you say, "Don't worry about me. I'll be better than ever!"

And the doors close, and the train starts to roll away, and goes faster, and faster, and gets smaller, and smaller, until it's alllll gone.

And pretty soon you're walking down the street without a care in the world, happy. Your Worry is gone! And, you took care of it yourself! Congratulations!

Remember that being happy is a very good way to be. Because after all, life is good, and all is well.

And if you ever happen to find yourself with Worry by your side again, and I'm not saying you will, but if you ever do, just go to the station, and buy a one way ticket for Way Far Away, and take Worry down to track 12. There will be another train along any minute.

(The author thanks Betty Mehling for her editing suggestions for this script.)

LIGHTBEING

You are about to embark upon a journey into the far, uncharted reaches of your imagination. For the time being, I invite you to suspend all that you know to be true about physical reality, and through your mind's eye, reach beyond, and if for only moments, glimpse a reality even greater.

Find a place where you'll not be disturbed, place your body in a comfortable position, and close your eyes. Become aware of your breathing, and as you do, notice your breathing becoming deeper and slower. Observe each breath, as you inhale, and exhale, and notice the pause between each breath. You're becoming more and more comfortable and relaxed, and letting those good feeling stay with you, as you become lighter, and lighter.

Imagine you're going to your front door, and stepping outside. As you look down at your feet, you see that the ground is quite different than you expect. And when you look up, you see that the entire scene has been transformed. You're now high in the mountains, standing at the edge of a small clearing. It's a beautiful sunny day, and the air is fresh and clear, as if there had just been a light summer rain. The subtle fragrance of wildflowers is here, and you see their delicate blossoms, amid mossy rocks and grass.

Take a full deep breath, and feel your whole body loosen and relax. Your cares and concerns are melting away in the warm sunlight, as each new breath carries you deeper, and deeper into the comfort of this place.

As you feel your breath gently rise and fall, look out at the beautiful scenery before you. From where you stand, you can see far into the distance on all sides, with nothing overhead but the infinite blue sky, and perhaps an eagle soaring silently above.

Something else is approaching overhead, that's hard to identify at first. But as it draws nearer, it appears to be a saucer-like vehicle, at times silver, and at other times clear, or sparkling white, as if made out of light. The flying ship comes closer and closer, until it noiselessly settles down in the middle of the clearing where you stand. The vessel opens, and after a moment, a very kind looking being comes toward you.

You see that his body is not solid, but a light-form, like the ship. His face is peaceful and friendly looking, and when he greets you, saying your name, his voice has a warm, pleasing quality. He asks if you're ready for an adventure, and when you reply that you are, he cordially invites you aboard his ship.

As you enter this unusual vehicle, your host bids you to make yourself comfortable and at home. Soon you feel the ship gently lift off the ground, and in another moment you're traveling high above the land, and heading deep into space.

Look out at the vast galaxy appearing before you. The infinite points of light spread out across the sky, and you marvel at the performance of this flying ship, with its ride so amazingly fast, yet so smooth and comfortable. There's a feeling of total security here, and of new possibilities yet to be discovered, as you travel deeper, and deeper.

Your guide now begins to tell you about himself, and his planet. "I'm very glad you've chosen to join me," he says, "for it will give me great pleasure to show you my home, and to offer you energy, for what you would call 'healing'."

His words seem to flow into you, without actually being said aloud, and resonate inside your mind.

"I am a Lightbeing," he says. "I exist in a dimension less dense than your physical world, and so I'm able to move much more freely than a physical body would allow. Because of this, I can also communicate with you through your mind. This ship is really an extension of myself, formed of the same light-matter as I. And within it, we can travel safely to my home, and when you are ready, return.

"Upon my planet, my race has evolved in a different, parallel life form to that of your race on Earth. But whereas your race is centered in physical matter, our race dwells entirely within the higher vibrations of light and sound. Our bodies are made of this vibration, as are our cities. On your planet you create with physical matter. We use our mind energy to create in the higher realms. When you're in a state of higher consciousness, as you are in this journey, you can experience our reality."

As your guide finishes these words, you begin to hear an unusual and very pleasant sound, quite unlike anything you've ever heard. It's as if your ears begin to hear in a new way, allowing you to receive this higher frequency. You become aware of sounds within sounds, and are amazed at the complexity of what you're able to perceive. Where the sounds seem as if they couldn't possibly become any more complex, they transform into visual images, forming the outline of a fantastic landscape.

As this landscape comes more fully into view, you find it unlike any you've ever seen, its colors alive and practically singing out to you. "This is my planet," you hear your guide say, "and you are beginning to experience the world I've described."

As the ship gently lands, you realize that you've come to a setting in some ways similar to a country meadow on earth. Here, however, everything appears more fully vibrant and alive. And when you focus on the images before you, you discover that they're also filled with sound. Your guide leads you to a nearby structure, appearing to be made of crystal.

"This is one of our healing places," he says. "On our planet, we've come to understand health as the balanced flow of life's energy, as illness as merely a blockage of that flow."

"Then, how do you heal a blockage of energy," you ask.

"With light and sound," he replies, "and with love."

As you stand in the center of this crystal structure, be aware of your own body and its flow of energy. While on this planet, you've become almost translucent, like the Lightbeing, and able to see, hear, and feel movement of color and sound within your own body.

Before long, you also feel a gentle warmth flowing into the healing structure, joining with your own energy. The crystal is beginning to activate, sending in a series of colors, beginning with a beautiful rich red hue. The red color swirls and flows all around and though you, bringing a wonderful feeling of strength and vitality.

Now the light begins to flow orange, and you can feel yourself merge with this color, as it brings you a stabilizing quality.

Soon the orange color begins to lighten, until it becomes golden yellow, a color that flows into your mind, bringing perfect clarity to all your thoughts.

Now a beautiful emerald green pours forth from the crystal walls. Feel the harmony and balance of this color, as you let it fill your entire being.

The green light changes to blue, and you feel this color's cool serenity permeate your emotions, and lift your thoughts higher and higher.

Now the crystal light glows a deep purple, and its energy flows gently through you, transmuting all negativity into love.

Finally, the light turns a pale golden light that contains all the colors, and it flows through you, bringing healing and balance wherever needed, for your highest good.

Feel this light caressing your face, allowing it to remove all traces of tension, leaving in its place peace, and tranquility.

Experience the light filling your head, and flowing down into your neck.

And feel it wash over your shoulders, arms, and hands, bringing deep comfort and calm, wherever it touches.

Now feel your chest, back, and abdomen open to receive this gentle flow of color, as it finds its way wherever needed. Take a deep breath, and release all negativity into the light.

Let this gentle, multicolored energy flow into your hips and follow it into your upper legs, knees, lower legs, and feet, as these parts of your body come into perfect balance, and peace.

Take a few moments to experience this transformation in any part of you that you wish, as the crystal light energy surrounds and fills you, clearing away any impurity, bringing movement, wherever there is stagnation and lending balance and harmony wherever it touches.

Now tune into the sound of this healing energy, and hear whatever messages its positive vibrations may hold for you.

Your guide appears in front of you and is extending his hands. With his touch comes the most beautiful outpouring of color and sound imaginable, flowing directly into your heart. Drink deeply of this offering of love.

As you and your guide quietly walk back into the meadow, you hear his voice once again resonate in your mind. "Your creative imagination has tremendous power," he says. "Never underestimate that power, and always use it lovingly. For the sounds and images within your mind are truly the music and scenery of your world."

It's time to begin your return home. You and your guide enter the ship, and lift silently into the air. As you travel back across the galaxy, give thanks to the one who has guided you. And give thanks to yourself, for giving yourself this opportunity to relax, and discover new, more positive ways of being.

The lightship approaches your original departure point. And as it settles down in the clearing, notice that you've returned feeling lighter, clearer, and stronger than before. Step out onto the ground, and wave goodbye to the Lightbeing, knowing that you can return to his world whenever you wish.

Look down at your feet once again, and recognize the familiar environment in which your journey began. Feel your physical energy becoming more and more present. Let all the benefits of this experience stay with you, and when you're ready, open your eyes and feel completely awake, alert, and refreshed.

PART TEN

12-STEP GUIDED MEDITATIONS

12-STEP GUIDED MEDITATIONS

INTRODUCTION

The guided meditations in this program are based upon the 12 Steps as described in the Big Book of Alcoholics Anonymous, and as practiced in 12-Step recovery groups all over the world. These meditations are not intended to take the place of meetings, sponsors, or any existing 12-Step practices, but have been designed to further support your recovery while you're actively engaged in such programs.

Much of the work in any 12-Step program is about self examination and change from within. But when looking inward, it's all too easy to fall into confusion, self-deception, and a host of distractions.

Guided meditation can be especially helpful here. The scripts included in this program are each designed to help you stay focused on a particular area of concern, related to the Step you're currently working on, from a deeply relaxed state. In each guided meditation, you're given a highly optimized opportunity to uncover truth, and let go of any negativity that might otherwise hold you back.

At the same time, this program can reinforce the positive, wholesome aspects of your character, while strengthening your relationship to your Higher Power. The deep support offered through these meditations can help you experience your own spirituality in a genuine, direct way.

Each of these guided meditations builds upon your work with the prior

Step, and the meditations for those steps. You'll want to use each meditation only after you've thoroughly explored the Steps before, and the learning they hold for you.

Take your time, work with each meditation carefully, and make the most of it. Set aside time where you'll have privacy and comfort, and can focus only on that guided meditation. Have pen and paper nearby, so that after each meditation, you can write about what you've discovered.

Work with each meditation at least several times over several days, to insure you've learned what you can, at that point in time. Later on, after you've completed the series and your life has progressed, come back to revisit the series, and learn more.

You'll find that the beginning several paragraphs of each meditation in this series is identical.

INTRODUCTION: STEP ONE MEDITATION
I admit I am powerless over my addiction—that my life has become unmanageable.

Everyone has blind a blind spot, something too close to see. The meditation for Step One is designed to help you uncover your own blind spot, so you'll know more about yourself, and how you might be getting in your own way.

There is a natural tendency at the beginning to avoid looking carefully, to jump ahead and try to fix things. But that very tendency is often part of the problem. As with the 12 Steps, each of the 12 meditations in this series will build upon the prior ones. So, don't short change yourself by glossing over this meditation. Take your time, work with it carefully, and make the most of it.

Set aside time where you'll have privacy and comfort, and can focus only on this guided meditation. Have pen and paper nearby, so that after the meditation, you can write about what you have discovered. Work with this meditation at least several times over several days, to insure you've learned what you can at this point in time. Later on, after you've completed the series and your life has progressed, come back to revisit it, and learn more.

GUIDED MEDITATION

Make yourself comfortable, and close your eyes. Take a slow deep breath, and let go of any tension in your body, as you feel yourself sinking into the surface you're resting on, becoming still more comfortable and relaxed.

Take another slow, deep breath, and feel a sense of calm and peace begin to fill you, as you relax further. And take another slow, deep breath, and let your thinking begin wind down and smooth out, as you become still comfortable, and relaxed.

Imagine you've been sleeping a deep, sound sleep for many hours, and you're just beginning to stir awake. And the first thing you notice, is that you're waking up on a soft bed of pine needles, on the ground, surrounded by ancient fir trees. It's just before dawn, and the air is quite cool, the light is dim, and there's a foggy mist in the air. You can smell the scent of pine, and the damp coolness of the earth. It's quiet, and any sound is blanketed by the mist. Everything is a palette of soft greens, browns, and grays.

Standing up, you begin to walk along a path through the trees, and you can feel the spongy ground beneath your feet. Perhaps you still feel a bit foggy from your sleep, but soon you come to a little spring, cup your hands to get a drink, and splash some of the cool, clear water on your face. Now you're beginning to wake up a bit, and see the trees and plants that surround you more clearly.

Walking along further, you come to an outcropping of rocks, in the shape of a small, natural amphitheater, surrounded by trees. It seems as if nature had prepared this place just for you, to rest and contemplate. Find a place to sit, and make yourself comfortable. As you look out at the small stage formed by the rocks in front of you, settle in and feel the peace and tranquility that seems to embrace you here.

As the show before you opens, a holographic image begins to appear on the stage, in the form of a banner displaying your name, and just below it, the word, *Clarity*.

The banner fades, and a moderator walks up on the stage, and begins to speak, saying:

"You are about to see a documentary about you and your life, presented to show you things you may not have been aware of, or things you might have glimpsed but then quickly blocked out. The producers wish to point out that this documentary contains only information, with no judgment or moral conclusion. Any decisions you might make as a result, are entirely up to you. We simply present the information. How you see and respond to it is your own choice."

The moderator leaves the stage, and a hologram again appears, this time in the form of a movie. The movie begins with scenes from your last 48 hours, and highlights something about you that had a negative impact on you or the people around you. This might have been something you said or didn't say, something you did or didn't do, or it may have stemmed from your a mood or state of mind. See, hear, and feel this scene unfold clearly, and watch carefully for the impact it has on you and any other people involved.

Watch that scene again, and see, hear, and feel it with as much clarity as possible, as everything comes into sharper focus. Make sure to notice if it included the use of any substance, habitual behavior, or mental/emotional pattern you held that contributed to the negative outcome.

Watch that scene one more time, and this time notice how automatically you slipped into your part. Be aware of how you might have been either unconscious of what you were doing, or might have known what you were doing, but were unable to alter your course, as if the matter were out of your hands.

As that scene fades, another appears, this time from the past two weeks. It again highlights something about you or what you did that had a negative impact on you or the people around you. Watch this scene unfold clearly on the screen, and look and listen carefully for the impact it had on you and others.

Watch that scene again as it comes into clearer focus, and notice the use of any substance, habitual behavior, or mental/emotional pattern.

Watch that scene once more, and notice how you automatically slipped into your part. Perhaps it seems as if you already knew what you were going to do before it happened, and you were simply following a script.

The movie changes again, and goes back further in your history. Look for a scene from as far back as you can recall, when you exhibited a similar pattern of behavior to the first two scenes. Notice how it seems you were somehow programmed to respond the way you did, as if the matter was almost out of your hands.

Watch that scene once more, and this time see it from the angle of the people around you. Notice how they felt about you, and how they reacted.

The last scene fades away, and the moderator reappears.

"This movie has been an attempt to help you recognize a pattern that might otherwise be hard for you to see, and even harder for you to admit. Although you may have been caught in this pattern for quite a long time, and despite all the negative consequences that may have occurred as a result, you've never able to change it, even up until the last 48 hours. This is what is meant by the sentence, "I am powerless over my addiction—that my life has become unmanageable.""

The moderator leaves the stage, and the holographic banner reappears to close the performance. Written there is the sentence, *I admit that I am powerless over my addiction—that my life has become unmanageable.* The words of the first of the 12 Steps remain, until they are finally replaced once again by your own name, and the word, *Clarity.*

It's almost time to bring this inner journey to a close. So gather together anything you have learned, that you'd like to bring with you.

Gradually bring your awareness back into your body, and your physical surroundings.

Take your time, and when you're ready, open your eyes, and feel awake, alert, and refreshed.

Pick up your pen and paper, and write about your experience now, while it's still fresh in your mind.

SECOND STEP

INTRODUCTION

I came to believe that a power greater than myself could restore me to sanity.

Please read the introduction to this series, in Step One.

In this meditation, you'll have the opportunity to address some of the issues you may have with authority figures, spirituality, religion, and other related topics. In order to be successful with this step, you're asked to be open to the idea that a power greater than yourself could help you, and to allow for the possibility that there's more to life than you might currently perceive. If you can say, "Maybe there's something or someone out there who's more powerful than myself, and I'm open to experiencing that," then you posses the attitude necessary to do the work of Step Two.

GUIDED MEDITATION

Make yourself comfortable, and close your eyes. Take a slow deep breath, and let go of any tension in your body, as you feel yourself sinking into the surface you're resting on, becoming still more comfortable and relaxed.

Take another slow, deep breath, and feel a sense of calm and peace begin to fill you, as you relax further. And take another slow, deep breath, and let your thinking begin wind down and smooth out, as you become still comfortable, and relaxed.

Imagine you've been sleeping a deep, sound sleep for many hours, and you're just beginning to stir awake. And the first thing you notice, is

that you're waking up on a soft bed of pine needles, on the ground, surrounded by ancient fir trees. It's just before dawn, and the air is quite cool, the light is dim, and there's a foggy mist in the air. You can smell the scent of pine, and the damp coolness of the earth. It's quiet, and any sound is blanketed by the mist. Everything is a palette of soft greens, browns, and grays.

Standing up, you begin to walk along a path through the trees, and you can feel the spongy ground beneath your feet. Perhaps you still feel a bit foggy from your sleep, but soon you come to a little spring, cup your hands to get a drink, and splash some of the cool, clear water on your face. Now you're beginning to wake up a bit, and see the trees and plants that surround you more clearly.

Walking along further, you come to the natural amphitheater you discovered not long ago; a small stage formed by rocks surrounded by trees, with places to sit and watch the stage, rest, and contemplate. Find a place to sit, and make yourself comfortable. Nature has prepared this place just for you, so settle in, and feel the peace and tranquility that seems to embrace you here.

Imagine a hologram is appearing before you on the stage, and as it becomes clearer, you see it's you, as a child, in a time when you were happy, and were learning something new. Watch as a positive scene from your young life begins to unfold, where you were engaged in learning, and someone was there to teach or guide you whom you liked, respected, and perhaps admired. Maybe it was a parent showing you how to play a game, or ride a bike, or a teacher helping you learn how to read or write. Find the most positive memory you can, and watch it unfold. If you're unable to remember a positive learning experience, use your imagination to make one up. Take a few moments for this now.

Now imagine that same scene, and this time tap into the feeling of wanting to learn, of how it felt to listen and follow directions, and the good feeling of having someone you could depend on to help you. Take a few minutes to experience this.

The hologram changes, and you now see yourself in a positive learning situation when you were a bit older. Perhaps you were in a class in middle or high school, studying a subject you enjoyed, or learning about a sport, art or music, or even how to drive a car. And someone was there with you as a teacher, whom you liked and respected, perhaps even admired. If you don't remember a positive learning experience like this, then imagine one. Take a few moments for this now.

Now imagine that same scene, and this time tap into the feeling of being open to someone's help, wanting to learn, and feeling that you could rely on them to help you. Take a few minutes to experience this.

As the hologram changes again, this time you see a positive learning experience as an adult. Here, you're learning either a skill you now use in your work, or something to enrich or improve your adult life. Again, someone is there to help you whom you like, appreciate and respect. Remember such a situation, or imagine one. Take a few moments for this now.

Be in touch with the feeling of openness, of wanting to learn, and of gratitude toward another person for helping you. Take a few minutes to experience this.

The positive feelings you've associated with receiving support, help, and instruction from someone who knew more than you did, form the attitude you need to move forward. So as you continue to sit in this amphitheater, get in touch with those feelings right now, inside yourself, in the clearest and deepest way you can, and allow them to grow stronger, and more real. As you do this, in place of the hologram a doorway begins to materialize before you, on the amphitheater stage, surrounded with light.

Get up from your seat, and approach the door, and as you come closer you'll see it opens onto a little stairway, with five steps leading up to a landing with another door, from which a great deal more light seems to be pouring out. This stairway represents an opportunity for you gain perspective, receive support, and release hardship.

As you step upon the first stair, feel the light surround you, as you begin to let go of any notion that you know everything there is to know about yourself, and there's nothing more to learn. Feel that idea falling away from your body as if it were an old skin, and open to possibility, as you become lighter.

As you step upon the second stair, feel more of the light surround you, as you begin to let go of any notion that no one can help you. Feel it dropping away from your body like a heavy cloak, and open to possibility, as you become lighter.

As you step upon the third stair, feel more of the light surround you, and set aside of any prejudice you may hold about God, religion, or spirituality. For now, simply be willing to let it go, feel it melt away, and release.

As you step upon the forth stair, feel more of the light surround you, and let go of any doubt, skepticism, or cynicism about any existence beyond the physical level. Simply release, open, and feel a wave of possibility sweep over you.

As you step upon the fifth stair, feel more of the light surround you, and set aside the obsessive, oppressive need to control your life. Embrace the possibility of letting go and floating freely, and feel lighter.

As you come up to the landing, you'll see a basket in front of the door at the top. This basket represents an opportunity to make a symbolic offering of peace and humility toward your own higher power. So, go into your heart, and find something within you to leave in this basket. This might be as simple as a flower, or it might be something that only you would know about that has particular meaning to you. Perhaps it's something you would really like to be free of. Leave whatever feels most appropriate for you.

Step through the doorway, and feel embraced by light, love, and compassion. Simply be open to receive, and do your best to let go, and allow. Whatever you're experiencing at this point, positive, negative, or in between, is just fine. Ask within you, in deepest sincerity, that if a higher power does exist, that it please help you become restored to sanity. Take some time to relax, receive, and be at peace.

It's almost time to bring this inner journey to a close. So gather together anything you have learned, that you'd like to bring with you.

Gradually bring your awareness back into your body, and your physical surroundings.

Take your time, and when you're ready, open your eyes, and feel awake, alert, and refreshed.

Pick up your pen and paper, and write about your experience now, while it's still fresh in your mind. Later on, revisit this meditation and learn more.

THIRD STEP

INTRODUCTION

I make a decision to turn my will and my life over to the care of God, as I understand God.

Please read the introduction to this series, in Step One.

In this meditation, you'll have the opportunity to examine the difference between your will and God's will, and begin to make a major shift in attitude. Turning your will and your life over to God is something that you do not do once and for all, but must happen many times, as your life unfolds and each new situation present itself. Step Three, and this meditation, represent the beginning of what can become an increasingly wholesome and fulfilling life.

GUIDED MEDITATION

Make yourself comfortable, and close your eyes. Take a slow deep breath, and let go of any tension in your body, as you feel yourself sinking into the surface you're resting on, becoming still more comfortable and relaxed. Take another slow, deep breath, and feel a sense of calm and peace begin to fill you, as you relax further. And take another slow, deep breath, and let your thinking begin wind down and smooth out, as you become still comfortable, and relaxed.

Imagine you've been sleeping a deep, sound sleep for many hours, and you're just beginning to stir awake. And the first thing you notice, is that you're waking up on a soft bed of pine needles, on the ground, surrounded by ancient fir trees. It's just before dawn, and the air is quite cool, the light is dim, and there's a foggy mist in the air. You can smell the scent of pine, and the damp coolness of the earth. It's quiet, and any sound is blanketed by the mist. Everything is a palette of soft greens, browns, and grays.

Standing up, you begin to walk along a path through the trees, and you can feel the spongy ground beneath your feet. Perhaps you still feel a bit foggy from your sleep, but soon you come to a little spring, cup your hands to get a drink, and splash some of the cool, clear water on your face. Now you're beginning to wake up a bit, and see the trees and plants that surround you more clearly.

Walking along further, you find that the ground gradually becomes more sandy, and the air more humid, and soon you can smell the sea, and hear the sound of seagulls, and ocean waves breaking along a shoreline. Before long, you emerge from the forest upon a deserted sandy beach.

There are some boulders nearby, and you easily find a comfortable spot to sit and rest. You can feel the mist and the sea breeze on your face, and the warmth of the sun, as you contemplate the beach, the sea, and the sky before you.

Watching a pair of seagulls arguing over a scrap of food, you begin to consider your own desires, the stress in your life, and your need to control. Based upon fear, insecurity, and a host of turbulent emotions, what has your own will brought to you?

Certainly there were many times you decided you wanted something, and found you could get it if you tried hard enough. But often what you wanted was out of reach, or ultimately proved unsatisfying. And in some cases your decisions had a negative impact on those around you. Take in the ocean before you. Thousands of miles wide, a vast, intelligent system, supporting countless forms of life, all interrelated and interdependent. And yet this ocean is just one small part of a much greater system of creation, reaching in all directions farther than the mind can comprehend.

You have a choice, to continue to live your life from your own will, from one desire to the next; or to open up to a much greater influence, one that oversees all creation, and knows how to help bring you true fulfillment. The opportunity is here, the means are available, and you've already decided that what you've been doing so far isn't working.

Direct your focus toward your spiritual heart, in the center of your chest. Take a deep breath, and begin to breathe in the word God, and breathe out the word Love. Here, in your own heart is where you may find your own connection to all of creation, all of life; and where you may find God. Not a strange man in the sky, or an angry force of nature, but a part of you, at your deepest level. God is all loving, all knowing, all powerful. God is in your heart, and you are in God's heart. In your own heart you can begin to listen and know God's will, and begin to follow it.

Continue to focus in your heart, and breathe in the word God, and breathe out the word Love. Make a decision, now, to turn your will and your life over to the care of God, in whatever way you understand God. If you wish, go down to the water's edge, where the sea meets the land. Listen, look, and feel within your heart, to decide whether you'd like to get your feet wet, wade in gradually, or dive into the waves with full abandon. Whatever choice you make is just fine, as long as it comes from your heart. Take some time, relax, and be with God.

It's almost time to bring this inner journey to a close. So gather together anything you have learned, that you'd like to bring with you.

Gradually bring your awareness back into your body, and your physical surroundings.

Take your time, and when you're ready, open your eyes, and feel awake, alert, and refreshed.

Pick up your pen and paper, and write about your experience now, while it's still fresh in your mind. Later on, revisit this meditation and learn more.

FOURTH STEP

INTRODUCTION

I make a searching and fearless moral inventory of myself.

Please read the introduction to this series, in Step One.

In this meditation, you'll have the opportunity to explore what it means to come to terms with your personal shortcomings, face the truth about yourself, and thrive as a result.

GUIDED MEDITATION

Make yourself comfortable, and close your eyes. Take a slow deep breath, and let go of any tension in your body, as you feel yourself sinking into the surface you're resting on, becoming still more comfortable and relaxed. Take another slow, deep breath, and feel a sense of calm and peace begin to fill you, as you relax further. And take another slow, deep breath, and let your thinking begin wind down and smooth out, as you become still comfortable, and relaxed.

Imagine you've been sleeping a deep, sound sleep for many hours, and you're just beginning to stir awake. And the first thing you notice, is that you're waking up on a soft bed of pine needles, on the ground, surrounded by ancient fir trees. It's just before dawn, and the air is quite cool, the light is dim, and there's a foggy mist in the air. You can smell the scent of pine, and the damp coolness of the earth. It's quiet, and any sound is blanketed by the mist. Everything is a palette of soft greens, browns, and grays.

Standing up, you begin to walk along a path through the trees, and you can feel the spongy ground beneath your feet. Perhaps you still feel a bit foggy from your sleep, but soon you come to a little spring, cup your hands to get a drink, and splash some of the cool, clear water on your face. Now you're beginning to wake up a bit, and see the trees and plants that surround you more clearly.

Take another look at the spring, and you'll notice the pool of water formed just below it, clear and bright. As you look into the pool, you see your face, reflected back. Look more closely at your reflection, and you may notice a mask you often wear: One that pretends that all is well, and you're not bothered by how your life has been going. This mask helps you hide from others how you truly feel; so you won't have to see true own feelings reflected back to you in their eyes.

As you continue to look at your reflection, something disturbs the water, and your mask disappears. Your face changes, and you watch as a whole series of emotions pass over it. Fear, sadness, anger, resentment, shame, jealousy... Not things you enjoy being aware of, but then, the time has come in your journey for you to finally uncover the truth, so you have the opportunity to change. It's time to get real, and you're ready to do that now.

Walking along further, you come to the natural amphitheater you discovered not so long ago; a small stage formed by rocks surrounded by trees, with places to sit and watch the stage, rest, and contemplate. Find a place to sit, and make yourself comfortable. Nature has prepared this place just for you, so settle in, and feel the peace and tranquility that seems to embrace you here.

A hologram begins to form on the stage, and soon you see it's a scene from your life, in which you were in conflict with one or more other people. Watch this scene unfold as clearly and completely as you possibly can. Take a few moments to do this.

They say that no two people experience the same event in the same way. So now watch that same scene, and this time see it unfold as if it were entirely from the others' point of view, from their experience. Pay particular care to how they felt about you, and how they may have felt you were responsible for the conflict. Take a few moments with this.

Now the scene fades, and you disappear from the stage, but the others who were involved turn and face you in the audience. If they were angry or upset before, you can see that now they have softened, and are looking at you with neutrality, or even with love, and compassion. They have no ill will toward you at this point, and simply want to help you in any way they can. Allow them to speak to you now with kindness, but also with total honesty, and tell you the truth about yourself. Let them say the things you may have known, but have been afraid to really hear. Take a few moments to listen carefully to what they have to say, and simply let it in.

As you continue to sit in the amphitheater, you begin to notice that you're not alone in the audience. Other people are sitting with you, as they silently materializing around you one by one. Before long, there are so many people in the audience they overflow beyond the amphitheater, and soon stretch out as far as the eye can see. The reason there seem to be so many, is that the whole human race is in the same position you're in. Every one of us is flawed. Every one of us is imperfect. And all of us have made mistakes, and will continue to do so. And sooner or later we all have to face the truth, in order to change for the better. To err is to be human. It's time to know your imperfections, accept them, and move on.

Take another look at the stage, and you'll see another hologram of yourself. In this image you are sitting at a desk, perhaps with pen and paper, or at a computer screen typing. Can you listen deeply within, know the truth about yourself, and survive? With less to hide, with fewer masks to wear, it's so much easier to live. A dark and heavy cloud surrounds you, as you write a list of your own shortcomings. But as you continue, and come to the end of your list, the cloud begins to lift. Watch yourself on stage as you learn and know your truth, face it, and come out of the experience lighter, simpler, and freer. Take some time to watch this scene unfold.

It's almost time to bring this inner journey to a close. So gather together anything you have learned, that you'd like to bring with you.

Gradually bring your awareness back into your body, and your physical surroundings.

Take your time, and when you're ready, open your eyes, and feel awake, alert, and refreshed.

Pick up your pen and paper, and write about your experience now, while it's still fresh in your mind. Later on, revisit this meditation and learn more.

FIFTH STEP

INTRODUCTION

I admit to God, myself and another human being the exact nature of my wrongs.

Please read the introduction to this series, in Step One.

The fifth step is one that's often difficult, because it involves talking out loud about things we may feel deeply embarrassed about or ashamed of. We've often put a lot of effort into keeping these things secret, acting as if they never happened, and in some cases even denying their existence to ourselves, so that a lot of armor becomes built up within us around them.

For those and other reasons, a Fifth Step can be hard to approach, but it does need to be done, and done wholeheartedly. So in this meditation you'll have the opportunity to inwardly prepare for your Fifth Step, to ease your way into the work you'll need to do.

GUIDED MEDITATION

Make yourself comfortable, and close your eyes. Take a slow deep breath, and let go of any tension in your body, as you feel yourself sinking into the surface you're resting on, becoming still more comfortable and relaxed. Take another slow, deep breath, and feel a sense of calm and peace begin to fill you, as you relax further. And take another slow, deep breath, and let your thinking begin wind down and smooth out, as you become still comfortable, and relaxed.

Imagine you've been sleeping a deep, sound sleep for many hours, and you're just beginning to stir awake. And the first thing you notice, is that you're waking up on a soft bed of pine needles, on the ground, surrounded by ancient fir trees. It's just before dawn, and the air is quite cool, the light is dim, and there's a foggy mist in the air. You can smell the scent of pine, and the damp coolness of the earth. It's quiet, and any sound is blanketed by the mist. Everything is a palette of soft greens, browns, and grays.

Standing up, you begin to walk along a path through the trees, and you can feel the spongy ground beneath your feet. Perhaps you still feel a bit foggy from your sleep, but soon you come to a little spring, cup your hands to get a drink, and splash some of the cool, clear water on your face. Now you're beginning to wake up a bit, and see the trees and plants that surround you more clearly.

As you continue along your path, you find that the mist begins to lift, and the day becomes brighter, and clearer. And soon you emerge from the forest into a beautiful meadow, full of lush grass, and wildflowers. There's a welcoming feeling in the air, as if this setting had been created just for you, and simply being here seems to make you feel more relaxed, and comfortable.

You'll notice that in the middle of the meadow are two comfortable chairs, facing each other, and so you quietly walk over to them, and have a seat. As soon as you sit down, someone begins to materialize in the other chair. This might be the person with whom you've already planned to do your Fifth Step; someone you know, trust, and feel safe with. But if you don't yet know whom that will be, the person sitting with you could be someone else you know and trust, or an historical or a beloved spiritual figure. Let this be someone you'd feel most comfortable speaking to very honestly about your life.

Allow that person to come fully into your presence now, seated before you, in this beautiful, natural setting. Soon, you're also aware of a cone of golden light coming down around you and this person. This cone of light emanates from the highest heavens, and represents God's presence and grace, as a support and witness for you, in your Fifth Step. You can feel the warmth, love, and beauty of this light as it surrounds and fills you, helping you to know that all is well.

In this environment, you're entirely safe, and welcome to be completely open, honest, and forthcoming. This is a rare opportunity for you to release and lay down any burden of guilt or shame you may have been carrying.

As you face your partner, notice a warm, soft glow that emanates from their heart. Their attitude toward you is one of complete empathy, and there's nothing you can say to them that would cause them to judge or reject you. They are there for you and you alone, 100%.

As that glow continues to come from their heart toward yours, your own heart begins to warm, and soften, and to open as well. Soon that comfortable, warm feeling extends upward to your throat, and now you know you're now ready to tell all there is to say about your life, and there's no need to hold anything back.

With God watching over you, in this environment of safety and support, take some time now, as you observe yourself opening up to this person before you, letting go, and releasing anything within you that needs to be spoken about.

It's almost time to bring this inner journey to a close. So gather together anything you have learned, that you'd like to bring with you.

Gradually bring your awareness back into your body, and your physical surroundings.

Take your time, and when you're ready, open your eyes, and feel awake, alert, and refreshed.

Pick up your pen and paper, and write about your experience now, while it's still fresh in your mind. Later on, revisit this meditation and learn more.

SIXTH STEP

INTRODUCTION

I am entirely ready to have God remove all these defects of character.

Please read the introduction to this series, in Step One.

The sixth step is about reflection on all that's come before, and preparation for what is to come next. In this step, you ask yourself, in deepest sincerity, "Am I ready to surrender control of my life, and place myself fully into God's care." This meditation provides an opportunity to focus upon that question, and all it implies.

GUIDED MEDITATION

Make yourself comfortable, and close your eyes. Take a slow deep breath, and let go of any tension in your body, as you feel yourself sinking into the surface you're resting on, becoming still more comfortable and relaxed. Take another slow, deep breath, and feel a sense of calm and peace begin to fill you, as you relax further. And take another slow, deep breath, and let your thinking begin wind down and smooth out, as you become still comfortable, and relaxed.

Imagine you've been sleeping a deep, sound sleep for many hours, and you're just beginning to stir awake. And the first thing you notice, is that you're waking up on a soft bed of pine needles, on the ground, surrounded by ancient fir trees. It's just before dawn, and the air is quite cool, the light is dim, and there's a foggy mist in the air. You can smell the scent of pine, and the damp coolness of the earth. It's quiet, and any sound is blanketed by the mist. Everything is a palette of soft greens, browns, and grays.

Standing up, you begin to walk along a path through the trees, and you can feel the spongy ground beneath your feet. Perhaps you still feel a bit foggy from your sleep, but soon you come to a little spring, cup your hands to get a drink, and splash some of the cool, clear water on your face. Now you're beginning to wake up a bit, and see the trees and plants that surround you more clearly.

Walking along further, you find yourself once again on the path to the beach you visited, not so long ago. Soon the ground becomes sandy, and the air more humid. Now you can smell the sea, and hear the sound of seagulls, and ocean waves breaking along the shore. Finally, you emerge from the forest into the beach where earlier, you made a decision to turn your will, and your life, over to God. Now it's time to revisit that decision, and examine it in a deeper way.

Walking across the sandy beach toward the shoreline, you notice it's low tide. You may wish to remove your shoes and socks, and walk along the water's edge. Because the tide is out, much more of the shore is exposed, and you can see pretty shells scattered here and there, bits of seaweed, and little sand crabs scurrying across the packed sand. Here and there sandpipers scamper back and forth with the foam, finding their meals hidden in the sand.

Just as low tide exposes what's been hidden under water, times of deep reflection help us discover what's emerging within us. Look down, and you'll notice just in front of you, a piece of sea glass. Pick it up, and feel how it's surface has been textured by the ocean floor, its edges softened. Who can say how long it's been at the mercy of the tides, shaped by the sand and salt water?

Are you ready now, to be shaped and by God's will; to set your own will aside and allow yourself to be re-formed? Have you spent enough time, trying unsuccessfully to control your destiny, to the point where you're finally ready to begin living your life a new way?

As you continue to walk along the shore, take some time to consider the following questions.

Am I ready to fully expose all of my personal defects to the light?

Am I ready to stop pretending I'm invincible, and unconcerned about how I might appear?

Am I willing to just be a normal human being with defects, struggles, and difficulties, like everyone else?

Am I ready to turn my recovery over to God, instead of trying to control what happens, every step of the way?

Am I ready to face the truth about myself, recognize my defects of character as they appear in my daily life, and keep turning them over to God, again and again?

Am I ready to make this a life-long process?

If you were able to say yes to these questions, your Sixth Step is complete for now, and you're ready to move on to your next step. If you were uncertain or had to say no, then you now have good, useful information about where to focus your attention next, so that you can become fully ready.

If you know you're now ready, take a few moments to humbly and sincerely thank God for helping you come this far. And if you know you are not yet ready, then take a few moments to humbly and sincerely ask God to help you to let go of anything within you that needs to be released, to prepare you to become ready.

As you turn around and begin to find your way back along the shore, you might notice a school of dolphins swimming by. Only you can know what their presence at this particular moment might symbolize to you. But the fact is, if you've been working your steps with purpose, at this point your life is truly turning around, changing for the better. And as long as you continue to say yes to God, your life will continue to unfold in ways you might never have thought possible, by the grace of God.

It's almost time to bring this inner journey to a close. So gather together anything you have learned, that you'd like to bring with you.

Gradually bring your awareness back into your body, and your physical surroundings.

Take your time, and when you're ready, open your eyes, and feel awake, alert, and refreshed.

Pick up your pen and paper, and write about your experience now, while it's still fresh in your mind. Later on, revisit this meditation and learn more.

SEVENTH STEP

INTRODUCTION

I humbly ask God to remove my shortcomings.

Please read the introduction to this series, in Step One.

Step Seven is all about putting ourself in the right relationship to God, through humility. Here we humbly recognize and acknowledge that we can't change without God's help, and we accept that our recovery must proceed according to God's will, in God's timing. We set aside our egotistical belief that we're in control, and place our lives and our healing into God's hands. In this meditation, you'll have the opportunity to face God, ask for his help, explore the part you're to play in receiving it.

GUIDED MEDITATION

Make yourself comfortable, and close your eyes. Take a slow deep breath, and let go of any tension in your body, as you feel yourself sinking into the surface you're resting on, becoming still more comfortable and relaxed. Take another slow, deep breath, and feel a sense of calm and peace begin to fill you, as you relax further. And take another slow, deep breath, and let your thinking begin wind down and smooth out, as you become still comfortable, and relaxed.

Imagine you've been sleeping a deep, sound sleep for many hours, and you're just beginning to stir awake. And the first thing you notice, is that you're waking up on a soft bed of pine needles, on the ground, surrounded by ancient fir trees. It's just before dawn, and the air is quite cool, the light is dim, and there's a foggy mist in the air. You can smell the scent of pine, and the damp coolness of the earth. It's quiet, and any sound is blanketed by the mist. Everything is a palette of soft greens, browns, and grays.

Standing up, you begin to walk along a path through the trees, and you can feel the spongy ground beneath your feet. Perhaps you still feel a bit foggy from your sleep, but soon you come to a little spring, cup your hands to get a drink, and splash some of the cool, clear water on your face. Now you're beginning to wake up a bit, and see the trees and plants that surround you more clearly.

You begin to continue down the forest path, when a column of light descends from the heavens, through the trees, and directly in front of you, going straight down into the earth. Having completed Step Six earlier on, you know you're ready, and so you step forward into the light and are immediately transported into another world, in which you are naked in body, mind, and spirit before the throne of God.

You may or may not be aware of the visual details of the setting in which you now find yourself, but you know you're in the presence of your creator, and are here for a very important reason: To ask for God's help. If you wish, bow down as a symbolic gesture, and in deepest humility, you now make the following prayer:

Dear God,

I turn my life over to you, and ask that you reform me, according to your will, that I might better serve you and your Creation. Please remove from me all my defects as you see fit, in the manner and timing that pleases you, and best serves the highest good of all concerned, as only you can. Please bring me the awareness to know when I am behaving out of my defects, and the strength of character to let go when that occurs, so that you might mold me in your hands.

Take some time to absorb the meaning of this prayer, and to add whatever you may need to say to God, now.

As the scene changes, you find yourself back in the natural, stone amphitheater you've visited during previous meditations. On the stage, you're laying face up on an operating table, surrounded by a cone of light. God's love is all around you, as changes occur in your body, mind, and spirit. Negative attitudes and other energies are leaving your system, while positive ones are being instilled, all according to God's grace. Take some time to experience this.

Again the scene changes, and you now see yourself going about your day, and coming to a point where you're acting out of a defect of character; one of the things you've asked God to help you remove. And just as you're exhibiting this behavior, a ray of light comes down from the heavens, touching softly into your mind. Although in the scene you're not aware of this ray of light, you do instantly recognize that you've behaved in a way that doesn't serve you or the others involved, and doesn't reflect the person God would have you be. Immediately upon receiving this awareness you shift your attitude, let go, and correct your behavior.

And so this is how God has begun to answer your prayer. By providing awareness, you're given the opportunity to change. Every time you recognize the need to change, then let go, and come into alignment with your Higher Power, your prayer is being answered. God brings you the circumstances and the opportunity to see your imperfections, and gives you the choice to let them go. Your path is provided for you by God. Your only job is to say yes at every step. In doing so, you're placing yourself in God's hands, and humbly allowing him to mold you as he sees fit.

It's almost time to bring this inner journey to a close. So gather together anything you have learned, that you'd like to bring with you.

Gradually bring your awareness back into your body, and your physical surroundings.

Take your time, and when you're ready, open your eyes, and feel awake, alert, and refreshed.

Pick up your pen and paper, and write about your experience now, while it's still fresh in your mind. Later on, revisit this meditation and learn more.

EIGHTH STEP

INTRODUCTION

I make a list of all those I have harmed, and become willing to make amends to them all.

Please read the introduction to this series in Step One.

Step Eight is about becoming willing to do whatever it takes to make amends, and involves the necessary mental and emotional preparation for the actions you will take in Step Nine. The difficulty in Step Eight is in thinking about someone we don't want to approach, and expecting the worst. But dread is not a necessary component of this step, and you can leave it out. "Drop Dread," as the saying goes. This meditation can help prepare you to do just that. Once you've worked through Step Eight, the meditation for Step Nine will take you further in the process.

GUIDED MEDITATION

Make yourself comfortable, and close your eyes. Take a slow deep breath, and let go of any tension in your body, as you feel yourself sinking into the surface you're resting on, becoming still more comfortable and relaxed. Take another slow, deep breath, and feel a sense of calm and peace begin to fill you, as you relax further. And take another slow, deep breath, and let your thinking begin wind down and smooth out, as you become still comfortable, and relaxed.

Imagine you've been sleeping a deep, sound sleep for many hours, and you're just beginning to stir awake. And the first thing you notice, is

that you're waking up on a soft bed of pine needles, on the ground, surrounded by ancient fir trees. It's just before dawn, and the air is quite cool, the light is dim, and there's a foggy mist in the air. You can smell the scent of pine, and the damp coolness of the earth. It's quiet, and any sound is blanketed by the mist. Everything is a palette of soft greens, browns, and grays.

Standing up, you begin to walk along a path through the trees, and you can feel the spongy ground beneath your feet. Perhaps you still feel a bit foggy from your sleep, but soon you come to a little spring, cup your hands to get a drink, and splash some of the cool, clear water on your face. Now you're beginning to wake up a bit, and see the trees and plants that surround you more clearly.

Nearby is a fallen log that would make a good place to sit and rest for a while. So find a comfortable spot, have a seat, and enjoy the peace and quiet here. Run your hands along the surface of the bark, and you might marvel at how beautifully nature has made this tree trunk. Not long ago it was firmly rooted and tall, stretching upward to the sky to take in the sunlight. Once a home for birds and other creatures, now it's a bench for a passerby. And later it will become mulch and then soil for new growth.

Drop down from your thinking self into your feeling self, and go deeply into your own heart. Here, in your heart, you can set aside worries and concerns, and focus on the essential qualities in life that are most important, and most supportive to your wellbeing. Things like love, honesty, and compassion for yourself and others. At your core, in your heart, these qualities are as natural to you as breathing.

Consider one of the people you need to make amends to, perhaps someone you already feel willing to approach. For a moment, put yourself in their position and tune into what it might feel like to experience the injury you caused them. How do you think they felt, and what was the effect on their life; emotionally, physically, financially, or otherwise. As honestly as possible, consider how would you have felt in their place.

Imagine yourself approaching that person to make amends, taking it on a moment to moment, step by step basis. Imagine yourself proceeding with total honesty and humility, without excuses or blame, and experience them responding either with neutrality or appreciation. Take a few moments with this.

Consider someone else with whom you know you'll need to make amends, perhaps this time someone who may be more of a challenge for you. Again, put yourself in their position and tune into what it might feel like to experience the injury you caused them. How do you think they felt, and what was the effect on their life; emotionally, physically, financially, or otherwise. As honestly as possible, consider how would you have felt in their place.

Imagine yourself approaching that person to make amends, taking it on a moment to moment, step by step basis. Imagine yourself proceeding with total honesty and humility, without excuses or blame, and experience them responding either with neutrality or appreciation. Take a few moments with this.

And consider one other person with whom you know you'll need to make amends. Again, put yourself in their position and tune into what it might feel like to experience the injury you caused them. How do you think they felt, and what was the effect on their life; emotionally, physically, financially, or otherwise. As honestly as possible, consider how would you have felt in their place.

Imagine yourself approaching that person to make amends, taking it on a moment to moment, step by step basis. Imagine yourself proceeding with total honesty and humility, without excuses or blame, and experience them responding either with neutrality or appreciation. Take a few moments with this.

As you continue to work with Step 8, understand that your job at this point is to simply become as willing as possible to communicate clearly with each person on your list. As you continue, you'll come to realize that there is no need to dwell on trepidation or fear. All you need do is become willing to move forward, moment by moment step by step. The rest will unfold accordingly.

It's almost time to bring this inner journey to a close. So gather together anything you have learned, that you'd like to bring with you.

Gradually bring your awareness back into your body, and your physical surroundings.

Take your time, and when you're ready, open your eyes, and feel awake, alert, and refreshed.

Pick up your pen and paper, and write about your experience now, while it's still fresh in your mind. Later on, revisit this meditation and learn more.

NINTH STEP

INTRODUCTION

I make direct amends wherever possible, except when to do so would cause injury.

Please read the introduction to this series in Step One.

In Step Nine you'll approach those on your list whom you've injured, and do your best to make amends in ways most appropriate to each person and situation. It may be that some people on your list will present a challenge, because of your feelings that they've also caused injury to you. But Step Nine is not about soliciting apologies or amends from others, it's about you making amends for your own actions. In order for you to sincerely apologize, it may be necessary for you to first release any anger or resentment you hold toward those on your list, and come into neutrality toward them. This meditation will help you do that.

GUIDED MEDITATION

Make yourself comfortable, and close your eyes. Take a slow deep breath, and let go of any tension in your body, as you feel yourself sinking into the surface you're resting on, becoming still more comfortable and relaxed. Take another slow, deep breath, and feel a sense of calm and peace begin to fill you, as you relax further. And take another slow, deep breath, and let your thinking begin wind down and smooth out, as you become still comfortable, and relaxed.

Imagine you've been sleeping a deep, sound sleep for many hours, and you're just beginning to stir awake. And the first thing you notice, is that you're waking up on a soft bed of pine needles, on the ground, surrounded by ancient fir trees. It's just before dawn, and the air is quite cool, the light is dim, and there's a foggy mist in the air. You can smell the scent of pine, and the damp coolness of the earth. It's quiet, and any sound is blanketed by the mist. Everything is a palette of soft greens, browns, and grays.

Standing up, you begin to walk along a path through the trees, and you can feel the spongy ground beneath your feet. Perhaps you still feel a bit foggy from your sleep, but soon you come to a little spring, cup your hands to get a drink, and splash some of the cool, clear water on your face. Now you're beginning to wake up a bit, and see the trees and plants that surround you more clearly.

Look for the fallen log you found in the previous meditation, and you'll see it nearby. Find a comfortable spot, and have a seat. Enjoy the beauty and quiet here, and allow this peaceful place to support you, as you begin your inner work.

Drop down from your thinking self into your feeling self, and go deeply into your own heart. Here, in your heart, you can set aside worries and concerns, and focus on the essential qualities in life that are most important, and most supportive to your wellbeing. Things like love, honesty, and compassion for yourself and others. At your core, in your heart, these qualities are as natural as breathing. And here, in your heart, you may also find your connection to God.

In the Step 8 Meditation, you made preparations to make amends. Now it's time to make sure you're ready to proceed. Consider one of the people with whom you need to make amends, toward whom you may hold some form of animosity. In order for you to complete this step and become free, you must first let go of any anger, resentment, judgment jealousy, or any other negative feelings toward that person. With God's help, you can do that, now.

Imagine that person as a small child, of about 3 - 5 years old. Take a good look at them, and you'll notice someone innocent, vulnerable, and in need of love, just as you were at that age. No matter what they may have done as they grew older, that small child is still living within them, as yours lives within you. We've all made mistakes, but as different from one another we may seem, inside we're all just about the same.

The past is past, and it's time to forgive that person now, and move on. It's not your job to change or fix anyone, only God can do that. God forgives, and you can as well. Ask for God's help for you to forgive that person now, and take a deep breath. Soon, you'll feel a wave of light begin to pass through you. Take some time now to experience that wave of light moving through you from head to foot, and allow any negativity within you toward that person to be dissolved by the light, and release. Breathe deeply, and let it go.

Consider another person with whom you need to make amends, toward whom you may hold some form of animosity. Imagine that person as a small child. Notice that they are innocent, vulnerable, and in need of love, just as you were at that age. And realize that inside, today you and that person share the same basic needs for love, safety, and support.

Set aside any need you may have to harm, change or fix that person, now. Ask for God's help for you to forgive that them, and take a deep breath. Soon, you'll feel a wave of light begin to pass through you. Take some time now to experience that wave of light moving through you from head to foot, and allow any negativity within you to be dissolved by the light, and release. Breathe deeply, and let it go.

Consider one more person with whom you need to make amends, toward whom you may hold some form of animosity. Imagine that person as a small child, of about 3 - 5 years old. Notice that they are innocent, vulnerable, and in need of love, just as you were at that age. And realize that inside, today you and that person share the same basic needs for love, safety, and support.

Set aside any need you may have to harm, change or fix that person, now. Ask for God's help for you to forgive that them, and take a deep breath. Soon, you'll feel a wave of light begin to pass through you. Take some time now to experience that wave of light moving through you from head to foot, and allow any negativity within you to be dissolved by the light, and release. Breathe deeply, and let it go.

It's almost time to bring this inner journey to a close. So gather together anything you have learned, that you'd like to bring with you.

Gradually bring your awareness back into your body, and your physical surroundings.

Take your time, and when you're ready, open your eyes, and feel awake, alert, and refreshed.

Pick up your pen and paper, and write about your experience now, while it's still fresh in your mind. Later on, revisit this meditation and learn more.

TENTH STEP

INTRODUCTION

I continue to take personal inventory, and when wrong, promptly admit it.

Please read the introduction to this series in Step One.

Step Ten is one you'll use on a regular basis from now on, along with Steps 11 and 12, to help maintain your "Spiritual Fitness." Step Ten requires that you continue to watch for character defects within you, and ask God to help you let them go as they appear. This meditation is one you can use to tune in and assess how you're responding to life, in other words, "take your inventory." You'll want to use it especially when you feel negatively triggered, to quickly identify what's going on, and turn it over to your Higher Power.

GUIDED MEDITATION

Make yourself comfortable, and close your eyes. Take a slow deep breath, and let go of any tension in your body, as you feel yourself sinking into the surface you're resting on, becoming still more comfortable and relaxed. Take another slow, deep breath, and feel a sense of calm and peace begin to fill you, as you relax further. And take another slow, deep breath, and let your thinking begin wind down and smooth out, as you become still comfortable, and relaxed.

Imagine you've been sleeping a deep, sound sleep for many hours, and you're just beginning to stir awake. And the first thing you notice, is that you're waking up on a soft bed of pine needles, on the ground, surrounded by ancient fir trees. It's just before dawn, and the air is quite cool, the light is dim, and there's a foggy mist in the air. You can smell the scent of pine, and the damp coolness of the earth. It's quiet, and any sound is blanketed by the mist. Everything is a palette of soft greens, browns, and grays.

Standing up, you begin to walk along a path through the trees, and you can feel the spongy ground beneath your feet. Perhaps you still feel a bit foggy from your sleep, but soon you come to a little spring, cup your hands to get a drink, and splash some of the cool, clear water on your face. Now you're beginning to wake up a bit, and see the trees and plants that surround you more clearly.

Walking along further, you find yourself once again on the path to the beach you visited, not so long ago. Soon the ground becomes sandy, and the air more humid. Now you can smell the sea, and hear the sound of seagulls, and ocean waves breaking along the shore. Finally, you emerge from the forest into the beach where earlier, you made a decision to turn over your will, and your life, to God. There are some boulders nearby, and you easily find a comfortable spot to sit and rest. You can feel the mist and the sea breeze on your face, and the warmth of the sun, as you contemplate the beach, the sea, and the sky before you.

Drop down from your thinking self into your feeling self, and go deeply into your own heart. Your heart specializes in honesty, and can rely on your heart for honest feedback about how you're responding to life, without having to sort through the excuses and justifications your head generally offers.

Become aware of your current inner climate, taking a moment to look within you for any upset, or disturbance. If you feel perfectly fine, go a bit deeper within and notice whether there is anything further down that needs attention.

If you find any disturbance, see if you can identify the source of your disturbance, including any people, circumstances, or situations that might be involved.

Now separate the other people, circumstances, or situations involved, and focus solely on yourself, taking full responsibility for your own part, your own actions, and your own inner responses. Stay in your heart, leave out any excuses or blame, and become completely honest about how you've responded to life.

Now ask God to come into your heart with you. Ask God to help you release any defects of character that may have played a part within you, in this situation. Take a series of very slow, full, deep breaths. As you breath in, simply receive God's love and support, and as you breath out, let go of any negativity within you. Be sure to thank God for your life. Take some time with this.

Stay in your heart, and take a few moments to consider what actions, if any, you might need to take, in order to make amends at this time, to balance the situation.

Stay in your heart, and take a few moments to refocus on how you can best be of service to others.

It's almost time to bring this inner journey to a close. So gather together anything you have learned, that you'd like to bring with you.

Gradually bring your awareness back into your body, and your physical surroundings.

Take your time, and when you're ready, open your eyes, and feel awake, alert, and refreshed.

Pick up your pen and paper, and write about your experience now, while it's still fresh in your mind. Later on, revisit this meditation and learn more.

ELEVENTH STEP

INTRODUCTION

I seek through prayer and meditation to improve my conscious contact with God as I understand God, praying only for knowledge of God's will for me, and the power to carry that out.

Please read the introduction to this series in Step One.

Step Eleven is part of your "Spiritual Fitness" regimen, and along with Steps Ten and Twelve, something you'll want to practice on a regular, perhaps daily basis. It has been said that prayer is talking to God, and meditation is listening to God, and the Eleventh Step is about both listening for God's guidance about how to live, and asking for the strength to follow directions. The meditation for Step Eleven makes it easy to ask, listen, and receive.

GUIDED MEDITATION

Make yourself comfortable, and close your eyes. Take a slow deep breath, and let go of any tension in your body, as you feel yourself sinking into the surface you're resting on, becoming still more comfortable and relaxed. Take another slow, deep breath, and feel a sense of calm and peace begin to fill you, as you relax further. And take another slow, deep breath, and let your thinking begin wind down and smooth out, as you become still comfortable, and relaxed.

Imagine you've been sleeping a deep, sound sleep for many hours, and you're just beginning to stir awake. And the first thing you notice, is

that you're waking up on a soft bed of pine needles, on the ground, surrounded by ancient fir trees. It's just before dawn, and the air is quite cool, the light is dim, and there's a foggy mist in the air. You can smell the scent of pine, and the damp coolness of the earth. It's quiet, and any sound is blanketed by the mist. Everything is a palette of soft greens, browns, and grays.

Standing up, you begin to walk along a path through the trees, and you can feel the spongy ground beneath your feet. Perhaps you still feel a bit foggy from your sleep, but soon you come to a little spring, cup your hands to get a drink, and splash some of the cool, clear water on your face. Now you're beginning to wake up a bit, and see the trees and plants that surround you more clearly.

Walking along further, you find yourself once again on the familiar path to the beach you've visited earlier. Soon the ground becomes sandy, and the air more humid. Now you can smell the sea, and hear the sound of seagulls, and ocean waves breaking along the shore. Finally, you emerge from the forest into the beach, where you made a decision to turn over your will, and your life, to God. Find a comfortable spot to sit and rest on the boulders nearby. You can feel the mist and the sea breeze on your face, and the warmth of the sun, as you contemplate the beach, the sea, and the sky before you.

Drop down from your thinking self, and bring your focus into your heart. Begin to take a series of slow, deep breaths. As you breath in, breath in God, and as you breathe out, breathe out Love.

Feel God's presence all around you, and within your heart, or simply know that God is with you now, as always.

Consider any question you may have about your life today. If this is a question that comes more from your head than your heart, then let it go for now. Look, listen, and feel for a deeper question within you. If you don't have a question today that's perfectly fine.

Turn any question you may have over to God, and come into stillness.

Breathe in God, and breathe out love.

As you sit quietly, allow any answer or information from God to come to you, however God wants it to appear. You may hear, see, feel, or simply know what God has for you today. And it may be that the best answer for now, is to simply be at peace. Take some time to relax, focus in your heart, and be with God, now.

It's almost time to bring this inner journey to a close. So gather together anything you have learned, that you'd like to bring with you.

Gradually bring your awareness back into your body, and your physical surroundings.

Take your time, and when you're ready, open your eyes, and feel awake, alert, and refreshed.

Pick up your pen and paper, and write about your experience now, while it's still fresh in your mind. Later on, revisit this meditation and learn more.

TWELFTH STEP

INTRODUCTION

Having had a spiritual awakening as the result of these steps, I try to carry this message to other addicts, and to practice these principles in all my affairs.

Please read the introduction to this series in Step One.

Step Twelve asks us to step outside ourselves, and bring the message and the essence of all we've leaned to others. Many of us at this point will question whether we are ready or qualified to help other people, and if we have anything to offer. But those are questions best left to God to decide. Our task at this point is to be open to the opportunity to serve, and available to others as the need arises. The meditation for Step 12 will help you adopt the attitude of openness and availability, and know what to do when the time comes.

GUIDED MEDITATION

Make yourself comfortable, and close your eyes. Take a slow deep breath, and let go of any tension in your body, as you feel yourself sinking into the surface you're resting on, becoming still more comfortable and relaxed. Take another slow, deep breath, and feel a sense of calm and peace begin to fill you, as you relax further. And take another slow, deep breath, and let your thinking begin wind down and smooth out, as you become still comfortable, and relaxed.

Imagine you've been sleeping a deep, sound sleep for many hours, and you're just beginning to stir awake. And the first thing you notice, is

that you're waking up on a soft bed of pine needles, on the ground, surrounded by ancient fir trees. It's just before dawn, and the air is quite cool, the light is dim, and there's a foggy mist in the air. You can smell the scent of pine, and the damp coolness of the earth. It's quiet, and any sound is blanketed by the mist. Everything is a palette of soft greens, browns, and grays.

Standing up, you begin to walk along a path through the trees, and you can feel the spongy ground beneath your feet. Perhaps you still feel a bit foggy from your sleep, but soon you come to a little spring, cup your hands to get a drink, and splash some of the cool, clear water on your face. Now you're beginning to wake up a bit, and see the trees and plants that surround you more clearly.

Look for the fallen log you found in a previous meditation, and you'll see it nearby. Find a comfortable spot, and have a seat. Enjoy the beauty and quiet here, and allow this peaceful place to support you, as you begin your inner work.

Drop down from your thinking self into your feeling self, and go deeply into your own heart. Begin to take a series of slow, deep breaths. As you breath in, breath in God, and as you breathe out, breathe out Love.

Consider someone you know whom you feel might need the kind of support you've been receiving from the 12 Steps.

Imagine that person together with you in your heart, as if the two of you were in a beautiful chamber, full of light.

As you stand together, imagine opening your heart to that person, so that a wave of love and support emanates from your heart to theirs. Take a few moments to experience this taking place.

Ask God to help you know how and when to best approach that person. How can you best be of service to them at this point in time, without offering too little, or too much. Do your best to distinguish between what your head might be saying, and what your heart is saying. Take some time to listen deeply, and receive.

Ask God to help you know the best way to be of service to others in your life, both in general, and in any specific areas, and be open to anything that comes up. Take some time to listen deeply, and receive.

Allow the meaning of the following Prayer of Saint Francis of Assisi to find its way deep within:

Lord, make me an instrument of your peace.
Where there is hatred, let me sow love.
Where there is injury, pardon.
Where there is doubt, faith.
Where there is despair, hope.
Where there is darkness, light.
And where there is sadness, joy.
Oh, Divine Master,
Grant that I may not so much seek to be consoled, as to console;
To be understood, as to understand To be loved, as to love.
For it is in giving that I receive In pardoning that I am pardoned.
And it is in dying that I am born to eternal life.

It's almost time to bring this inner journey to a close. So gather together anything you have learned, that you'd like to bring with you.

Gradually bring your awareness back into your body, and your physical surroundings.

Take your time, and when you're ready, open your eyes, and feel awake, alert, and refreshed.

Pick up your pen and paper, and write about your experience now, while it's still fresh in your mind. Later on, revisit this meditation and learn more.